WarFair4

M.Stow11

Published by M.Stow11 Smashwords Edition

Part One: The Day The Markets stood still...

It has been said that love of money is the root of (many) evil(s) and a wandering from the path which has brought- upon us much pain. The lack (need) of money is so quite as truly.

Samuel Butler (1835-1902 ME) EREWHON Ch. 20 (amended after: The Old Testament: 1Timothy, and before Mark Twain (Mark Twain's Notebook 1909 ME).

Life is a series of natural and spontaneous changes. Don't resist them - that only creates sorrow. Let reality be reality. Let things flow naturally forward in whatever way they like.

Lao Tzu (531-604 BME)

WarFair4: Part One: The Day The Markets stood still...

1.

'It's like living in a rabbit hutch' She often said metaphorically and He replied with a shrug. *Nothing to say in reply. It was; and it would take long enough to pay for. Eight-floors up. Looking over the street below, now starting to become busy with traffic.*

They had lived with his parents for a time, and then after they were married in a small rented flat in The City, before they needed to afford somewhere to live together, and to bring-up their two small children.

They had both saved, and with some financial help from a relative (deceased) they had managed to get this place. When the housing market was 'buoyant' and home loan mortgages easy to get if you were in work. The home was bought with a loan, a promissory note, deposited and co-lateraled together with the home itself. They were afloat.

Both worked to pay-off the loan, which although it was supposed to reduce each year, did not seem ever to keep up with pay and prices. The loan would anyway be paid-off, many times over, if they were ever to pay off the debt. If this place was ever to become their own. If they managed to keep paying-off for 'the shelter from the storm', as they called it, from everyday life. A life or home that they did not now own, and may not ever actually own, if foreclosed to sell-back at Market Price the difference between the buying and selling-price of which along with the interest paid they would have lost to The Mortgage Company, employer, overlord. No recourse, and be homeless. On The Street. Refugees. Like wartime. Leave the land. Return to parents, and over-crowding as before. Or with friends similarly fixed. Their home, such as it was theirs, re-possessed. Their lives dispossessed.

Their home: a two-bedroom cabin apartment she thought of: *kitchen-lounge, bathroom and toilet, and tiny balcony between them, and the sky above, and onto the world below. Each day, each month, and each successive year into the unthinkable future; no-deposit but interest-only nearly two-thirds every month of what they both earned. She did the household accounts, and she knew. Of every week, every month, every year, every decade...two thirds of two lifetimes...the Loan would have been paid for several times over by the time and if ever it became theirs or The Children's; and perhaps even their Grandchildren's...paid-for with extortionate charges and zero-security...but that is the nature of the human animal, is it not? To do over; and be done over again and again?* she thought: *wanting more and more for less and less and prepared to do anything for it. Break the rules...even murder, in effect? A walking nightmare, as if a daydream* of violent retribution or suicidal; and in the quiet mind wandering moment of pillared door, a room, a table, *a bed let go and a bed sheet left behind ready to be buried with as they did in the olden times, shrouded* as now by window curtains *thinly* pulled-back.

Each worked to pay off the loan on the house, and to pay for food and bills and extras, clothes, and nights out, occasionally. Maybe once a month, or not at all. Then He had been laid-off work at The Bakery: three-day-week, and three days' wages. The mortgage was renegotiated, and they continued struggling to pay-off the loan and other loans, credited and debited from what they both earned together for the basics of life. There was never an issue of who should earn more and be the main breadwinner, and who would do the most caring of each other and the children: the unpaid responsibilities shared around the home and in the world of work, and good times with other friends and family out there, made do.

They were equal, without even having to think about it or confront societies' and other's false expectations of gender and family. They were equal, and supported each other's frail and fragile egos with a natural equanimity. Respectful, and loving, each contributing their best and differently according to their means, to make the whole: It's not all doom and gloom she did often think, and he tried not to think on it. *The homely claustrophobia only had to be relieved by going out. To the cinema, to a bar or restaurant. But that was not very often. Now there were children as well. Seldom did extras make their mark. Clothes bought carefully a piece at a time replacement rather than extravagance . The cupboards filled with groceries, and emptied by the time the next weeks shopping is needed, and the next weeks earnings spent.* She was awake first this morning, and she got up from the bed on which he still lay awake but not yet awake enough to leave its night-time warmth.

She went through to the next room. The bedroom led across the narrow passage to the living room which led directly to the tiny gallery kitchen and balcony on one side and the door to the front room on the other. Except it wasn't the *front*-room, exactly, the 'front-room' of her childhood *playing on the street and door directly to the matted rugged smell of cooking from the stone wall white-washed country kitchen upstairs two bedrooms, on the gallery landing for the parents and children, and grandparents in the loft. An outside closet room to flush away into the ground, with a zinc-metal bucket of water...into the slurry sump* she thought *where you could hear it 'slurry' all the way down; and then to wash out and replace from the outside tap pumped-up from the well refilling the bucket, and the decorated fired china clay bowl for washing, ready for the next use. At bedtime children first, then the adults.*

Rat nested runs beetles and cockroaches were kept away by the domesticated cats and dogs that no-one owned but all fed and looked after; and there were horses at the local stables, to ride at week-ends and holidays. Each week by cart, then by car or truck into The Market Town for food supplies and treats for The Children with whatever they had to sell, their whole world a living market place of work and play. Now great enclosed superstores and supermarkets and factory outlet warehouse parked. Where goods are now transported she thought of: *to and from, by railway train and motor vehicle, by great tanker lorries and container freight ship and aircraft to and from The Docks and airport at The City Harbour hub. Humming away, remotely yet directing everyday life, everywhere.*

Freight-cargo and tourist passenger with the affordable flight to get away from it all: necessary, a change, a necessary move, once in a while, not every year but to visit family here and there and elsewhere, or else you'd go stir-crazy; do a night-time flit, leave the rent, the mortgage, unpaid. Only to keep on fighting another day, for the bargain, cheapest within budget, to get through the next day; and the day after that.

*When debts and fines could not be paid, the debt collector, bailiffs, the selling off of the personal possessions, and then the person...*the laptop computer on sleep and awakened placed on the table booted-up and she blogged instantaneously her thoughts:

'We all need a roof over our heads and put food on the table! How?!' Without any other word or contextual continuity that did not remain obvious to this early morning. *Everyone, and anyone in the same and similar circumstances...*getting the hastily tapped-out message (140 letters) *excluding those without, sooner dead; and those with patently far too much and who had administration to do their messages for them.* And her thought continued in the context of the mindful moment *and that which we all have to pay extortionately for over and again even when the food is eaten and the crap washed away there remains a nasty stain, a nasty taste. The original wages sweated over, wasted away, and the loans ever in negative equity! To who? Them!* Looking up, and down again now, not in dejection, but

circumspection against ever apparent possible failure, with optimism, with perfectibility warning, waning. Below the window, only mechanised traffic building-up, soon into a busy rush-hour congestion. Cars and buses, bicycles, motorbike and motorised delivery truck *from here, and there only another view of the same. From two-sides; and every all sides...*the bedrooms along the passage corridor, the sleeping children slept.

Earlier peeked into *soundless in beautiful dream or dreamless seeming startling worrying death* of self, and other...checked for breathing.

Crossing from night into daytime TV, remotely automatically turned on, confirmation, that *life goes on.* The *living* room, as She entered bore all the chatter and the silence of one who listens, still and safe, cosy and secure.

The other rooms took over the emotions and needs: sleep and food, love, and arguments. The central room, the central chamber looked on and awaited eventual almost inevitable, but never certain, or taken for granted, reconciliation and rest. Indulged in social events, noisy chatter and quiet evenings indoors:

'*You have to work at it everyday...*' she heard her mother saying, about marriage, children, and life in general.

The furniture was adequate and filled the room. Table, chairs, television, a draw and shelved cabinet standing against a wall, displaying various icons. Family photographs in frames: a portrait of a famous film star, or a print of an oil painting, ornaments, statuettes, figures of worship and of novelty. The furniture the infrastructure, from the livelihoods, and eventually:

'The roof *over our heads...'*

'In over our heads...' heard as originally spoken. There were opened envelopes and cajoling leaflet advertisement *Kill your debts! Die debts!* she saw and thought of the remarkable coincidence between her vision, and thoughts.

Letters and bills for payment, propped up behind a ticking clock. There was a picture postcard from someone-else's holiday, forming a picturesque frontage to hide the stack of demands for reply and payment which lay beyond.

She drew back the curtains and looked out of the window across the balcony, with its unflowering plants growing in flower-pots. It was still misty outside from the early morning warming; and she gazed over an area where many lived and it seemed to her, this morning, where they too lived out their lives *day to day, week to week.*

They too thought to themselves as she looked-out onto the dawn of a gradually opening new day *that the world must have always been this way.*

2.

Soon the television was blaring as usual in the morning, in the main room that was empty again for the moment, and beyond where she was now dressing hurriedly, and he was brushing his hair frantically.

There was the noise of children getting washed and dressed, with incessant commentary and conversation to each other, and any other, or just to themselves. To each other as a one-way argument older to younger, incited over some triviality, shouted back in frustration. At that point the only-game-in-town and to be fought-out until one of them is crying, and the other shouting-the-odds; before calm brings *even loving fun again* at least while they all got ready for work, school and pre-school-nursery. The sound of the kettle screaming on the kitchen cooker and television advertisements conveying to deaf ears, and blind eyes, but perhaps receptive memory:

'The Best in the World',

or:

'Longer-lasting',

or whatever the dubious selling point perhaps to be *unconsciously* recalled later that day at the supermarket.

At present they seemed to be of no avail. Both rushed to get the children to school, and themselves out to work. To earn the pay that would pay the prices at the supermarket later that day:

'Where is my shirt?'

he called:

'Where you last put it!' she retorted.

As she entered the living room she found her shoes under a chair, and stopped in front of the television. The networked advertisements ended, and the programme returned to the main story of the day:

> 'Today there is no money to pay share dividends, or to buy shares with...'

She flicked a channel and got:

> 'Individual and group share prices have collapsed or become so high that they have become worthless.
>
> Confidence has collapsed. Debt undiminished price increases have been blamed, increases in pay and pensions have been blamed. Increases in interest-rates and profit-levels have all been blamed.
>
> Each of these has pushed share prices ever upwards. As share prices and shop prices overtake the customer's ability to pay, and the ability to pay pushes prices-up profit margins recaptured by increases in interest rates on banking and other loans, these have pushed share prices up even further...'

A view passed across the TV screen: *to locked factory-gates, ports and land borders closed to traffic or trade.*

It did not seem too bad, or even unusual: the television experts and announcers liked to make a big deal out of anything she thought: *it was their jobs after all.*

The pictures shifted to *City office-buildings, that only a few were being allowed into and then to the squares and circus's around Town and City centres all over the globe, all the streets and roads and highways leading there...*

The TV reporter turned away from the camera, and let the scene somewhere else *could be anywhere*, speak for itself. In the kitchen radio reports followed from The Stock-

Markets around the world: The Tokyo Nikkei, Shanghai,

Shenzhen Hang Seng, Bangkok, Delhi, Bombay, and Saudi and

Egypt Stock Exchanges. RTS Moscow, Frankfurt, Cape Town.

London and Canada Stock Exchanges: New York Wall Street

and Rio...Buenos Aires to Lima.

JSE Securities Nairobi and the Nigerian and Sydney Stock Exchanges...as she went to look for tea-bags. He got the cups out and put some bread under the grill to toast. As the cups were emptied and the door was opened to go out The Stock-Market Reports were interrupted by the radio-announcer:

> 'We have heard in the last few minutes that The International Conference of the Leaders of Governments and World-Banks meeting in Geneva are to make statements at midday mean-time on the current state of financial affairs across the globe. The Economic Crisis' around the world...'

They stopped and looked at each other as they heard the announcement:

'What will they come up with this time I wonder..?

she asked, aloud to him and to the radio speaker, and as she went to the bathroom door:

'Come on you two! ' to the children, and to him in the same breath:

'What time are you finishing today?'

'On-lates' his reply; with a shrug, noticed, as she said:

'I'll have to clock off early then', (and she thought, *another opportunity to sack me for not doing overtime, but if school finishes before work what are we supposed to do?*).

'I'm taking them in, anyway ..!' he called.

'I know!', she replied,

'... we will have to go to the supermarket tonight' added knowingly *a reluctant necessity when it came to it*:

'Or tomorrow anyway...' as she kissed him on the lips, quickly, tantalisingly, knowingly *these weekly and often daily shopping trips for basics, food and water, with a shelter over their heads, is what they did all this for.*

Along with the mortgage-rent, and love of their family and children smiling he went out of the door, and onto the communal balcony and hallway:

'Another financial crisis!' he called out, with more than a note of sarcasm, which did not need any reply, other than a disinterested:

'Is there?'

She went back inside the living room, and went to turn the television off, as the announcement of the impending declaration from Government-Leaders and World-Banks was being repeated:

'Won't make any difference..!',

she shouted, over the noise of the television:

'...never does!'

and she left the house, soon afterwards.

3.

He took the down stairs with the children two-at-a-time one in a pushchair the other just learning to walk, and turning outside pulling the buggy *up* steps to the road level they headed off together for The Corner Shop.

Turning at the top of the road, pushing the baby buggy uphill, the almost unmade pavement now in disrepair, showing the lack of maintenance through *the good times* as well as the now financial recession.

Telling *The Walker* (as He and She said to each other in jest *the children laughed at that...*) but *The Walker no longer holding on to the buggy* called-out to:

'Hold on to the buggy' *answering the constant questions*:

'What is this?' and:

'What is that?' *and having to say*

'Be careful!' *every second, and*:

'Stop!...making me have to say 'Be Careful!' every second!' and they giggling together, at what, he knew not what.

Not even imagining a time when He and She would not be going to work, and they to school and nursery, and then *keeping them in our dotage probably!*

Going to pick up the fallen walking running-off child, grabbing the perambulator again, and continuing walking on the uneven pavement road:

'Do Not Run! You'll *tripover...*'

The walking child hearing only the middle word:

'Run!'; and wondering what all the shouting was about, and running:

'Stop! at the edge!' hearing all the words this time: *thoughtfully*:

'O.K?'

'O.K.!'

trying out these new words heard from them and at school.

'Stop!', The Walker running now and stopping at the pedestrian-crossing to get collided in to and rolling on the ground giggling *The Road!* getting up and running off laughing, looking backwards,

'STOP!'

Having crossed the crossing turning confidently the opposite way,

'This way!' onto the next junction,

'Stop! at the kerb!'

He catching up, pushing the pushchair ahead, The Walker hanging on, over the kerb and into the road.

Looking both ways, and then both ways again. Then back again, one last way this time: *too quickly...going to Run!* The way the traffic was headed, moving slowly, one car stopped, and let them across to a wave returned. Watching-out, for all three and to the oncoming traffic split, by traffic lights commanding: *Stop, Start, or Pause...*

To the other side safely chasing on ahead to The Shop. The 'Little-'un' in the buggy trying to get out to follow, screaming and pointing with one then both index-fingers toward the road,

'Taxi!'

swivelling around almost falling-out. Pointing, ahead:

'Bus!' the other returning, giggling:

'A. Bus!' correcting, and then as they passed The Shop pleading verbally and non-verbally tugging and whining for sugary sweets:

'Helicopter!' singing, and pointing and swivelling around again:

'The Shop!' the other:

'Sweets! categorically. *Usually not until they came home from school and nursery. Even then only some days, and if they had been good at school or nursery. But always worth a try....*pointing, jumping up-and-down, on the buggy, the other falling out, buckles unbuckled, by the older one:

'As long as you behave yourselves today, and they're not too bad for your teeth, and you clean your teeth!' *they knew that.*

Giggling all the more, at some reference only they knew. To the words, the noises, and the tone of voice, the bedtime:

'Clean your teeth! Properly!!' the older one repeated, and they went into more fits of giggles. Into the newsagent-come-grocers and confectionary shop and sometime licensed off-licence. Where He, and She, and They stopped each morning, for bread, or a newspaper.

On the way to nursery and school, when it was his turn, always the possibility of sweets as well. As they crashed through the door the older one getting deliberately, or so it seemed, in the way of the baby-buggy. Asserting rights over the other smaller and weaker, and released both leaning up at The Shop counter.

Not unusually but always predictably in the morning rush *with so many other things to think about* the only thought, unable to think about anything else: *Food shopping tonight? Newspaper? Sweets?*

The buggy almost tipped over in the raucous, the older one falling over the younger, strapped in, strained at the straps, snapping painfully back.

Letting out an ear piercing yell.

The older one still giggling, until the younger lashed-*out as only younger siblings know how too* and the older one let out a *Yell!* then a *Scream!*; apparently exaggerated explication of pain from both now, and claims of *unfairness idiot! etc.*

'Come-on you're the older one, you should know better! Do you have to have to fight and argue over everything! No sweets!' and then he knew, as soon as he said that that he was *A Beaten Man.*

A yet louder exclamation set-up.

While the younger looking on in glee, quieted and puzzled, twisted turned looking upwards to *The Father* for some resolution to the questioning plea, and fell out of the buggy, unbuckled:

'Me a' well?'

Looking up from the floor, the older standing and going to stamp on the younger, smiling sweetly now, the other sprawled on the floor as if felled:

'The Smiling Assassin!' he called-out from the front of The Shop in common reference to the older child and to The Shopkeeper grinning in collaboration, and who was stacking shelves from remaining stock.

He, holding-up the regular National *Financial*-Newspaper, the shopkeeper called:

'You may as well keep that!'

to the loose change being handed over the counter:

'...it will be like one of those free ones!'

Hearing and not listened-to until later, scanning the headlines:

STOCK-MARKETS IN CHAOS!

The money left on the shop-counter chuckling, when the remark realised:

'No, I got it!' minding: 'The Children...' who were not fighting but pretending to steal sweets *not knowing any better yet*, knowing better, laughing and looking palpable.

The Shopkeeper bagged and handed over most of what it was they-wanted:

'There you are, for later...your Dads' change!'

the customary sweets as a gift now *in-change sometimes anyway* for a small note passed across the counter. From the Shopkeeper, to them, and then him:

'Daddy keep it...for later'

The children looking pleased, and anxious also, that they too might have to 'keep it for later' with only then the conditional:

'And only if you are Good today!'

The emotional and ethical merged into puzzlement. Sweets given to The Father patiently waiting to get off to nursery, school and work.

Again consternation, put-on, by the older child, to the younger. Pouting, dropped lower-lip. Acting-out, pretending, face pulling. Puzzled at, and copied by the younger. Both laughing at this, and between themselves, at something they did not really know: what it was *to Be Good*...or: *all day*; or how or what it was to attain this.

They had stayed together and with two little ones, one of each, girl and boy by the time they're both about to be in school, they could not risk another to bring up, and the cost of it. They only hoped they would hold on to their jobs, and worked hard. Difficult hours, and few days-off. Where the rota's didn't workout for childcare, family, or neighbours, parents now friends of the children's friends who lived conveniently nearby: The Social Network...from the cradle to school. Diapers to Diploma.

They had met when things were starting to get a bit tight, get difficult again. Meaning the situation for most working families, for those looking for work, and those in work, things had not got any better, any easier really during the so-called good-times, and both parents were needed to work to keep the family going.

Voluntary social networks became all the more significant, and reciprocal. Shared-care with child and adult interaction, thereby social and meaningful: shared lives between people, and gender.

They had both kept their jobs in, more or less essential services, although not without their job-cuts and reduced hours, or expected overtime at the same or no pay, ever-the-less, never the more, in real terms. When The Bakery factory went on three-days week, and pay to match. He had more time to be with the children, and helped the same with others still in fulltime work, or Her awkward shiftwork.

He had done some untaxed building work on the odd-days to fill-in. She had done some shop and garment-making work before, then when they were no-longer hiring, took retraining, her current work she hurried toward, as did He.

Then they had moved to his folks in The City: suburbs really, inner-urban, something-like-that. His mother had worked at The Old Mill and got her a job there; and then with him at The Bakers' Factory at the top of the road, near the nursery and school, when they had moved in together; and had kids. Turn right, then left, and a few more turns, before The Factory Gates.

His father's family had been millers too, before that. Gypsies. Did well. Moving around (funnily enough He thought *like Business People nowadays do...*looking across the busy roads beyond, leading to The-City.

To The-Airport *to visit salespeople to the retail outlets, shops in other words: Big Business. Marketing, and sales.*

By plane to meet clients meetings here and there and everywhere. Cities all over, to do deals on a massive Global-Scale worth millions, now worth billions and trillions of whatever the currency.

Sometimes, dealing even with the currency itself.

In the past when the work dried-up his' family 'moved along' or stayed with their stores, shares of the crops of the fields and water, natural and free from the well.

Waiting for more or different labour or better paid to the costs of running the household...

He thought *of them, and his own family. Out of work, they always found something. When the work was finished, they moved on. Along the waterways, they not dissimilar, but also different from her family. They had a farm in the countryside for a while, and the parents still lived there. Hers. he and She, now, through the Industrial Future. To The Soul of The City. Across The River, across the tram tracks, and railway, by the station.*

From The Heart of the City, the Financial Quarter. Settling in The City outskirts. His self-employed, their own bosses, worked on the building sites of towering sky-scrapers, lining The River. Then employed. Not their own boss. Both their families on some land, renting from their pay together.

Then they, He and She eventually, buying: homeowners now. Investors in their own future, and their children's' children...

She had pressed the OFF switch, and They all had left for school and work. *Now,* closing all the windows and door behind her, a short while later and going where those others' had left, and others were still leaving front doors, for the days school and work and buying and selling activity ahead.

Outside and downstairs, through the piles of discarded rubbish and the door wedged open. To the blocked refuse-chute, to the stairs and the *If-it's-working* lift down to the ground floor: t*he worst thing standing inside the open lift door not being sure if the elevator was going to work, or not. Or go crashing to the ground, like everything else today,* she thought. He was *on-a-late* and so *he was taking the children to school and nursery. He would not be collecting them later today.*

When her shift finished she could normally do overtime, but today to clock-off, to collect them. *If there were no emergencies, that was*. Then she would have to phone one of the other mothers or fathers to collect their children as well, *if they could...*She entered the same shop He had recently departed with The Children only a few minutes, but crucial lateness seconds, earlier:

'Got any bread in?'.

'You may as well take one there, only one-day-stale!', climbing-down off a stool-from-stacking-shelves:

'It's gone stale already hasn't it!? Never mind the bakery! Haven't seen them yet today!' Today the shop was open as usual ready to stock-up again with the usual days-supplies that had been 'phoned in the day before *or rather*:

'It looks like it is *whenever The Delivery turns up*!

Then, not for the first time:

'Your better-half works at The Bakery doesn't He?

Then:

'My other-half went out early enough today to The Cash and Carry, and not back yet! I phoned-in the order. They said: 'No Deliveries yet today!' nothings' moving yet...'

Then: 'Gone to see if we can collect...in the food-queue probably!' pointing at the dry loaves on the shelf:

'Going stale!' momentarily paused, then:

'No Cash, No Carry!'

exclaimed.

'Fresh is best' concluded.

The Shopkeeper continued to her:

'But this we get from Your Bakery, you know, it doesn't last! Gets chuckled. Have to *Health and Safety* it, or give it to *The Bin-Raiders* out the back. They have it! Still, can't blame them can you? Poor beggars. I leave it for those that take it. Homeless, you know, or out of work, on The Benefits that go nowhere, poor and hungry and homeless...'

'That's where we'll all finish-up...if we're not careful! She called, The Shopkeeper replying:

'They take it home, or toast it on one of those outdoors braziers, you know? They sleep under the bridge arches you know. Don't seem to worry them...'

'All yesterday's bread has gone? Panic buying!'

'Panic buying? What already?'

'Only that one left now. We won't get another delivery today I dare say. And I am told: 'We don't know when!' Well, if they don't know?! Only the 'papers delivered so far, and I haven't paid for them yet. Only pay for what I sell. How's that!!' doubly surprised at the apparent revelation: *that not everything had to be paid for up-front credit?*

The shopkeeper came towards the counter of the shop, and continued:

'You can give me all the money you've got if you like. No change though, more sweets instead, like the last time! Your kids have got something to last them! The Banks are not open, so you won't be able to get any notes or cash out anyway. Never be able to sell this place now. You know, I've been trying to sell-off The-Shop and its stock to pay off loans and bills on the shop *and* on the stock; but no buyers. Not yet. Not now. I'd have to sell-off at too low a price…or too high...maybe...'

'I'll just up-and-go sometime, leave it all behind'.

'Any buyers yet?', she asked, not listening, heard it before; *and not just this shopkeeper. All the local shops were known either by the name on the front of the shop, or the nationality or ethnic-identity of the family that owned, or rented that shop, and its' stocks and shares, and did their business there small retailers, family run businesses across the globe, despite the Supermalls and Hypermarkets still the way most trade finishes up, from the roadside, to and from The Town and The-City market-places and lined the streets and roads out...*

*And, of course, the Stock-Markets and Money-Markets...*she pondered.

She looked at the front page of the newspaper unfolded, and thrown onto the worn-*light* dark varnished and metal-trimmed wooded surface. She glanced at a cartoon which depicted The Finance Ministers heads in hands sitting on stacks of money; no words needed, but a comment she read for free, without intending to buy, on the inside page:

The Inside Page:

In the last weeks and months there have been queues in shops for scarce goods, rationed by ability to pay, there have been queues to spend, instead of investing, pay, pensions, and profits, before they became worthless.

The prices of goods and services have increased week by week and day by day, as more…

She pondered again: *Don't we just know it! So what's so different!* she wondered, and said:

'So what's so different!' to no-one in particular: *how the small shops and retailers and service providers like health and social care, whether small cottage hospital or fast-food chain.*

How the small shops managed at all. With all the out of town shopping malls, and giant chain stores. That everyone shopped at, because they could not better afford the prices and special offers.

The supermarkets paid up-front, but cheaply, and only what they thought they could sell at a good profit, and what people could afford...

The Shopkeeper had continued without stopping hardly, and stocking the shelves and the final aisle way, finished:

'...that's it! Everything is out. I'm now officially out of stock!' *apart from what I've got in the back for me and the family for a few days...*

'...and that's it!'

The train of thought returning, to re-stacking the meagre shelves with the remaining stock, and with some finality:

'Not stock-piling…not getting in even enough customers to cover the household ourselves! Existing loans on capital, stock and shop; rent is unpaid for the year...'

Back at the counter, handing the money-back:

'Go-on, you may as well take it! Here, why don't your Hubby bring us some nice freshly baked bread to stock up the shop with?!'

'That is where He works, it is isn't it? They 've closed the works. Again, did you know?! I owe them anyway, The Bakery, The Cash and Carry, you name it! I'm well into negative equity now! The amount the shop owes...is owed. Never sell up now, have to give it away!' Then:

'That is where he *works* 'though, isn't it? The Bakery?'

'Not any more it seems...' her sullen answer.

The Shop Keeper then with a renewed finality:

'How about a free newspaper then!? Everything else has been taken from us, they've bled us dry!!' She exclaimed, without irony; restrained and mixed with anxious mirth. She said to stem the merriment:

'HaHa...You know We can't even get bread retail nevermind free! They are that tight with their profits and credit! Like you have buy food before you can eat it even if you're starving!'

'Even although He works there?!' The Shop Keeper and She added together:

'How stupid is that?!'

'Or uncaring-for-your-staff and workers...'

'The Bakery wants to make as much profit out of us as they can!'

'Out of all of us! Never mind the measly pay! Anyway...' pointing a thumb back through the door:

'If the works are closed, no bread...'

'And no cakes either; not today, at least!'

The money for a small loaf was put on the counter and the large sliced loaf in its *mould-inducing plastic wrapper* and the newspaper with its banner headline declaring:

was carried off.

'Will you be going into the rally?' texted, when she had left the shop, and called his mobile 'phone, with photograph stored number gazed at longingly, but without answer, voice-message ready as he texted back:

'No point going in beforehand. I'll not be getting paid, anyway!'

4.

The-train moved slowly out from the glass and steel raised slab of the new edge-of-The-Town main-line high-speed railway-platform running alongside the banking blank back of high-street shops, and the station car-park, awaiting return.

Into harvested-fields and open-grazed pastures. Below remaining precipitous pine-forest, planted-poplar windbreak shielded. Through the trees, the new days' sun appeared. Speared, blinking-awake burst! through the carriage. Breaking-beyond the blue-grey staggered and staged, rolled and ranged. From the east-*peaked* settling yellow-orange, onto the western-hills shadow-flanking purple-green valleys; and up-country, the farmed grid-framed plains, where the day was already begun.

As steam grey white lifted across a dried-up estuary. In *thinrain* spluttering, over an elevated iron-riveted red ochre painted girder-bridge built. On pillars of a deep-red local stone and brickwork arched, and breached. With the Suns'-rays the train rattled-on emergent as through a fog over a beached river, onto the other-side, of a ravenous, gaping-gorge.

Over-spilling through the outskirts of a recently built-up ancient sea-harbour, and river port Town. Sub-Urban High-rise housing-project and industrial-units. Business-Park, and Shopping-Mall. Home-furniture, and motor-car showrooms sales-rooms, cheap-Hotel and motel link razor-wire fenced, chained-in. A horse-paddock, gated, and padlocked adjacent to a blue-green to red-waiting train-crossing signal a freight-train privileged-over passenger passaged prerogative *thundering*-by *that* morning.

The passenger commuter-train trundling along, for now. Beside a chequered black and yellow train-crossing, arterial hot-tar-road, weighted-heavy and ever busy with traffic. Coach and Omnibus, cycle and motorcycle, car and caravan-trailer. Articulated-juggernaut, container-shipment on-board onto and beneath the over-passing concrete-highway into, and out-of Town. All traffic travelling with one accord. To-and-from galvanized corrugated iron steel and zinc tin roofing roving between brick and-cinderblock doorways...loading and un-loading bay's beneath canopy entrance-coded and secured, air-extracting to the outside world-*unseen* windowless. Between belching cooling-tower pylon-linking electric-welding workshop engineering factory-crafted machined and manufactured goods. Human resources, food and furniture packaged warehoused shipped to-and-from The Town harbours and The-City port and portals co-modifying in-return.

Stock-yards stacked-up, exchange value-assured on the money- Market's awaiting transport to-and-from Home and Abroad. The *investment* merchant-Banker sat-back and glanced across at the *administrative* accounts-Clerk sat in the opposite seat, fixed-table between. Travelling on this same-train same-time, same-carriage. For the-Clerk the *same*-seat, if that or any other was to be had amongst the everyday commuters seated *and a few standing today. Usually crammed-in each weekday, early-morning* into The City.

For the-Banker *this* day too-early for the usual-reservation. With, or today without, waiter-served breakfast or a free-morning newspaper. *only those freely given-away* and piled-up in the station forecourt to be taken-away.

That had to be paid-for anyway, by publicising the events and latest product model and version and the most *reasonably*-priced. Like copies of The Big Issue sold-on by homeless-people in Metropolis' around the world: *no such thing as a free-lunch* the-Banker reasoned.

In First-Class The Financial-Newspaper paid-for anyway by The Railway Company ticket-seated and breakfasted with The-*Financial Newspaper* at massively *discounted* market-rate or cost-price *freely* as-advertising encouraging in-someway paid-for, and for: *returns*...The Newspaper could be easily afforded, anyway, from today's loss-leader, tomorrow's winner paid-for upfront from the station kiosk. The newspapers' corporate-investment at-least *knowingly borrowed on perma-credit: staff-costs paid-off and on continuing steady-sales, to be recouped, shorted, and long-term investment...achieved...Today, The newspaper not given-away with the extortionately and exclusively permissive over-priced pass this day* into The City: *The Stock-Exchanges and Financial-Markets.*

The Annual-Executive rail-ticket paid-for, whether used or-not. This day the first train out and apparently only Standard-class available. A single First-class carriage was filled-up quickly by anyone who had a ticket and *conceivably some who did-not:* there were no-tickets being checked or paid-for *apparently* the barriers left-open and *inviting all-comers.*

For The-Banker, for another-time that morning, something mildly, now-seconded, and *markedly* unusual. The earlier, when the radio alarm-clock had switched-on routinely with the early-morning fishing, farming, road, and rail, airline and shipping delays, arrivals and departures and speculative *forecasts:* weather-reports, from around the world. Local, and global, political-economic, and media-news with the previous-nights' *closing* market-prices from around The-World: there had been developments, overnight, from around The World that needed attending-to.

From the emptying platform The-Banker and The-Clerk boarded the train together more or less equal. The-Clerk with a free newspaper, and headphones plugged-in to a mobile Media-Centre. The-Banker for the first time in a long-while with a bought-copy of The *Financial-Newspaper* from The Trains' limited refreshments-trolley.

Having taken the first seat-available in the nearest Standard-Class compartment coupled with a foul-stench reeking drain-leaking latrine *literally* retching between the brown and grey-green patterned seats. Along the narrow aisle way the-Banker waving the newspaper ahead *as if to clear-the-air*. Unwavering, when shunted across by the next-passenger inline to the only *vacant* window-seat glanced across-to, and sedentarily leaned-forward across the table between them, asked of The-Clerk, already sat down-opposite:

'So what do you make of it all then..?' in the customary easy clear voice of one born with the interrogative confidence of swift appraisal. As to The-Banker, as to The Newspaper headline shaken-out: the *whole*-carriage and The World beyond...to The City could now be viewed and as to what was initially referred to, that too, was soon made obvious:

The-Banker sat-back purposefully, purportedly, and provocatively to-unfold *The Financial-Newspaper* with the headline outer-most, upper-most:

WORLD MARKETS IN TURMOIL!

and *seen* again *that* photograph, taking up the whole of the rest of the *grey*-top printed front-page. Remaindered, pictured in the *mind*s' eye. Now, turned inside-out and with a staring squeezed blink of the eyes, fumbled as if in a freak storm, a blown umbrella, folded quickly-away.

To the-Clerk: hung-out to dry: having seen earlier the front-page photograph and one-liner, top headed:

re-conceived on-line and *connected...down-loading* and *updating*...milli-second minute-to-minute mobile-version *uploading* freely...with-advertising: optional: *freeview* choice or fee...*skipping*...as instantly as if mysteriously-*accusatory*...as if with some felt need for *validation, valediction, justification, testimony, guilt? Even before any evidential fact, or fiction?* With a self and another-deceiving finality justifying, with instant-conviction...*but of who? By whom?* Despite the original opening-question, it seemed as if with no real right-of-reply. The initial conversational-question asked as if not-*intended* to be replied-to or any other-mindedly *mitigating* circumstances or any-answer-at –all particularly, or generally listened-to.

Or so the younger-Clerk, surprised to be spoken-to then considered: *perhaps like a nurture-nature kind of thing? Possibly a-Plebeian enquiry? Selected-standard flagged with no-probation* the-Clerk decided: *more likely a command, to make something of IT, and to-be-taken-notice-of.* Notice-given of anyway, disregarding of the possibly-paranoid maniacal rhetorical-answer awaited or not, by either, or Both.

Regardless of the-Other*: The subtler -Inquisitor? The Quickest to-the- Draw?* The original-*recipient* by-assumption looking-up from a streaming mobile smart-phone camera and video-games-console: 4slot-machine...game...*downloading*...PER (personal electronic reader)/de-pocketed-*information*-recorded singularly removing the ear-phone microphone-socketed-lead off-line *searching*...for the source of the *mildly-irritating openly questive-words' spoke...* as directly-to or so it seemed. The-Clerk, in almost immediate reply:

'Senseless.'

The-Clerk looking-down and into the same recently concealed picture, and slowly re-storing from *browsing*-history as accurately *acutely*-historically as-depicted, as veritably untampered-with mobile cell-phone-photographed: syndicated and World-Wide-Web *network*ed-scene: as at the end of the previous day: City: stocks and bonds' markets as then as now: seen *news*-printed and pictured from the evening before: a *litter*-strewn like old ticker-tape across *The Trading-Room* floor. Forsaken, and an *unforgivingly* blankly waiting-screen strap-line: *Markets closed.*

The single-slogan as about to go up or down was not possible to tell. Diagonally, from one corner of the screen to the other, perhaps *tangentially*-to slip-backwards...smoothly-across continuously stuttering across, only-slightly *blurred* from the-top aloft, above, or below, the perfect: the-*normal* midway *ideally*-positioned not at the-*extreme* outer-fielded or even ever truly-*centred:* but as *inside-out,* and now, as stilled.

As then, as now: as no-longer identically existent: *or*

ever again exactly the same. Except, now: and as everywhere in The World and *nowhere* at all. Except: now, there, only as stop-framed cinematographically stilled, to be recorded and repeated looped...any movement as any-moment only *impendent* occurred of pixels printed and glowing in The-*Cloud...*: that bold bland statement *flickering* nonetheless-memory *fuzzily* held in-abeyance:

Markets closed

shimmering grid-table mapping diagrammatic…a *flickering*…a coming-together. As a dawn held rising, over The Worlds' edge.

As a vertiginous horizontally remote-geometrically sited Cityscape *skyline...diverting...*to:

<Banking- *details...scams of undeclared-bribery and corruption and fraud: on-consultancy and management-only contracts hostage taking hi-jacking debt-ransoming deals projected unfounded optimism or pessimistically threateningly unthroated or keeping quiet: the-public purse: tax-dodging as if this would be enough to boost-confidence on-fixed, and violin-fiddled jigging burning-figures in columns revealed above a dialogue-box:..*

<Options:...*with-structure and series arcade-style deviation from the normal...too complex-to-control, if at all...cutting-edge:*

'Perhaps, bringing The-City down?'

'The-*Country*!'

'The-City? The-Country?! Being brought-down?!' tapped-into:

<The-City *news: ethno-linguistically gender and ability driven plutocracy strategically falsely declared promoted tactics shouted-out:*

'Why?' *grotesque over-Investment in Property...*

'Over-valued...'

Dot-Comm. Construction...Banking- Bubble...to take them out of the marker...on a whim...restructuring below value...above-value market dependent on actual returns...

'*Private-Equity...*'

'And Public?'

'Equity...'

'Funded by incomprehensible *debt*-instrument...inequity...'

'Irrational...it turns out...Residential and Commercial Retail that never gets built...No ground-plans even! The-Mortgage never gets paid-off...Money...*scarcity*...**Boom! Boom!** and **Bang**! Again!'

'**Bang**!! And ***Bust*!** Again!'

'Credit-Crunched collapsed on everything!'

'Government of course...'

'Of course? The Core-Corporations...'

'Global: Big-Business...'

'Everyone! The Banks...'

'Building-Societies...'

'Grown too quickly...'

'Too greedy!'

'*Too much growth without collateral...*' in-camera *secret parallel accounting:* 'Without the *actual* goods delivered to back them up...'

'Only the *false*-figures...they are *all*-false!'

'At any Time?'

'Perhaps the-Price of Civilisation?-Keep moving…same as I.T.'s ever been! Bringing in the-Harvest? Or not...Global-failure!'

'Of The-Banking-System...*this-time...'*

'Prices-war now...'

'Scarcity...low-production…'

'Trade-wars…' *list...bubble-popped...*

'Buy-low Sell-high doesn't work anymore…'

'People want quality and low prices…'

'You got It! Double-bubble saw Nothing like this! Triple, quadruple...*many* times over-rated...'

'And with bonus on top of that!'

'Paying Taxes!'

'Who pays Taxes in their right-mind?!'

'Who can get away with 'I.T.' No-one does...except...unless You're the-Revenue?! Police or Thief, eh?'

'Both.'

'Us and Them.'

'Off-shore?'

'You? The-*Revenue*? I don't *owe...*

'With The-Peoples' *futures investment...*'

'Pensions, social-security…insurance..' Both now in the knowledge assumed of the other. Both assumingly knowingly, unknowingly yet simply *pictorially*- imagining that morning, the scene as unchanged from the night before.

The same now, as far as either of them or anyone on The Train there or anywhere-else knew of: as of dealings of commerce and business, small, medium and large, as that evening previous, ceased. Then, as now inside the City Stock-Market building heavy-teakwood mahogany door's tightly-closed hermetically-sealed. A normally *fluorescent* glow turned-off. Except for a single computer-screen presence there remaining:

Markets closed

as if readied for all time previously, ready for this day.

As if this had never happened before.

Yet it had.

From the evening-before, as in pointless pointed *dire*-warning: *installed once, and now as if permanently. Equivocally unequivocally however automatically not to be taken too-literally, or indefinitely: normally meaning: before the cleaners had cleaned-up and some...but then everyone- else had been cleaned-out*:

Markets closed.

Before, *nightlife* restaurant and T.V. cabaret, the latest news and repose-taken. The *on*-message only that:

'The-Markets will be open again and sooner rather than later...'

'This Day?'

'As any other day...'

'The Day *today*...you mean?'

'Name Your Price...'

'My Price?'

'Unsecured then? What are you worth? In debt?'

'Of course!'

Looking down:

'Between one-price spiral and another:...' *and downright-incorrectly dis-honestly and non-rightly irresponsibly sealing stealing The-Deal...ceiling passed...all stays put and stayed:* 'It is all down to The Tactics...'

'You know of any?'

'Good, or Bad?'

'Any permissible…'

'By what means?'

'Any possible...An Act of God.' *circumstances unfathomable...Into living-obliteration, nevertheless, unconstrained. Imposing, the investment...*

'The-Banker's Bank…' *assuming and ensuring but not insuring but re-insuring the highest value's of private-equity stock in Government and Peoples' currency-bonds individually personally self-owned, by self, or other...*

'And Clerk's Clerk…' *As Other...*

'Priced-out of The Market'...Cash-back credit-borrowed on inter-bank foreign-exchange payday everyday loans...trillions of them...'*Generic-key: designer-rip-off: online: taking-over the competing computer-programmes co-operatively collectively collaboratively algorithmically metering like- a taxi-cab carrying and insuring business-plan's financially under-written and over-insured. Under-insured, over-written, or not-insured at all*:

'On Auto-Selling unchecked...' *pre-programmed virtual-win, lose, or draw, cancelled postponed, and re-negotiated. The animal-urge to risk, and win or destroy, through mistake, error...non-negotiable...The* Accounts-Clerk: *savings-account pension and insurance and Home-Loan, as and always country clear profit-to Corporate and Government-taxes paid-in or not...paid-breaks taken-abroad suitcases full of cash, it may as well be.*

Except digitally electronically and to-be taken-back with repayment in compensation yet hardly covering the original-crime in sin in-bribes and back-handers' dodgy-deals millions of them or a few in the billions and trillions of fixed-rates' false-accounting...unreal today unavailable unassailable unviable cashed-in...

'The-Bank's ill-liquidated...'

'Governments too...' to stay-in:...

'Stays-out. Stashed-away: unavailable to The Government or to The-People to spend. On the-family-business and as of small-Company...' names seen briefly as painted hoarding pasted on the side-of-buildings painted advertising as along the embankment railway-track. Alongside-sidings and stations to be passed-through at high-speed non-stopping. *All else stopped...*

The-Clerk *thought: closed, shrunk, and engulfed by-globular enlarged Corporations' advertising-hoardings:* Banks' currency economic-zone and another Country-Town passed-through. High-street branches, shops and currency-exchanges as-*laundering* domestic clearing-houses for returns or no-return:

'This morning...'

'Standstill. Quits? Then? Eh? Who wins does not lose...'

'Who loses does not win...'

'Really?' *all investing higher-and-higher with insecure unsecured funds in stocks and insurances: inter-bank loans re-insurances, and re-sales...within (closed-text) the listings...*

'What's Your Price?'

'Last night?'

'This morning...'

'Stayed Put.' *Over and into... almost as suddenly as the whole front-page picture re-pasted into-memory...*

For the-Clerk far from *assuaging* the culpability of the-other, now exposed as the deplorably irresponsible and *reckless* lender. Not as yet wrecked-borrower *wreaked* havoc-upon to The-Banker, The-Clerk cast now as the likely irresponsible yet hapless helplessly indebted no-deposit poor credit-*rating* history *first*-time *mortgaged* and-*possibly employee...*

As in: *Bank-loaned salaried monthly paid-off...and to be paid-back payday pay-check paper-money on-screen backed, and banked-*

on. The-Bankers' newspaper front-page pictorial held-out taut-and-proud, as a flag of convenience:

WORLD MARKETS IN TURMOIL!

As a *crumpled* bank-note opened as to The *Light*. As checking the veracity of F*...oldin'* money *billfold bank-account* the-Clerk knew and returned momentarily to the hand-held now re-opening news-*filtering*-screen...

The Newspaper heard again, as the rustling of dry-leaf cadaver.

The Newspaper turned crisply inside-out and halved-again. Both now newly to the same page *skim*-read by The-Clerk earlier: *pre-registered up-front...next page*...and as world-wide-web free and as-*expected* to be paid-for not-*freely-enabled* seen with advertisements scamming and both *skipped*...to:

The *Insider*-Report:

'There will be winners, and there will be-losers...'

As of today, there is so much owed, by so many, that cannot start to be paid-out or paid-back, this day, or next. This morning the stock-markets are closed. Once more world-trade has ground a halt. All credit and trading, has been suspended. The trading of stocks and shares in recent times, has left prices at such all time high-levels, that, overnight, have collapsed. We are yet again in the grip of the greatest global-*fiasco*, the greatest fiscal financial crisis again, ever.

Further down The Page:

This morning in Geneva there is to be an announcement of the International Conference on Monetary Compliance (ICMC). There is to be a declaration of economic policy and *intent*. This announcement is expected to stabilise major-global currencies and exchange-rates, at some *mutually*-agreed rate, to boost confidence in the banking-system, and in Fiscal-policy, and World-trade. A shared-protocol, at Midday, world mean-time today, by the International Date-Line will...

Looking-up The-Banker as from The-Clerks' *laid-back* attitude drawn from the impending appended silence. The-Bankers' now self-imposed imposing *imaged* point-of-view...the close-up pictured *closed-markets* again:

'The-*Barrel*... AKA: The-*Cage*:...Join the-game? C*alculated*-risk?'

<**Rational-Equitable?'**

'What? Rational and Equitable? You?'

'What am I? Petitioning-*supplicant?* Equitable equal elections? Of who, by who, for what?'

'Defrauders!' *corrupt de-frauding people...customers share-holders and for good measure insurance and pension-funds:* 'The top five or six together…whole countries, families, people…Cabal! think on: 'It': Economics-rules! Always has done. Nothing wrong with that…' *as if scrawled along a wall on screen on the street wall…*

'On your wall!'

'If you wish...*with the graffiti and cartoons, newspaper print sheets and template…sprayed on the:* News-Screen:

'As Kings and Queens now others as Rich and Corrupt...' *as the once Colonial-Elite...*

<Establishment<:...list:...*list...*

'And for-*Peace* and Stability...

'Peace of mind...buy-weak sell-strong…no-liquidity? To pay staff or creditors indebted and severed: bankrupted out of business…'

'Generally…not-*greed...*then?'

'No-more Greed. Greed is then: the enemy of the good-management of the-economy...Let the river flow every which way it will…'

'Not stepping in the same river twice, then?'

'Without intervention…' *damning ironically noted…*

'In more ways than one way…' looking down into the handheld screen:

>**Rational-Equitable:** Import-Export: Logistics' facilities:…

'Goods in-and-out then?'

'Stocks...and Shares...and Services...Health and Social Care…To and From...'

'But then never-equitably...eh?'

'Or even rationally...on a whim…' threat grasping…grabbing…

'Despite the faultless algorithms...' as if invading the very land and buildings passed…between the corn fields and water-wells starved and thirsted without resolve…bellyfull...the strongest...while One is starving...another is getting rich…on International-Aid for…!

'Even in *money*-itself! Big-**Bang** Credit-**Crash!** Cash-in now!! The Great-Prize is within our grasp...' The querist paused, then as with an iron-fisted *velvet*-glove...

'Moderate growth only to start with…'

'Re-regulation?'

'The-Government...beyond our means...*Open*-Markets...'

'Society?'

'Secretive...is how *IT* works...' looking into one screen or another including the window scene outside inside the-scene people:

'Civilisation!'

'If only there were such a thing...'

'There is not? It would be a good idea! Don't you watch The News?'' *professional business confidential secrets kept from competitors:*

'How would we operate otherwise? *'It' is customary...on-commission, evaluation, and management-fee on every bring and buy sale...easy...keeping The-Government out of IT...and other Corporations in-line.*

On-line...The-Traders grouped...sometimes-in sometimes-out...headed-up...until one breaks through...Anti-trust! Cabal! Section...faction..sect!...like...

'We've had regulation and *de*-regulation...and re-regulation...and de-regulation again...see them all out!'

'Bread and Bandages...eh?'

Cotton-wool wrapped:

>***Rational-Equitable***:...

' Technocratic-ally-speaking, technically *broke*...'

'Lost?!: at sea or pirating-stolen?'

'Or on-price spreading rumours… and secretive dealing…'

'Insured? On the high-seas?:

<Bio-Technology:list:Social-Healthcare:list...

' Sovereign **Ruling**-*classes*...Soviet-**Mafia**-Oligarch…'

'**Families**...' *Blood*-**Feud**...**Population** *polluter-pays*...*perverse*-incentive...to break the law by the law-enforcers broken...

'Oil-wells blown-up…'

'Blown-up!'

'Martyrdom!

'Crucified!'

'Sacrifice!'

'Hero!'

'SuperHero!!'

'You get blown-up?'

'Or You blow yourself-up! And…'

Silence.

On The Wheel-of-Fortune:

>Barons and **Serf**s...

<Lottery...

>Capital-**City** flight...fighting and peaceful remonstration between brother's sister's squabbling over the kitchen...the bedroom, bathroom-raiding corporate pirate hostile-takeover...*speech:*

'Sliced like bread...'

'In *dis*-proportionate-proportion...'

'Value-added...deaths...'

'To buy-out cheap and sell-on...' *regardless...almost...*

'If you can sell crap you do right?'

'If you can save life you do, right? If you can buy lives..you can sell lives..'

'Wealth and Social-care? Education? Health? Who are?'

'Armaments...you only have to look there:...'

'Who spends most?'

'Who makes the most?'

'Armed...and legged...*Shit for-brains* though...'

'No brains at all…' *keep them in the dark and feed them shit…*

'Mushrooms! All of *Us*?!

'But You need The-Goods...The Stocks in The First Place!'

'That is what The People want...at least in principle...what we need! Bread and Bandages. All the time and if not?'

'Over-Optimism *spread like wildfires...'*

'As pessimism now cooling-off…virtually...trust...confidence...*breaks-down...'*

'*As mis-Trust?'*

' Mostly over-reaction based on *bad* information…no-confidence…'

'All the time. Trust is what keeps everything going…but a little *mis*-trust may save your soul…A little *false*-information and then coming up with The Goods?'

'Is that all this is? Lies that don't pan-out long term?'

'Crashed! Money-deals, only, really...You want shares? *Virtual- Transaction-Cost...Price?'*

'For what we *have* to have to buy? Staples: of course, energy, food and water and roof over our heads...Shares? For what? To who?'

'US!'

'All of Us?

'Not-likely...not if We can help IT!'

'Zero for some then?'

'How about it? Allies?

'You? Rational or Equitable or both?'

'One of five or or six really...in any sector…Globally…WorldWide…'

'Ally? Right here? Right now?'

'The-*City*?'

'Specifically?'

'SMART? Me? You?'

' How do we get there?'

'Not how…Where?'

'Apart from on this-Train? The-*City*?'

'Share-Prices? Dropping like rocks…

'Or bombs…'

'Nuclear-bombs…no-confidence…confusion…benefit from the confusion buy-out then stabilise and…Business as usual?'

'What about the bought out?'

'Costs analysis: Placement and Promotion! Penetration, development and *diversification...*'

'Product?'

'That as well...Money. The-City...Society...'

'*Civilisation*?'

'Where brokers and jobbers…buyers' and seller's Buy and Sell...and make IT!' And *gophers' runner's-rumoured and listened-in whistles-blown. Bells wrung. Trumpets, horns blew from afar. Behind-self and other-construed cloud constructed amorphous as from behind closed-door newspaper-screening curtained-off* then heard from back behind The-Newspaper.

The-Banker peering out asked:

'It is all a Great-Game!'

'No-*real*-risk...then? Serious consequences? Limited-liability? Responsibility? To Your Shareholders?

'Only To Myself. You too?'

The-Banker avoided eye-contact now on ear-piece bartered furtively and openly and loudly and confidently *confidentially flashed* a look across and down into the opened laptop tablet as if commanding from the top of a mysterious money mountain…swapped hand-signals and *punched* the air...*slapped both*-palms together:

'High-fives!: We are in the ten's...six...seven-Billion if you will…' and holding a-hand over the heart openly-palmed, and as sat bowed slightly winked, a single staring- eye, as stooped to conquer:

'Deal!' with *on-screen* confirmation apparently…*re-directing...confirming...* password…and printed-off paper-copy waved-frantically financial-agreement-stipulating:

'Only to be signed-off...' brief-case revealed laptop lapped as reading-off as The-Clerk now speaking:

'But The Markets are shut-down, closed?

'Only to the outside world...details only to be added then...*Complex completio*n…simple really but make I.T. look complex…'

'When the markets open again…The International Conference?'

'Details…Love The Small Things! Anyone can...'

'All 7-billion of US?! One for Every One of US on this Planet...'

'Mutually insured…trust…'

'Mutually Assured Destruction: Hellism!'

'Heavenly! Recovery!'

Recovering, The-Clerk continuing:

'Not The Grand Things...that can only lead to disaster...'

'Buying-up…all the little people? Like you?'

'Not you, not like you…'

'All of us Supermen! And SuperWomen…of course…If we want to be…Shares? People? That is *The Name of the Game...Buying-up and* selling-off?'

'People? Bought-off...as in *slavery*? Servitude?'

'Same...difference... Certitude… New-Slave-Drivers:...*list*:...and over-seers...foreman- and-women...servants, and savants...Certifiable! To the-Buyer...or to the-Seller…That's you…'

'Buyers' market?'

'And the Seller equally…get 'em out of shit borrowing…'

'Equally?'

'Dealt-with. Killed-off...'

'Bought-off? Me?'

'No, not you. For you we have a special arrangement…tell me what you know…or-not? Raw materials in, Goods-out...get me?'

‘What?’

‘Money...*itself*...*The* Information…’

‘You…have?’

‘Shit in...Shit-out...’

‘Prediction? Analysis? Plus or minus...that is all IT is...Deals...regardless of what IT is…’

‘Shit.’ hitting a button-key:

>Deals:list:...Done.> *and with a nod, laterally entrusted, undisputed, and further endorsed over-lengthy client midday luncheon tied-in gifted as* Charity: *by-guilt-association...pending…*

Expense-account accounted-for, and through electronic-signatory: password name and number recognition and as a matter of public-record details:

'No longer negotiable...or ever-were. And only the final - *details* to be added...’

The-Banker:

'Then...’

'Then? Renaging?'

Then:

‘All to-be *ironed*-out today.’ *By the all The-Clerks' of all the-worlds' works?: information-kwiki:..transparent liquid-like, solicited.* Solid as an assignment. Proposal. Proposition. Projected through The *Cloud*...pending *thieving conspiracy that is where the mistrust lies…*

Station-stop pulled-up.

The last one before the-bell was rung for-departure for:

<The-City: Then as a *warning* to anyone last-boarding the train doors’ closed the train-carriage sealed and seated *up-front* aside again facefully faithfully fatefully:

'I don’t know what to make of ‘It’ yet…’ *pause*...pregnant.

Then from The Clerk: 'But I'll *bet* we will find out soon-enough anyway? Don't you?’ the-thought snickered *slightingly* to-self. As if spoken to self then: that *sarcastic* thought, or was it sardonic?

Outlined *out loud* sounded differently. As if someone-else had spoken the words instead. As a gauntlet thrown-down to be picked-up. Only as instantly-*realised* now, and as at the time-of-speaking, and that short-moment-later as-spoken now irritatingly *intimating* only-now at the-*gamble* seemingly already *commit*ted-to.

The *uncertainty* now at such a private yet communally and now seemingly *un*shared shared-venture. This seemingly reasonable, or unreasonably as yet un-priced, as yet only a projected proposal. There would be a price though; and a cost too:

‘Your Price?’

‘Yours?’

‘If The Price is right...Purchase-price and re-sale onward, that’s all you need to know’*...as yet, an un-bidden offer in-prospect.*

To follow-up the seemingly automatically-accepted challenge, as yet to be fully realised:

'O.K.’ as well as the-other, each spoken now and heard, and now seen: ‘No going-back now.’ Both now considering the import of these words, the more thoroughly, thoughtfully, perhaps, than said and heard; those out-spoken, aloud, as to the-*enterprising* enquiry requiring further-reply? In-turns? Or not?

Now the previously *saved* in-memory and as the *first respondent* again The-Clerk ignoring the possibility again of turn-taking, with another supplementary yet elementary question:

'Why?’

‘Why? Who?...is...What?'

‘Me? Now?’

‘Business is not-as-*usual...*’

Puzzlement seconded now by both-speakers triplicated as almost-identically *mindfully* apart...reflected against all The Others' on The Train. In The Train-compartment *visible* through adjoining compartments and conversation and music tinkling and thudding social and financial networking and attempting quietitude eyes closed as if neither further-apart or closer to, as to The-Clerk and The-Banker from each *others'* Truth and in Each-Others' *minds*: and *all this meant what? Exactly? And how soon? How soon, is now? How much is-enough?* And: *How much is at stake here? Exactly?* as instantly both now regretting the opening-given to the exclusion of anyone-else in the carriage. As both-enjoined, as advertently now in a two-way dialogue, of which at that immediate-point there was persisting, yet only limited-*information...*

5.

She worked nights, evenings, day shifts. This week it was the late-day shift; or *the day late!* as some liked to call it. From the ambulance station she arrived at and clocked-on. From where she drove the ambulance, maintenance engineering and assisted at incidents as the *First Aider* but not as a so-called *SuperMedic* like some of the other crews had and she was training now towards:

'Be careful, today' he had said to her 'I love you', and she had replied 'ditto.' a*ccident and emergency crew, trained up in skills and procedures, assessment of injuries, life or death sometimes. Observing vital signs...moving patients safely, onto stretcher or aided walking, checking for any changes. To report to The Qualified Clinician and taking relevant information, from carers, and others at the scene.*

Administering first-aid and supportive emergency medical procedures, transporting people to and from hospital, accident and emergency, the elderly and frail to The-Hospital for check-ups and appointments.

Could be anything: road accident, multiple severe injuries, or just a scratch. Taking notes for the medics, and the insurance, and police, if there had been A Criminal Act.

They would be on the scene-of-the-crime. Alleged. Or the Fire-Service if there had been a fire, or if someone needed cutting out of a car. Rescuing from a roof. You name it. Anything, and everything could happen, and did. Never a dull moment. A good job, a great job, She enjoyed and was paid, well, reasonably well. Not poor. Definitely not rich! More poor it seemed daily recently, what with rising prices...could be a pedestrian, or housebound, head wound, heart attack, to a broken toe-bone.

In a busy shopping centre, or on a country lane. Sick baby and worried parent, or elderly infirm, worried well, or unconcerned brawler wanting to carry the wound back into the bar, to show-off, not realising how much blood was being lost

That's when you needed back-up.

Sometimes a suicide. Under a train, not much you could do them, bag them up and the undertakers take them away, to the morgue. Maybe later just find out the official-cause-of-death: 'crushed' or 'shattered body' and 'body parts...' in the jargon. May have been pushed? On the roof, threatening to jump...

'Go on then!' you always feel like saying:

'If you're going to! I've got children to collect from school!' Before thinking about the possibly seriously painful mess to clear up. For the public, family, not the suicide. Maybe they would kill someone else rather than themselves. Make a public show turn the hurt on themselves, or to be carted off and made safe in prison and their own death eventually...

Once The Bouncy Castle (as they called the safety bag) is set up against the wall, and the suicide gets bored and tired and decides to walk the stairs.

Could be someone fallen down stairs. Beaten-up in their own home. Domestic violence, denying, screaming the odds. Unruly, intractable, recalcitrant, not well-behaved. Not well-mannered. Not biddable, broken-bones, not funny. It would all be reported, had to be. To the Social Care Agency, The Housing Project, The Police. They would press criminal-charges, if necessary. Must do, ought to. Some of the things you see....abuse...self and others...

We pitch-up and patch-up and tell their story as well as our own: witness. Sometimes threatened as well. You had to stand your ground. Emergency blue light, siren wailing. Steering in and out of that traffic, that never seemed to thin out, or even give way sometimes.

Still, that was the job. Worth hanging onto. Going on to take the medic and paramedic exams in our own time; evenings and weekends, and bringing-up the children! Check out the vehicle, like it is a patient; stocked with bandages, medical and life-support equipment. Ventilator and de-fibrillator, stored properly and in good working order. Communication equipment, to the control-room...

Where she had started-out. Learning how to differentiate one emergency from another. Over mobile radio-T.V. Video-link, inside and out the vehicle, and *The patients!*

They would joke...

Heckling themselves, in their shared pain and agony. Checking mileage, speed, safety, on the road, and in situ...clean. New documentation: date, time report charts, name... address if known, distinguishing features...

Check the fuel and oil and water, start up, at the start, and end of each shift...

Driving licence of course, passenger public service classification, different gross weights and bearing gear shifts and light and heavy goods for the larger vehicles used in public events...now, though, the regular chat, only if there was time...

When she got in this morning-shift the morning newspaper, with the Lotto numbers and television and radio pages: *this job you could make more than a TV drama any day of the week. Fiction and drama* she liked *a murder, thriller; or a biography. Not many of them write their own do they?* she thought to herself. *What next? I know: Nothing! or The rest of my life I haven't lived yet!* The accident and emergency department and hospital wings were as quiet as usual first thing in the morning: *there's always time for things to change...she thought...in my life:*

'It always gets busy as soon as I think it's going to be a quiet day!' she called to a colleague, and thought to herself: *turn around and something happens, then it all starts happening! You hardly have time to think until the shift is ended, and no overtime-pay!:*

'When did I last finish on the dot, the bell?' she asked herself rhetorically and then outloud to the others repeated:

'When did I last finish on the dot, the bell!!?' answering herself in response with a thoughtful but blank thought:

'Never!' they all chanted as if they had does this routine before. *Waiting for the first call. That's when it always happened. Commuters driving from home, to work. A van, or lorry, at work, driven recklessly. Someone in a car crash. On the way to work, domestic, accident, or not. On their way to early-morning deliveries. Or to a job...not anyone's fault that they are late for but they blame everyone and put their own as well as everyone else's life at risk...*

As if they are the only ones on the road. Who does not have an appointment to reach?! With fate, and a social duty ahead: Slow Down! You are not the only one! Think Safety! The imperative to keep working too ridiculous, time-set time-frames, shifts.

So She could feed self and family; and others could be fed, and stay alive. Referrals from night-doctors; there was always work waiting anyway. No later than sooner, the first call of the day: the drunks, and *Homeless* who slipped-in and slept in the waiting rooms during the night-shift and had to be moved-on; for the *earlyday shift* to start. *It was not any different today no day ever the same...*

Although the last call out had been a disturbance.

Some missiles thrown, and one person injured, the police were on the scene. When the ambulance crew arrived, the crowd had been moved away the nightshift Ambulance-crew told them all about it when they got back:

The Bank had not opened. A queue, a line had formed outside many metres long and wide, a crowd really. Of staff locked-out, and angry, upset, worried, scared, lackadaisical customers, with people trying to get wages and savings out The Bank was closed:

Until further notice.

There had been a scuffle between two of the waiting customers over an unpaid unwritten loan, and eventually, after others had got embroiled, two or three lay injured.

Someone, bystander, onlooker, passer-by had called an ambulance. Several on-lookers came up to them, as they went to see to the injured customer, or patient-to-be; and the crowd, realising The Bank was not likely to open had dispersed to await the further news. To see if The Bank might open that afternoon.

She was on next call but was not needed. The injuries were only slight, but the scene was ominous, an *omen it seemed for the day. If any real disaster did strike* she often thought *only enough bandages and fuel for the ambulance for a few days, and only if that is rationed from The Start.*

Only enough food at home, the same. The closer to the monthly Big Shop time, the less there was at home. Nothing-left-in-the house'(as they called it: the apartment really...nothing left, at home!) Not stocked up recently, and can hardly afford to go more than for a few days at a time. Sometimes, only one day at a time, for bread and milk, without replenishing need, and staple-goods…basics, nevermind the ordinary luxuries...

Everyone was talking about the crash of The Stock-Markets and the announcement expected at midday:

'We'll have to go to the supermarket tonight!'

She had called after him as he had left; and *he collecting the children later, or she? With certain familial protective panic immediate: after her first shift was done without overtime she would be on second shift later in the day hand-over to the evening-nightshift split-shifts it would have to be: He going to work, or the rally, now? Midday? Finished-by...She collecting The Children?* Suddenly, everything seemed more uncertain. And She really did start to wonder, what this day would bring.

The 'Open for the day' notice pinned on the school-gate re-passed on the way to work, and now brought back to mind*: thank goodness*...had been His immediate response. Although there were mutterings and mumblings about *whether The Teachers and Nursery-Nurses would actually see their pay and pensions this month. How long The Parents would be able to keep on paying for The Basic Education never mind the extra trips and activities equipment for this and that...*at *least The School was open, and The Children did not need collecting until She finished her first-shift and He finished his at The Bakery early evening so that she could return to the Ambulance Station and she start her second split-shift...while he took on The Children again:* 'Don't forget after-school!' the older-one had called after him.

'...half-day today' the school teacher had joked, and laughing together. After sending the text about going to The Rally as The Walker walked not ran toward the school-doors since the teacher was now in-charge, and he settled the younger child into nursery, and out through The School Gate. He met a work-mate going towards *The Works*: *The Factory* as it was known: The Bakery: The Factory-Gate. From the nursery school passed the old religious buildings at the top of the road. Now a Friend and Neighbour from the same Residential Housing Street walking in the opposite direction now shared the journey Home: 'No good going in ...' The other said: 'They've shut The Factory Gates again! Remember last time? Few more out of work, three day week again?'

'I Know only too well! What now? Zero-hours! Work for nothing!'

' The last time, and the time before that! 'It' has happened before!' was the blunt reply without irony. The Other replied:

'Its' Close-down Time for good this time we reckon. There's a meeting midday...'

The Other continued:

'The Factory-gates! We'll find out then!..' and laughing:

'See you there!'

shouted as they passed closed shops and each to their separate homes *laughing* at what they could not be sure *like The Children waving and laughing too, at what they knew not what.*

Awaiting midday afternoon when they would meet up again.

*Or would <u>The Rally</u> finally put pay to all their carefully laid plans for the day? The Children...half-day he remembered...*they had walked back towards their homes.

Passed by other shops, nodded and said : 'Hello' to The Shopkeepers and The Customers standing around inside and outside on The Street as they passed:

'What's going to happen then?' Another called over:

'Nothing!' He called back. Then to The Friendly Neighbour walking alongside:

'*Nothing*...again!'

Then up the stairs to the apartment along the balcony walkway. When he got indoors with the key, shouted:

‘’’llo!’

Only out of habit and out of habit switched on the T.V. and started to clear the breakfast things away. She had already set off for work, with a sandwich and the last of the bread remaining calling after him, and he then thinking: *Did I say I’d bring some bread home?*

She’d said earlier: ‘We need bread!’ laughing: ’ I don’t care if its stolen from work!’

‘ *‘I’ll bring some later anyway, in any case…’*

‘If they’ve got any left over anywhere!’ He had replied, and She then: ‘Don’t lose your job over a loaf of bread!’

*Lucky I got some in yesterday...H*e thought: *or sheer skill remembering what she’d told me before I went to work the same yesterday…and I* didn’t *forget!*

Then, to now: *and now it’s all gone!*

But this time...tomorrow... and as he settled-down with a *last of the bread* toasted-dry sandwich in front of the television to watch events unfold he wondered: *or did I just imagine that?*

*From some other time, yesterday? or at all, anyway...?! Anyway: What does it matter. We need bread...and I’ll get some later...*then mindful *of the midday meeting at work and collecting…no looking after The Children…shopping later at the supermarket* wondering: *what would happen if there was no bread*

No work? No money to pay for the bread, the shopping? The mortgage? worry reserved-not for what would occur anyway...which as yet he did not know for sure, for certain, what would happen today. Only what might occur, *could* not would occur, which was all he could really think about. Existential-angst...comprehension-essential...what should occur? Home, and a sandwich at this very moment…with whatever is left in the bottom of the breadbin and some *half-empty or half-full jar or a tub of something and back to work...*or not. *Before the meeting at midday…collecting The Children…half-day telling her…*reading quickly, scanning the front page of the newspaper paid-for:

STOCK-MARKETS IN CHAOS!

> Today, there is so much owed by so many, that cannot
> even start to be paid-out, or will ever be paid-back.
> This morning the stock-markets are closed. Once
> more world trade has ground a halt.
> All financial currency and credit/loans trading, the trading of
> stocks and shares that in recent times has left prices at
> all high time levels, overnight have collapsed.
> We are in the greatest fiscal and financial crisis ever; and yet
> again.

Sitting at home *no hurry yet* he realised: *get fed first then…again, if or if not before, this time: that he didn't have any cash.*

Only a couple of notes, the cash-card machines would be empty. If The Banks were closed, and there had been panic withdrawing, as well as buying yesterday, there would be none left, and anyway risk going around and topping them up with new notes now wouldn't there? Money riots? Pillaging Smash 'n' Grab! Striking-first!

On-Strike! Lightning! Wildcat! Same thing...something: stoppage looting...on TV already:

Going slowly the armoured security vehicle, bullet-proof cars, dark and light brown, black and silver striped, dusty rumbling over the go slow cobbled pedestrianised street as seen*: shops either side walking down the centre...*the *imagined* seen-crowds *emerged into the square had emptied: Automatic Teller Machine...emptied well before...so simply locked and bared barred empty.*

The security-vehicles will be headed-back or staying in base...keeping all the money for themselves!

Under-Orders no doubt. Police escort definitely; and The Supermarket would not be open anyway. Since most people paid by credit/debit card. There would be shortages already, on the shelves, after one day. They were all virtually 24/7 anyway, everyday of the week, month and year. It would all be gone. Or robbed. Or hoarded. Possibly with violence. No deliveries anymore...they'll be closed. Waiting with all their stock for the prices to rise! He exclaimed to himself. In-image of threatened looting, hundreds, thousands of shoppers stripping the shelves of everything *paying, or not. The Supermarket?*

Could be open tomorrow; if everything was sorted-out by then He wondered *If? And how much would everything cost, once it was all sorted out? With what pay? None? What about the food and everything? Ourselves? Our families? Our Mothers and Brothers…and Sisters…compadres…*

Duty bound, to each other and to Them to their *Stockholders ourselves anyway paid and pensioned-off if we are lucky in and finished work…putting the prices-up! They tell us! To their customers who are US! Trying to keep prices down they say…Price wars? Shopping Wars! or colliding…colluding?*

They themselves…*would have enough to stock at home and then be broke again and if we don't get paid into The Bank and then to The Shops, then what?!* and suddenly he thought less calmly.

He had to get some money from The Bank and The Mortgage had to be paid: *would the mortgage be paid if The Bank was closed? There was some food in the kitchen, and water in the tap. He had a little money. She always had some..usually... so they should be alright for a few days? Perhaps? The Banks had been shut before. Bank Holidays! That's all! It would get sorted out.*

After the enforced holiday...the shops always open the holidays to grab everyone's Cash while The Banks are closed anyway. The Banks are never closed…auto-money that is what it is now…online…go to The Supermarket tomorrow when The-Banks would all no doubt be open again and shelves and cash-machines re-filled like fuel-stops, and cards and online banking re-commence…again:

'After all, they are not going to want to lose business' he said outloud and to himself: 'I get paid so that They get paid and They pay people like me to pay The Prices to pay them back on Credit and so it goes around...everything-costs…' to no-one else there…except the TV screen in the background: *'Basics:staples:fuel and foodstuffs...health and social-care...when markets back in the black...from the red...credit…'* blues and yellows and greens *flashed* across the screen…

On the T.V. more reports from The Stock-Markets around the world. Those that had closed, or opened and then closed immediately: 'The City, the Financial Quarters...are awaiting instruction from Governments and Big Business...and: *The-Market, Street and International Experts to give their expert opinion…*

Minor officials from The Banks and The Governments' made statements to the effect that The Banks were closed today *as if anyone did not know that by* now. Unless they were brain- dead; or living in the middle of the jungle or the desert or on top of a mountain with no electricity, no radio-signal, no fuel for smoke-signals: 'Government officials are meeting to discuss the crisis around The World...' from the TV: 'The statement at midday would calm fears of looting...' *never mind looting that had already happened and was about to kick off again somewhere, maybe even here. Maybe our street, our home...food in the kitchen...water in the tap shut-off through non-payment*...The News continued to come in from around the world and was broadcast simultaneously.

Raw and unedited reports on audio and video from Cities and The Country-sides cataloguing *unfolding* events. The sound and pictures of people meeting, being interviewed. Ready to comment on the announcements and their responses: 'Temporary shelter tents etc. food and water...'

'Women and children are at The Railway Station fleeing...'

'Stock-piling…Food-Riots!'

'Water!...'

'In the dust and debris...' and the like

'In the fields homesteads and out houses...buildings on fire...' suddenly from The-City streets:

'Convoys blocking the way...'

'In some places Race and religious riots as sides taken…' by-*force: Hospital Doctors, and Electrical Engineers; Architects and Builders their work undone gone to help the last emergency emergency-services attacked for trying to save Police or Army casualties and The-Demonstrators!*

It didn't matter who they were. Misunderstood, language, perhaps, uniforms. Phrases, trying to make the situation more understandable, not less: *Any excuse* She thought, then heard:

'Shelling gunfire...fields land-mined...cluster-bombed...'

'Attacking or Defending?' *Attacking obviously* She thought:

'*It is Difficult to Tell...'* from the T.V. *not from here it isn't* she thought *fighting back against Governments, and The World Bank and Global Trade-Markets...as they see it. Necessary as they made themselves seem but it wasn't necessary at all except for themselves and the competition from the people:*

'No Surrender!'

'Freedom and Justice...' all specific and vague:

'World Governments and Big Business and Bank's leaders meeting face-face. Others via satellite links...' *telephones and facsimile machines whirring and humming helicopters buzzed in and out of The Conference site...this next solution was expected by each side or another...not whether, only when.*

Concrete-bollarded blockaded and surrounded by army vehicles in convoy with police protecting the buildings and streets beyond, helicopters landed and took-off:

'At the International Economic Conference...' the most well known and many totally unknown faces exchanged formalities; beckoning each other forward, back, or sideward's *in gestures of Power-Broking and Politicking: not even they know what is going-*

on…what is going-down…they were made to laugh, coyly in public; at comments made amongst each other, shook hands, and slapped-backs:

'Press-Conference and Delegate meetings *bull-dozed*-in...'

'Demonstrators' bull-dozed-out...'

'Behind barricades…'

'The Governments and Banks however cannot agree Privately or Publicly between themselves or each other...yet some developments *will* be made before midday...we are told…to stem uncertainty…violence and…' Lines were drawn, and withdrawn.

Re-drawn and drawn, anew; and still again it seems: 'There are still too many vested interests. That divide, that could not in one or the next session get resolved, yet...'

From The Studio above and below: 'The City Road and Railway Junctions and intersections...' *forked knifed and spooned to The City...seamlessly linked centre taped-off in yellow and black, blue and white, red and black, as through into a crime scene:*

'People coming into The City and towns and even village-centres gathered or emptied, travelling-out, and on motorbike and car. Coach, and Lorry…'

Like a crime scene, they were made out to be: 'The Demonstrators and The Security Forces...so-called…to avoid panic…' *causing panic by the looks…*

Outside, and inside CCTV cameras *reached the boardrooms leaking e-mails toxic enough, high-level Puts and Calls being put-in drop placed:* 'On Present-Index:...' *texting sexting*...unmoving defaults...commission interest-rates and credit-rebate altering payment and re-payment...

The News Broadcast *broadcast*:

'*And we seem to hold Our Collective breath...*To await further announcement:...' Blank screen for a moment, then:

'People arrived to work to join the Meetings and Demonstrations that are already gathering in great numbers at workplaces, towns squares and piazza and village-streets and roads and streets in City Centres...'

'As the whole world protests in Town and City-Square...Shopping-Mall…' and as cinematic as a musical theatre-hall on-line and in front of TV: The President's Face appeared:

'More and more elaborate excuses and blame.'

Conscionable, self and The Other. Not caring for Him! or anyone...anyway. More anger and blame. Self-satisfied, and lying, self-assured lustful delirium reaction:

'The-Crisis...' This Time it was difficult to tell if at the beginning or end or an almost endless sounding speech *perhaps on loop...*The-President looked drawn. But was adamant no-changes or some changes would be made, after the previous offer of limited

change had been ignored and *the speech went on and on, round and round* and faded-out. A TV-Journalist:

'The Presidential Security Forces...'

'The Secular Rebel Fighting Forces…' *as well as ostensibly Religious and with sophisticated Scientific technology...radio and TV press-releases...social-media...weaponry in the crowd:*

'Allied-with?'

'Religion and Science...'

'God help us!'

'Science help us!

'Common-sense! That is all that will Help us! Get us through this!' shouted into the screen. Reports and interviews, speeches, and the chants of gathering crowds.

The claims of Government-Officials, Politicians and Market Experts alike, were supplanted by declarations from people on the ground. From workplace meetings and city centre assemblies and world-wide television networks. In some places there was the sound of police sirens, and at others the rumble of water-cannon and Army Tanks and of Police Truncheons beating on Protective Shields as some shots rang-out from the partisan rooftops…

On the TV screen *blurred* and *faded*. On the rapidly re-booted Smart-phone *add-on* screen wi-fi: the T.V. picture *froze*...the personal phone-book quickly suddenly and unexpectedly emptied: Error message 303: *Invalid connection...connection closed...*

6.

All likewise: The Banker and The Clerk momentarily inadvertently, and actually advertorially making eye-contact: *flash*-framed each-other and through the closed shared-window as in bright- rainbow and sky-coloured mirrored; as through each of-themselves *enraptured* recklessly perhaps to be wrecked or saved as overcrossing The Estuary Bridge unnoticed perhaps by anyone-else in the carriage. *Uncared* if-noticed-or-not by anyone *else* at-all. Now each *in each others Thrall*:

'Connected?...'

'You too? Same. Diversification...*Innovation*...that is all what is needed...'

'Un-charted territory...'

'New-*product*?'

'Better? Or staples...'

'Doesn't much matter *what* It is...'

'As long as IT sells...'

'New functions...New markets...'

'New algorithm?'

'You?'

'Me?'

'You?'

'Both...' anyway-horizontally and vertically to the same outside-world moved-past *moving*-past and through, oppositely and thus as inevitably differently *viewed.* As if replicated refreshingly really...*relishing* as then focused-away both to the outside-world as indifferently similarly perhaps yet *inevitably* differently: from The Estuary-Town now staring beyond and both towards the as yet unseen rapidly oncoming *City:* 'Through-the-roof! Fell! Off The Bridge! There are the already *drowned* Hung from the-Bridge? Mental!'

'If You can *Getaway* with It!'

'Again!'

'The same! Again?!' *crafted* frozen legend on-screen: *names* and places...times, and as instantaneously:

'Meteoric!' *collisioning, folding downwards, and inward full-fell brown green mud-sliding and earth-quaking...shaking bursting volcanic red-flaming...livid:* 'Once-lived! Will Live! Again! Experimental! Always! Innovation...That's what make it exciting...Every Time! Each season brings...'

'Experimental? Food Health and Social-Care...'

'Education as ever! Like Religion...Science...'

'Farming?'

'Pharming?'

'Harming?'

'No!' *uncertainly* to: 'Phishing?'

'Do no harm...'

'Unless *harm* done to? Who?'

'Do harm in return? Where does it end? First-Principles...An Act of Trust! Not mistrust fixed in Advance. So, who wins?'

'We do.'

'Not all of us.'

'No, not all of us...'

'Fair-shares?'

'Not...'

'You and Me...perhaps?'

'Perhaps not…Maybe...did you hear the one about the starving Clerk who stole a chicken to feed the family? A stranger asked to share the chicken The Clerk asked: 'Who are you?' The Stranger answered 'I am God! Trust in me!' The Clerk said: 'Why should I? As you are unfair in life and do not share I have had to steal for me and my family to live...What have you done for me and my family?' The Clerk asked: 'What have *we* done to you to let us starve?'

'Another Stranger appeared and asks to share the chicken. The Clerk asks again: 'Who are you?' The Stranger says 'I am Death. The Clerk says: 'Sit down…as we shall all eventually starve and we shall all die…you are fair on all of us...sit down and eat! Fair shares, then?'

'Only when you're dead?!'

'Exactly…What is-*normal then*? Eh? Eh? Who is-*normal*, eh? You? Your Company:-*Plant*? Eh? Keeping the company-line? I was here first before You sat down...'

'Government-Officer? That's 'It' isn't it? Doing the-Governments' work: The-Peoples work! In The Tax-Office? Government-corridors? Got the ear?'

'Pigs' ear!'

'Sows. So? The purse? The purse-strings you mean?'

'In a barrel of our-own making...' *each stock and commodity and bonded share price passed...each sell-by date outdated...*

'Crashed!'

'Train? Blown-up? People killed?!'

'Yes, I know..' remembering as lower and lower price-marker losses move across electronic-boards against rows of banked fan-tail desktop screen-closing: listing: acronymical and apocryphal-foreign and unpronounceable...or home-grown, and familiar on-screen pictured read-off:

'Governments...'

'And *their* Peoples...'

'All falling into the same *raging*-pit...'

'The same *pithy* core of being...' that evening previously with prices continuously rising steadily being-bought and-sold *relentlessly* on-commission and on The-Management-*fee* taken already as socially contracted, suddenly, stilled:

'Taken each time on-inflated prospect...'

'*Deflating*-prospect now...that is all...de-valuing-with c*onfidence*-undone...' looking down and into a blank screen: with *realisation*-rising dropped in free-*fall:*

'Unprecedented rises...'

'Then: stagnation?'

'Now collapsing initiating unmitigated-disaster...'

'To the initiated: just another Day's Trading...' *strange, and unknown incantation of Capitation announced and de-capitation pronounced thereof: disproportionate-response record:*

'The Body Politik-Religiously hanging-on: The Scientific-Economic *split*: Price and cost that is all it is...'

'All you need to worry about…'

'All *we* all need to worry about…Who is going top make the...

'Profit...'

'Loss?'

'Exactly.' *simple as that announced with comparable lamentable-loss...laconic, iconic, as compared to a nano-second earlier, and no sooner or later than:*

'Timing...'

'Mis-timing?'

'Is no-timing...as Today...'

'Too-*late?'*

'Now! Immediate-closure. There, and Then...' *e*-photo taken:

'No warning-signs?' *and at that-place...as in each and every other Big-City-Exchange. In their own-time and place there was for a-change in the stifled stilled emptiness: an assumed and peculiar, and utter quiescence of now religious tragic almost comical, theatrical proportions. The Patronising*-secular promise: pictured: an unpromising condescending candescent screen-saver stilted stilled as on paper-writ:

Markets closed.

crumpled as some witticism *baiting* as some as yet *unrealised*-victim:

'Ignored.'

'By Greed! Blown-*up in your face*? Out of all proportion! What-for? Knocked-down *traitorous villainous UnHeroic Martyrdom*!' Dead. On-track, now *toward where dealers in-Global-commodities: wheat and gold, diamonds and cocoa, coffee and tea, corn and rice-fuels and rare-metals and mineral markets...frozen screened re-heated*:

'On *false*-Figures?'

'Official! False figures!'

'Or-*True*?'

'Accounted for?'

'Divide and rule?'

'How do you know?'

'Exactly! Not on your life! Fraudulent! Corruption is what keeps this whole caboodle going!'

'Traceable? Buys and Sells? Bought and sold...that's all...'

'All?'

'How about a share in the-*recovery*, then?'

'How's about *fair* shares then? 50/50?'

'One-to-One. Don't tell everyone!'

'Zero-sum? No chance...Time, and Money! Work, and then Pay! For Play!' looking-up into the eyes of the original protagonist now turned antagonist:

'*Nothing* is for Nothing.'

The-Banker, looking down into the screen of a half-opened briefcase then speaking into the blind yet not-deaf-space between them:

'If You don't...someone else will.'

Marshalling-prowess, and the-dark-arts horse-back ridden, risen over grass-roots green-shoots...actioning:

'Dark-*Mountain Project...*' mystifyingly undermining, transition-culture *collapsanomical...Drilling-down: optimism projected...against pessimism resurgent emotional climate-changing-inevitability...muddled spiritual-debate: of confident-faith-boosting happy gamma-decoding brainwaves...into abstract-reasoning memory...re-locating...after any event has passed pasted into-history:...acted-out as previously run-backwards before a backdrop of multiple-window screen-graphics: a patchy grey-hazing jagged-green shining outward sprouted trailblazing digital-numerically downward, taken-root.*

Re-routed, deeply-inside and on carbon black luminous background: pixilating-light screen black and white to-red-simmering onto a dark slate heat-light dotted...cooling-off warming pastel yellow grey cloud-softening over mountain and hillside and as The-City skyline re-imagined, as Logo:

'Markets closed.'

ridden-towards as at the start of *a brand new-day*.

The-Clerk asking now:

'So. How did 'We' get into this mess?'

'What mess?'

'This cycle of indebtedness again?

'This dis-*array*!' into the out of cloud screen device:

'Fast-Action...Slow- motion...saw It-coming?'

'Pile-up. Hit the buffers. Off-the-rails...'

'Slow-motion wreck...'

'Train-wreck?'

'This *little*-Turbulence...' The-Banker perhaps unexpectedly uncompromising, in response to the- Clerks' questioning:

'Wrecking-ball!'

Recovering, The-Banker:

‘There is a Market-Situation known as Demand and Supply…where if a company doesn't have enough shares in stock to distribute and sell...then this increases the price for these as a result...and this is known as a Bull-market...’

'And this is what we have?'

'Or perhaps had...’

‘Or perhaps a Dragon-market now...anyway...'

'A Tiger-market?'

'A growling Jaguar squawking screeching-Macaw-monkey market if you like!'

'A Liger! A Tion?’

‘A Lie-ter fire’

‘Bonfire?’

‘Of The Vanities! ‘It’ doesn't matter what you call 'It'’

‘The bigger picture...thinking outside the-box...’

‘The-Cage?'

‘Bigger picture box….’

‘This is..a moving film?’

Outside The Train-*carriage*...momentarily looked blankly thought and spoke the-Banker:

'If you like. The *reverse*-situation...'

'What? Supply...then Demand?' *Not getting the reverse-irony. From the pen-ultimately closing under a bridge continuing out the other end of the tunnel*:

'A *Bear*-market?'

'This is when there is an increase in sellers...'

'I know *that* too...'

'...and a fall-in...buyers...'

'For stocks...*and* shares?'

'Money...mostly.'

'Cash? Whose?'

'Yours?'

'Mine?'

Bluntly:

'Everybody's'*...savings, pension's, investment, salaries...and wages, day-rates...*

'This is now what we now have...'

'Risk?'

'Of course, that's what makes it exciting...'

'Responsibility?'

'That's what makes It boring! leave that To God!'

'Shared?'

'The International-Banks, and Economic-Zones, Governments and Corporations...it is a Global market!'

'Shared?'

'Now the bottom has fallen out of It.'

From the-Banker, a printed-card handed over with writing seen: **The Rational Equitable:** *Economic. Effective. Efficient*. Nothing else:

'The three-E's?'

'How about Easy?'

'Nice and Easy? You think this is *Easy* too?' *as if practiced before:*

'Rational...or Equitable?'

'Equitable versus Rational...'

'Rational versus Equitable...'

'Equitable or...'

The-Clerk considering...taking and reading <u>*The-Card*</u> noted online: *hearing:*

'You would take My=Debts…'

'No-debts, as such, you see? You? Owing...Others?'

'Of course...they would not be My-Debts otherwise...Credit-driven...Bought-up. See? Cheaply…' *falling*-in...gradually...

'Given <u>The-Remit</u> on-interest made...re-paid…and the cash-funds to draw-back on…' *free-running now.*

On all cylinders The-Banker let loose, re-covering, on the tracks next-steps: 'The Stock-Market prices although always at some point in the past...' *minimal seconded, in the seconds this will take* interrupted*:*

'Last night?'

'The-City?'

'Remains-high...'

'The Others?' *collapsed completely ready as spring chickens...*

'Buy *them* up? You got IT!'

'No, you got it.' *as the previous evening passed into-night and into this day* for The-Banker:

'From First-impact!' *trading instantly as a body collapsed. In the moment between open and closed...' fortunes- made...retained:*

'Cheaply are Fortunes-lost...'

'On paper...'

'On screen...' looking down:

'Virtual only! In that brief second It takes between The Opening...'

'The-Closure...' *the final roll of coins landing face-or tail-up* across...

The screened-Globe lit-up in letters and numbers:

'Without the *liquid* monetary-assets to pay, or re-pay, to cash-in...'

'For the *Asset*s to be bought-off...'

'What assets?'

'*Whole-Corporations...'*

'*B*rought-down!'

'Governments...even? Change the Name. New account. easy. To be sold-on....'

'With non-*existent* credit?'

'All Put's made must Stay-on! Stalled!'

'Precisely! Business as Usual! *Virtually...*'

'Only! Nothing is moving...' as if behind a paper curtain hidden, heard, *anger*:

'Except us...we are moving-in...*currency* currently…'

'And con-currently worthless in name…'

'But shares are not worth the value of the product...'

'*Virtual*-Money?'

'Of course!'

'Relative to others?'

'Not of-themselves *toxic...*'

'But *toxic* of whatever *noxious*-currency they are being bought and sold-for!'

'Exactly.'

'Or-*not*, as the case may be.'

'Nuclear!'

'Exactly!'

'Not Negotiable, shall we say?'

‘And the-goods?’

‘The-property of whoever has bought or been sold-out… unpropertied!’

‘As moneyed shares of the goods in the first place. Except now...’

‘Restructured...’

‘Out of the Box?’

‘Closed down? Locked-up? Out of work?’

‘ Take a Holiday? Stoppage? take your money abroad…’

‘Homeless? Worth *nothing* hardly...’ *Home-circle...going around...*

‘On Everything: The-Stocks and The-Goods...’

‘Got to get them moving...’

‘And the only way to do that?’

Looking-out of the window. Across oil-field pipeline, gravel-pitted hillsides, concrete cement-based conveyer-belt-brick-buildings smoke-stacked flues...venting:

'Buy?’

‘Shares?’

'They cannot sell! They have nothing!'

'Except to us!'

'We have…them?'

'By the balls…or tits if you prefer…'

'Knock-down?'

'How far?'

'Exactly!'

'Exactly, what?'

'With wider and wider differential-*ratings...leverage...*'

Deliberately looking again, forward through the window, directing the gaze:

'Between one-place and another...'

'Between one day and the-next...'

'Each milli-second…'

Looking out the window:

'Until this day...'

'When The-*Bear* laid-down?'

'Or clawed Its way back?'

'The-Bull! Goosing! Taken to the air...or whatever....

'Crash landed!' and any other animal-analogy thought-of *statuesque yet misrepresented, the otherwise rapidly turning-numbers turned-off and unrevealing shot-down drowned-out surfaced exploded in slow-motion...in-pieces*:

'Shot-down!' market-marker board, and screen-seen pictured, mobile-camera photographed: on the train-travelling from where The Worlds' Stock-Markets' early-day trading had, or would have already begun. With the hammering of ancient cast-metal a brazen-gong, as if heard. A knotted-tied rope-pulled a whistle and an air-horn, an electronic *buzzer* air-vibration-*releas*ed…warning-signal…

Red light. Black, as the night, yellow-red, to blue-green, as to the light of day. As when the field or factory-hooter: blasted pale pastel-*yellow* rising over the horizon. As at the-beginning, and then again the closing-of Business-Trading. The-previous-day, where-ever it was, trading-constantly throughout the world, around the globe, and then as with each evening. following-on, to the final-days' trade, and the next unstarted:

'*Final*-Trade?'

'What? Last-night?'

'Was it correct? Or not? What was the last thing you bought, that you could afford outright? A loaf of bread? A Home? Pension scheme or Insurance? Health, and...accidental-insurance...premium-protection nothing but…'

'Connection-back…'

'No-accident, this...'

'This first second accident?'

'Of many throughout history. Only when, where and who gets it worst…and can buy their way out.'

The-Clerk and most of the carriage back in business social-media newsbreaks and checking-account screen: clicking :

<Account(s)?*...closing...instantly* closed-down...

>Credit? *Advanced?*

<Profit? *in*…T1:T2…T3?

The-Banker:

'Commission...Aces-in-their-Places!'

'Done-deal?!'

'Almost...'

<Profit-*margins*..? Bonus! *Stays*...Stay-Put. Until they are Put. Again..?

'All this is now in the-past...'

'In the *Future?*'

‘Exactly. Now. So, now it doesn’t *matter*, see? Ker-ching! Blinging!' behind the scenes. Stabilising...then immediately back onto the Dealing-room floor...

'Leveraging core-competencies...'

'Play for-today?'

'Pay for today?!’

Back to The-Train-trolley-bought coffee and tea delivered paid-for to the table between:

'Well. Here’s the Deal...’unquestioning intention anymore:

'Further-loans at fixed-*assured* rates...’

‘Assured?’

‘To re-finance the debt?'

'What debt?’

‘Your debt: cover possible-*loss*es...’

‘Surely?'

'Insurance? Compensation-cover...'

'Guaranteed?’

'Never. Never use that word!’

‘What?’

'Surety of Inter-Bank *inter-governmental...*'

'Compensation?

'R*ate*-fixing?'

'The International Conference?'

'Fixing-interest and exchange rates will take care of that. A declaration.'

'Expected today. Midday... or...thereabouts...'

Re-called. Stepped-up...and in, again:

'I know *that* too!'

'At some lower fiscal rate agreed?'

'Or not? Zero?'

'Almost...'

'Yes. I know that! To stabilise major global-currencies, and...'

'Exchange-rates?'

'Higher?'

'And lower...You got it!'

'No, You got It.'

'At the same time, if *You got it, They got you...*'

'And if They cannot agree?'

'Globally?'

The-Banker looking-up sharply and out of the window as if there were nothing there. Where farms and factory-buildings, homes and retail-parks *flash*ed-by. Held. The-Clerk, as if sub-claused again, now.

Left out-in-the-cold. The- Sun *warming* the hillside outside shouldered out of the window reflection...moving-on. Attempting, open-jawed to fill the *void*...but no words came out.

Dry-mouthed, and with an intangible uncertainty, unfamiliar-*anxiety*, both, yet no so obviously one to the other, and again, anyway retorting to The-Bankers' incomplete statement, and asking again:

'...and if they cannot agree?' *paused.*

'Which they must Do! They will!' *only...not even thought about:*

'They will?'

'Their will, of course they must!'

'Otherwise?'

'We will prevail!' photo-shopped elastic-banded *sprung-back* missiles blasted into hoards of hired-mourners:

'Do not-*mourn...'*

'For What I never *had?' massed-crowds, gazing at a passing poster advertisement* Both:

'Stock-market, super-market, Hyper-Global markers, at points and places...'

'Gone. Bull…and Bear-drowned...'

'Making up the-odds?'

'In money?'

'Some may-not return from this?' *everyday shopping? Going to the cinema, theatre...*

'Bull-fight?'

'Bear-pit...'

'Fish out of water...'

'In the soup.'

'Some adapt...'

'Some do not.'

'There is the fight...and then it is over. Then, there is the *mental* fight...'

'Real or imagined?'

'The written word is a lie, so the silver screen too...'

'Depends. Reality one step, one-second away…'

'Repeated over and over in-*detail makes reality*? A lie?'

'Changing the-story...does not *bear*-witness…'

'Ohhh Bullish!'

'Only the-*Truth*!'

'*The* Truth will prevail...'

'Our Turf…Justice will-*prevail*...no-matter how *unlike*ly...' driven, as being still: waiting for things to happen. Re-action. Response. Consequences. Action. Unprepared. Prepared. Predictable: Unpredictable:

'Price-war...'

'Trade-war?'

'Averting disaster that is what The Conference is about...'

'By creating the conditions for...Disaster again!'

'Of the profits only?'

'And the losses...OK! Profit from Losses! You got It! Patent on Profit then:...patience…' *available worldwide, from shared-academy-styled: research:...*

'Payback time!'

>@>The Big-Banks…Royal-Houses…

<National and Private, International: Global Companies...

<The-Government...*so-called…*

>'The People in-Corporated'...in the background...foreground: *pulling the strings issuing-suggestions: modelling modest debt-reminders...*

<Cash-flow cut-off threats...

> If-necessary…

<Sanctions?

>Bargain-Basement Trade-agreement's:...

<Proportionate...fair…

>Not war then yet?

<War is never fair…

'You got your Trade-Ins?'

'Trade-ins?'

<Kill or get killed...<

>For what?<

<Food? For-Fuel-flow cut-off...subsidy...tax...<

>Call It what you will...<

<<It< gets more-*serious*...now...<

>Trade-*stop*page? Food-shortages, and water, how about that?!<

<Sanctions? Embargo? For what? Medical-supplies?<

>Bandages, yes could say that...Boots and Bandages...<

<Sticking-plaster...*skin-colour...caste:*

>Staples: food and water...<

<We are now *The-Yeast* you may say?<

>For a stable *healthy*-economy...again...<

>Whose?<

<Ours! Your<s and mine!<

>Sliced Social-Stability?<

<Purely-Financial-agreements...

>On the sly sky-line...*glanced, surreptitiously or openly simply-unchallenged...*

'That is down to The Others...'

'The Others?'

'Politicians. Buy? Or Sell? Boom! **BOOM!!**'

'...and **Bust**...'

'And **BOOM!!** Again!'

'Until it's time to go:...'

'**Bust!** again...'

'You?'

''It' is all about when you get-in and when you get-out...' in the background now:

'Natural-selection...'

'Buyers' or Sellers' market?'

'Depends, if you are a Buyer, or a Seller! Natural *de-*selection...' *for later-life: health and retirement from all this fucking work, for leisure...me...*

'Family?'

'Could be...'

'Family-farm or something? As a small-Business...*flourishing*?'

M*ocking:*

'Seriously?'

The-Banker accordingly *affordably, breaking-out of the cyclical-contortion, if for nothing-else in-particular, except attempting-testily an explanation of:*

'The 'Periodic-crises of social-Capitalism...'

'Collapse of Coca-Cola Communism…'

'Into *pure*-Capitalism…'

'Failure of secular both…'

'For religion…ideological faith and currency movements like troop movements…'

'Not yet as lethal yet but nearly…been *there* before…insurgence and retreat…'

'Of investment-banking...true everyday...peaceful mostly…relatively…within limits…'

'From where you start out…'

'So It seems...'

'It *seems...*'

'It is only having that Competitive-Edge....'

'Naturally.' *Naturally:*

'Naturally-fixed!'

'The customary re-normalising-*writ...' to be re-presented. Of what may be implied...not in Real-terms...*

'Unrealistic? Then...In *Monetary*-terms...'

'And that which will decide the-Day…I see it in you. You're a Natural!'

A bit too sarcastically, or was it ironical, or even:

'To be honest...'

'And otherwise?'

'To be honest...'

'You mean you haven't been up'til now?'

'Too honest, perhaps?'

'Who?'

'All of us?'

'Or none. Everything I say is false...you think?'

'Never mind…'

'Only if True?'

‘Eh?’

‘False? Only natural! Lyin’ and a-cheatin’...’

‘Human-Nature...’

‘Credited with *Animal*-Spirits…’ *self-recognised, self-fulfilling in the glow of a naturalistic-fallaciously held-privately...and publicly-renewed admiration*:

'We prepare for 'It.’

Meeting head-on:

‘Scheduled-in!’

'On what?’

‘*C*ommodities. This Stock-Market...debacle!’

‘Do you? Or could you have been? Prepared for this?’

‘No. Only in the correct place, at the correct time, with the correct amount of risk to...’

‘As in preparations for a failed-harvest? Software-crash? That’s it? Isn’t it?! Cover-up?! Conspiracy? You want Me to fix...’

‘The-hardware, replaced every eighteen...months, and going-down...monthly weekly daily..faster and *faster*...no-one notices...until the final second...’

‘What is that game you have there? WarFare4?’

'Prices war...Trade-war! WarFair4! Everytime!' *hit the target:*

'Battles Bullets and Bandages...'

'The Trading-Game...'

'All! Going down unless we catch IT!'

'Jobs and mortgages...homes and raw-*mart-erials*…food-supplies…'

'And savings...going-*down...*'

'What savings?! Family...is a business? L*ivelihood...Loans?...*and-**Home**? Credit?'

'Taken…'

'And the Credit-Debit *loyalty*-card?'

'And the pay-day shark loans and debts that go with…and so, what are the rest of us supposed to prepare-for? To be starved into submission like subservient pariah's? To be homeless? So, mortgaged. Credit/Debit card, or cards...'

'Own anything else? Shop-cards? Loyalty-cards?'

'You? Serving on the Board. Of several different...boards...Family? Executive, non-executive, you get me?'

'So. Down to trust again...*they* only want you to *owe*-them…'

'They? How many? Not only Rational or Equitable then? Irrational-inequitable more like...'

'As I say: The top five or six 'let 'em ins' globally trading in any sector…'

'The Banks? Investment houses?'

'We do not-*own* them with our investments…They owe us!' *with shares, and insurances, dropped- out now...floatation?*

'Cheap? Of course...To Big to Fail...The-Bank's:... do not want you to own them, they want you sink paying-off whatever It is for eternity...though...*bail-out* that is all they want...Bankrupt!'

'You? Bankrupt?'

'Of course! We are all bankrupt! Except the Banks won't let their money go…private-equity or Government!'

'Always owing and being owed, that is what makes us wealthy! You? Your debts? Your taxes, eh? Owed? Your Flat-screen TV? What about *that* gadget? Bought, or borrowed? Vehicle? Any other Property? Loans? Shares, and stocks? Insurance? Stock-up, each week?'

'What do *You* want to *know* that, for?'

'Advance? What You owe? Already? Plus? Business-Credit?'

'What?!' *to any cross-trading traffic immediately curtailing blue-green cross-trades parallel and crossing-tracks passed rattled and rolled-over passenger and freight-lines like ships in the-perhaps moonlit-dark starlit-passing that previous night*:

'Serial-Creditor? Debtor? Personal-Credit?'

'Your own Executive? Non-executive? What? Trading-partners? Margins-called...breaking-point...

'Braking-point?'

'Broking-point in and out of...' *timing...*

'Tipping-point...'

'Credit for raw-materials…For-goods and salaried services…*profits ploughed back in*…or lost?' and silenced, skulked, sunk, and lights turned-out. Screens left-on referenced:

'Markets-closed?'

The-Clerk, to the-Banker:

'Final-Trade? Close of play?'

'Time to Pay...'

The-Clerk:

'Time to Play...'

7.

The-Clerk now moving around tapping toes and hand mumbling to-self, or to the screen-talking unawares, into the earpiece-microphone replaced-lead: *talking to someone?*

Talking to Who? Listening to what? Is that, singing-along? To what song?

‘What-*game? Watching The-Game*?’

Watched-in window-manifestation: *manufactured on-line news-updated...*

The-Banker puzzled at The-Clerk head-down, no-further eye-balling body-contact and The-Banker *shuddered* at the *thought* of The-Clerk maybe getting ahead of The-*Game*:

'LoL’

'Ha-ha.'

'There, You have got it!’

'No, You have got it!'

‘What? The ball? the-outfield?’

‘The umpires whistle?’

‘Managing the game! Calling time...’

‘Time-out! Foul?!'

'Out-the-Park! Past The NN Metre-line!'

Dropping-down, the eyes, leaned slightly forward, looking into keenly:

<Enquire-upon…@...from the *Market-place*…

>Pricing…guidance…mortgage/rent…pay…skills C.V….fixed…fixing...overheads…Capital-amount: Your-Balance-sheet:…

>>Credit...plus/*minus*...Debit...*indebted*...to:...Bank of You:...*opening...*

<Capital-*assets*: list...*to sell-off...then*...to cover the Owed amounts: to: *lists*...out-goings...*that must be-paid...*

>Owed? By Who? When? Why?

<Need-*cash*?

>I know...because the-debt you *started*-with is the-one you're stuck-with...

<Live-*value*?

>May as well be...*already worth more, or less than one-second ago…not only increasing the-debt…but decreasing the chances...of-recovery...as the-likelihood probability, of that-debt ever being paid-off…*

<***Rational-Equitable:***...*forcing Your Currency to be devalued...*

>Which means?

<You get less-for-more: for-example:…when you spend your currency abroad on-Your-*Imports* to *You*...then Your-*Exports* are priced-high to Others' Exports to You...as to *yourself* named:...*list*:...imports that you need, are expensive, to you…

>Too expensive? Only what I need....

<Nevermind the-*Luxuries*...You *cannot afford them*...You *need: items:* ...*Basics list*...Your-Imports:...Nn...pay-off...that You need to pay-off:..Food and health...Your Loans: *outlist*...and Your Bank-overdraft...N/nnn...and buying the things you need to stock-up…Your shares worth:...

>Too expensive!…Nn...

<***Home!*** *Call...*

>Dead of night...*portable...sold-on...*

<Daylight robbery!...

>Loaning money to buy...*loading...*

<Losing-money...

>Your Bank?

<Casino!

>Pensions...insurances...

<Loans to pay-off loans...*mugged out cold then...*

>Break The Bank:...*then...*

<Currencies? Selling?:Yes/N0?:...

>Y! Cash-account...in The Bank...

<Cashed-in...*then:*

>Bust! Uncashable...

<Here maybe...*abroad...*

>The Value changed higher or lower? Why would I do that unless I was going on-holiday!

>Where? Get IT! On Holiday!@:? Exports/Imports: n/N not-N/n...

<Bonds? Travellers-cheques…*devalued* as other currency: Currency-Exchange against yours …N/nnn...*printing more currency?*

>Government-bonds?

>Other:…Quantitively-*easing*…*like printing money...*

<Inflationary? And *Devaluing-Other*! Yours…*buying:... privately owned government bonds/debts unlimited agreement for government to write-off...Done:...*

>Debts: Nn...*default with Dignity?*

<Defeat, with valour! Devalues yours against them…*in monetary-terms…*

>So the monetary value of the currency against *Others currency...*

<So I want to trade for currency alone?

>What do you want to trade-currency for? Currency? Y/N:...

<Y. >Currency-zone…Others-Banks:...reducing: N...n...Exports:...Importing...for currency and the goods and services currency buys...*this is different from and more-important than the actual goods' value.<*

>Currency *list*...GoTo:...

<The-Bank's:...list:...

>For Goods? Stocks? The-currency? Money?

<To pay-off the loan-debt-credit...

>On-paper? *Printing? Where?*

On-screen: **The Rational-Equitable**...*The Real-World*:

<Shares...*getting-there*...of the self-worth wealth...against...

>*Supersubs*:...Euro/Dollar/Yuan-*mindi*/Sterling-*silver*/Gold-Rand/new-Ruble/new-Dinar/convertible-Peso's/ Rea and Rupee...: *forbearance* of your...A-Z:...

Looking-up: The-Clerk:

'Zombie? Me?'...servicing-debt choking-off further lending be-heading, clean-cut ripping out the guts...in front of boggling-eyes...as they used to do...bartering? What? Nothing but money...numbers up and down every second...except now...except now...now:

<Settle All currency in *One deal*? *The next Big Thing*...OK....*rates*-available: *list...as above, or below, other short to long-term deposits may be made*...Savings:... Credit...in the-Bank *All* to be:...made...

>Lending-for *investment at a reasonable-return or simply-fore-going...foreigning...feigning..before fore-closing...*

The cash-till action:

'Going-down! Sinking-ship?!'

'Whole Nation-States! Titanic! In for The-Rescue!'

The-Banker held onto the newspaper, brief-cased opened screen.

Sat back, where had been leaning-forward, in some kind of *reverie*.

Looked-over, and stared the-Clerk directly in the eyes and between and around the other less-experienced in the ways of the world. Shiny-suited silver-grey not-dull-charcoal burnt-out only just glowing red.

The Banker: a sharp-suited dull charcoal-grey blue-flecked power-dresser rotund in-parts like a tailors' dummy sharp-suited, three-dimensional 4G strung-out as a puppet *as to the Invisible-Puppeteer* staged-and sound-designed as self-seen: *motivated moving synchronous photographic phonographic pornographic form...textured breathed-in...and breathed-out...flavoured movably moved: recruited:*

<**The Rational-Equitable:***...hostaged to fortune...exchanged:..loans....*

>Access Denied...

Terror-transformer: with Fear and Anger: revolt revulsion propelling political economic and media-pundit expert-citizen...per-citizen...

The-Clerk clicked looking-down, not into anguish or fear, but deprecation, with depreciation:

<**The Rational-Equitable:** password enter:*******:

<Test:letter/no./symbol/complexinthemix: *******

>Basics required...*restricted...password*:********...*simplified independent advice-orphans...*

<Charging-model: fair/unfair depending on:...

<Specific one-off advice (charged to offshoot company):*...inherit pension-portfolio managed-fees...no-Personal or Corporation-Tax if registered with:...*

>Fixed-retainer or percentage-fee? Y/N?: Y...for *larger-*amounts*...press:...*

<Less transaction-fee-deal*...through home and small-business and personal-credit...*

On-screen bundled-up again: obliterating...traceable credit and...mortgages and un-paid-loans...

<Swapping-loans/debts....send-to*: confidential....done:...*

>Food?...Water?...Air?...

<Evenly spread? Across Your Life...Lives? How many do You *wish* to Buy?:*list:...debt:...*

>Everyone's?

<Only Yours*...available at this time:...*

>Objective-*selfishism*?

<Does not-*compute...suicide? Self-murder? Does...Objective selfishness...Subjective unselfishness...unselfish Subjectivism...unselfish Objectivism...computing all possibilities: now: computing...>*

>The-Market: lists...of *lists...uploading..*

<*Market-Trades:**R/e:**?*

as elsewhere:

>*Deleting...*

The-Banker taken aback. Beneath-what were actually Gold-Gilt Bold CAPITAL-type caption-topping, and a clearly no longer tumultuous Stock-Market recalled. The-Banker gradually and all too quickly, and suddenly and readily now recalling: implicitly getting-now, the pitiful irony of the newspaper headline:

WORLD MARKETS IN TURMOIL!

and the photograph below. Taken, without permission *who would be-asked? For permissions?*

To the-Banker, now again, forcibly revealed, for the first-time by The-Clerk, *perhaps, notoriously, not only into short-term memory, but now also into The Newspapers' open-consciousness as of this morning awakening as in a pent-up fury, raging invoked from the vestige of the evening-prior*:

'A Phoenix, to rise out of the ashes...' speech-bubbled, spoken outloud. *Trimmed-wings* is what the-Clerk thought:

'Business-as-usual?'

Both looking out of the still moving-window:

'Business-as-usual:...

‘There is to be a Declaration this morning...’

'By midday...’

'Inter-National Meantime...’

'This-will stabilise the-markets…’

'At some-lower-rate...’

‘Others' automatically-*Higher...*’

'And, and that is the-thing! What 'We' will do is simply re-align currencies....’ The-Clerk interrupted, as if boring into the brain of the other. As if to satisfy some lust, or inbuilt hidden hatred unavoidable, as both, even as an idle- interlocutor:

‘You got it!’

'No, You got it!’

‘And start all-over again...’

‘At a lower-point?’

‘You give me the-nod on prices of one thing and another...and I will Do the Rest, get me?’

‘Financially speaking?’

‘Functionally-speaking…Now then, those debts, who they with?'

'*Errr…*'

'**The Rational-Equitable**?'

'Factionally, fictionally speaking…'

'O.K. **Right Here, Right Now! True!**' *as issuing some oratory declarative without clue of real-implication:* 'Anti Collateral-damage? Un-intentional consequences...so…' *like unusually honest politicians yet unaware of their truth, only that made up by others, themselves: ready to be barracked. Self-deprecating and yet, as anyone appreciating of themselves deceiving of-themselves implied depreciation of The-Other. Felt, believed. With the opportunity presented: as an explanation of the rise to glorification yet also thereby pre-emptive fall from grace albeit temporarily, and for this journey only:*

'C*urrency-account*?'

'As in *Current* circumstances...Business-charges…'

'As simplicity Itself…and with which 'It' will all be resolved today...'

'You? Banker? Politician? Of course! The warnings given...'

'Taken. Too-late. For that.'

'Warnings? Unheeded?'

'Unstoppable! After the event!' and *that* Front-page! That nevertheless now could only now be seen from The-Clerks' supposed and *likely derisive, and probably gloating, satirical perspective.*

Once the side-panels rapidly absorbed concerning the latest sports and business-media celebrity-star photo of stage and screen religiously-inoculated to:

'Keep up with The-Markets...'

'Keep up with the...'

'Other?' *through theft, and violence, on TV. The other 1% fiscal-psychopathic.*

In a consumer-hazed blazing marketing-characteristically: gentle/capitalism/rough/communism fluctuating gently and roughly in colour *as loan- sharks encircling the flotation-tank gas-chamber propitious-publicity canaries in cages...*

Of the photogenic IN-crowd the IT-crowd, and for the crowd of passengers generally-un-attainable. Unobtainable, and therefore to be utterly-loathed, or loved, in equal/ unequal measure. Perhaps, as well as envied for their art or wealth, or both, and thus taken a part-of.

For The-Banker: m*ost alarming of all, the guileless, seemingly-misguided Trusted bought The-Newspaper-Owner: Media-Magnate one of the five or six Globally...now with the even more incongruously and mischief-making paradox-inducing intent of a supposed-ally turned enemy?*

Anyway, not-yet, anyway: The Newspaper Tycoon-Proprietor: The Media-Mogul Magnate: Oligarch empirical pseudo-Economist. Fine old art wheeler-dealer and owner. With-whom Golf and Gold may have been shared-interests and at least a singularly badly-shared literary-joke: 'This is not charity! laughing together. Not laughing together:

'With influence...' *still marking cards, making-detergent soap, or string-balls. Media-Empire, whatever it was it mattered not.*

Although betrayal was. Betrayer, betraying even spiteful little-threat, whenever not-making-out. At the end of the day: when push-comes-to-shove, no-one is or ever was your-Ally. Not even, your best friend, not even your-family bailed-out, bailing-out from this false-accounting phone-tapping mess from Power*: Wealth corruption and lies...rate-setting, premium payment protection racket.*

Perhaps before anyone had rumbled...tumbled-in, could have at least perhaps seen it coming. Could-have, perhaps should-have, acted with even-handed propriety, perhaps? Got away with Murder! Acting, with assumed-impunity and as-usual uneven impropriety summonsed-up and convinced and therefore convicted in- their absence-of-wit...

The- Editorial Traitors!

The Public: Closing-in. Closing-in...

'Closed-them down! I would!' *and closed-down the print-run down and deliberately stopped the newspaper and the train-company from delivering...*

'For-Free!'

Then:

'No more Hand-outs?!' *let slip:*

'No more Bail-out's!' *back-handers re-cycling...*

'By and who For?' *super-power hotelier? Medical-expenses? Children's school? College? University? Food? A roof? A mobile media-centre:*

'Media social-communications...*suppliers...and re-tailors...'*

'The-Works...'

'The-Works?'

'International Times...Unfinished business...The Conference...what *They* will do...is...*simply* re-align currencies...'

'Will They?'

'Incontestably...Stabilise the-Global-markets at some lower-point and carry-on...' *everything will start moving...Again. No longer Universal finger games, but on paper...*

On-screens...The Clerk and The Banker both, looking-up:

'Buy or sell?'

'Simple...Buy? I suppose?'

'With what?'

'Money. If you've got it Eh? If you've got it?'

'Flaunt-it!'

'At **The Rational...Equitable!:** That is what we do not do!'

'*Naturally*…Alright?'

'Maybe you did not think CEO-Banker and President: *acting in their own self-interest* could be so…so…'

'So mean...So-selfish? Think they rule! Think that They are The-Gods...that made All the Living-Creatures!! So un-caring! That is not-what I would do. I would have watched the next one coming-along...The Next One to grab at the opportunity...To knock 'em-OutaCourt! I have got IT! That is all IT is...beat the competition…'

'*Naturally*...by co-operating in mutual self-interest?'

'Only partly…you get me? Never 50/50 either…'

'Zero-sum game? For both of us?'

'100-0 maybe…'

As if on automatic:

'Algorithm? The numbers? Frozen.'

'Names?'

'Pish!' Only following Rational-Equitable orders...as dropping-bomb on an unseen civilian-population:...

Looking through The Screen*: hostaged as distanced from...the thought...*the-pictures: destroying ancient ruins, bomb-crater *border-convoy approaching*:

'So...Stupid!

'*Damn*-lies...'

'Repeated endlessly…'

'Statistics…and...'

'Weather-reports…as unpredictable as each-other.'

'Without analysis.'

'See that is it…that is what You work with.'

An uncomfortable pause. For the-Clerk affronted, and taken. As-for-the-Banker:

'Not just, the-*Money*...you know?'

'I know.'

'But whatever stock and goods and services information you have…or think you have? Get my drift? And there is a lot of IT?'

'And it has to be the *correct*-information?'

'Got-it! At last!'

'The-Truth?'

'Truth?!'

'*Ethical?*'

'*Moral?*'

'Legitimate?'

'Even?'

'Of-course!'

'Even-handedness?'

'Rational? Regulatory...'

'At least...*Reasonable*...Equitable?'

'Not! On the *open*-information market…'course not…'

'Believe-it...Or not. What do you believe?'

'Not this…'

'Believe what you like! *Soft-news*...Hard-News?' *to charm, and almost-paralysed with fear...mis-placed awe, or not:*

'Does anyone else know this? Who has the-vote? Democrats?'

'Republican? Monarch? President? Dictator? CEO?'

'For a term? For good! With all these little-Big secrets…'

'Corruption and fraud…'

'Fixing only the exchange-rates!'

'Bought. Preaching to fix The Popular Vote by fear and *vanity!* And they know it! Crime-rates? Crime-rites? Rights? Am I right? Only reasonably equitably ethically morally legitimately-*hypocritical*...then?'

Head-phoned sarcastically scornfully-mordant:

'Only Natural, of course!'

'Saying your prayers, again, surely?'

'Wait until after prayers?'

'Of-course!'

'In the rough!'

'In the trough.'

'Out of bounds?!' *Prying...*

The-Clerk looked-up: on-screen:

'Serious numbers!'

'I don't usually ask twice…Do You want to take-a cut-in the Recovery, eh?'

'Cannot lose?'

'Be in on the next **Boom!!** Basic commodities and Rare *Metal*s?'

'Food and Furniture?'

'There is more:...Oil and Gas…under them there rocks...passed-generations...to use-up...'

'Generating? Energy?'

'Uranium? Plutonium…'

'*Polonium*...Industrial: *or* Military-use…'

'Business? To be *had*?'

'Keep IT *down*...mining-minerals from The Earth…'

'From Space? Eh?'

Satellites and Solar-panels perhaps? Who knows? Exciting-*possibilities*...and we do not think we have to be persuaded. Do you know what I mean? Just a simple 'Yes' is all 'We' need.'

'Who? Is 'We'?'

'For a *comfortable*-Peace?'

'Piece? Of What?!'@*Never...say: Never'*

Never...say: Never!'!'

'*What*?"

'Why-not?'

'Uncomfortable with War, then?'

'This is War!?'

'Is it? Why would you not w*ant* Peace?'

'Like we had before *this*? Cannot have *the*-same-again...'

'Everytime...is different?'

'Of-course.'

'Virtually…preserved…'

'By Madness!'

'Mutually Assisted Destruction assured!?'

'Insured?'

'You think you are? No? Your…' *breaking-point...snapped!...broken, into-pieces...the-Whole-Thing…collapsed...whether-designed to or not-to...*

'With Catastrophic-damage...'

'For some...'

Ignored:

'Not-All. See?'

'Cannot-be? Again?'

'Yet.

'Now.''

Suburban-edges, trimmed-hedges, overgrown woods, and peeling whitewash walls. Compound three or four-storied building alongside creosoted-fences before the graffiti-walled enclosed-ditch between poplar and ash-growing pastures, unharvested-fields. By the railway-track…*looking*-out:

'Business as Usual?'

'So...Stupid! Damn-lies...'

'Repeated endlessly…'

'Until now...it was all going so well...'

'Ostrich! Head in the sand...'

‘Ostracised Ostrich? So you knew?'

'What?! In the water? Slash?...’ *of course, understood, of didn’t understand into the paradoxical waters nonetheless:*

‘Boarding-Statistics…and...Harvest!’

‘Surfing *weather-reports…’*

‘Only as reliable as The Day before...’

‘Yesterday? The Same, some minor difference towards rain or shine...but...’

‘Stalled stilled…’

‘Stopped! Crashed! Collapsed! Yes! As unpredictable as each-other?’

‘What? Rain or Shine?’

‘Without proper-*analysis*...See that is it…*that* is what You have to work with...If You are not The Red Barbarian at the gate!’

‘You are The Big Green Giant? Hulk?! The-Executive bored...President-Monarch-Ruler…Party?’

‘Too.’

Turned away, and down into the-screen: playing the-Game:

<Media *Bluey*-Meanie...

<Magical-Mystery Tour…

>Alright. Don<t be-*stupid...*<

<If you like...<Insexts…The-Beatles?

>A-Soldier? Worker? Part-time Police and *thief?*

Declaiming:

<We all are. Expedient. Pragmatic...

>Fair? brick-*Bat*! *seen...*

<Building: Home:...

>***Home***: *Government-Corporation<s:...listing*:...

<The International-Conference: *insider-information:...*

>***The*** **Rational-Equitable:**...

<Done-dealing…

The Others' computer-case closed. Inadvertantly showing: *no-connection…*

'Closed?'

'Never! Stops! Could not-stop ourselves, could we? It...was just...too-Good...'

'To be-True!'

'The-Truth? The Game...'

'The Game-Over. Now. Enviably too-Big to Fail...' *too small to survive? Familiarly...Socially?:*

'Including *hoax*-loan's and *overdraft*-agreed:...*heard:*

'The-*Gambler* bets on what they *think* may happen...

'That Others *do not know...'*

'Are not *meant* to know?'

'Customer's? Share-holder's? The-People? Are not meant to know. That is why this is now between You...*hush-hush...clandestine...covert...*

'Playing-the-tables...' *broken-into:...a* finger over the mouth, glaring eyeballs:

'There are only individuals and families...' and with an *air of fulfilled destiny*, then:

'To not tell....'

'And The Conference?'

'And all the Chairs and Tables of that G*20*! 'We' are the 21's...getting *in-early...*'

'This century?'

'Today!'

‘Today!...Now!’ *peering into the day rising out of* The Screen*:*

‘Politics of Envy…You too? *envied all the same...*

‘Only arguably...too Big and too-*Bad* to Fail...’

‘Only winning-bids now...’ *assuming-absolution: The Lion-roars! When it gets Hungry! Roaming signal...lost:again…*

‘These *Loans*...then? You agreed them, didn’t you? Signed for them?’ o*nline...re-connecting...*eventually all other parts of the Ancient-land and Lands beyond the Oceans seen as yet from:

>‘**Rational-Equitable**...’ clicked into:

<To: Credit:...

>Store’s... and Stock’s...Good’s...and Service’s? Logistics...Wheat and Weapons’ facilities’ silos and runways…

<Military...*radio*-equipment...*opening*...Battleships? Tanks? Soldiers? *Non*-lethal...*supporting...Humanitarian...*

>No-Fly-zone:...*destroying the whole armaments' industries...Nations...*connecting...*connected…*

<Aircraft?: Tourism? Business-class. Freight? Military?

>Military?

<Weapons?

>Holiday Time!

Until things get back to normal, better, improve, not get-worse…answerphone-on...Inter-Phone...Out of Office assistant: not taking-calls…

Both. One *deleting:...emptying...:...*

The Other: *connected...re...disconnected...re-directing...*

<>Desktop: *we are sorry that you are not-able to...your connection has not worked properly...*go- online to find a solution to this problem?:y/n:?OK?: Y/N. *yes/no*?

<No? Yes?...*we are sorry that you are not-able to connect at this time...your connection has not worked properly...*

>I cannot get online to fix-this…

<Go- online to fix this problem…fixing?*...click.*

Double-click...fixed: *fixing...*

>Factional…*fictional…almost...*

<*Executive...non-Executive director...The Board of Directors...*

>*Protracted*-Capital...

<Value/Risk: N/n...deposit/investment covered.

>Utilising-maximum...

<Capital-*profit:...after* *Tax:...revenue-dividends:* *engineering and on top of that: economic infrastructure risk-cheated public-private sharing between...*

>Country to Country *place and people to people populations and actual-goods and buildings' routes and ways: visionary: To establish perpetual-growth in-proportion to inheritance and wealth earned... and taken disproportionately:*

<*Steel-girders and glass...*

Laughing, to self...

>Railway-Tracks and Engines! Steel! The Future!*...bringing out the past from sand and rock, water and wind and gas and oil...fractious...*

<For-Wealth!<

>And Health?<

<Health and Social-Security:...< *pragmatic-ideologue!*

Ethno-linguistically, gender and ability driven, strategic-falsely promoted tactics, using history:

<*Social*-Security? *Beat them down!* No-business operates on *Real*-Economy terms *you must know that?!*

>And...Education! *not-wanting to Lose: any of it on-Fiscal-Security...*

<Rather than on simply *Pure-*Monetary-Terms:...*doesn't matter what on?*

Not a Bit.

>Goods? Services?

<The-Banks? Real-markets? NN/nn:...

>Prices!: *Price-compare:...*

<Prices-War...

>Costs and Benefits:...

<Cost-Price war:...

>Shop for Armaments? *Cost-Price war:...*

<Weapons?

>Clash-of-Countries...

<Nation-States…Empires...Civilisations...Theocratic…

>As in Good vs. Evil?

<Evil vs. Good? Democratic? *Defined by their currencies…social-genocide...seeking:off-line…in-line…online:…*

>Business-centre: *Vanity*-Project:..*soaring!:*

<Name: **The Rational Equitable**: *Home:...*

>Your-**Business-Centre**:...

<*Vanity-project!*

>*The-Town named after You. The currency named after Your Town, Your-City...*

<**Equitable-Town**:...

>*Currency:...opening...*: Rational-City: O.K?: *Rational-Equitables*: **R/e**:'s...out by the airport appearance prompted by-*clicking*:

<Building-*materials:* Food Furniture…Media?

>…and Luxuries:... item's…including: Your Business-centre:…the-Bank of You...how many floors? (give a number up to 100) and a number-given:...

<Nnn…

The-Clerk entered another number, by speaking, saying the number word, flashed on-screen and clicked:

<Nnnn...Loan?:Nnnn...Agreed…*dropped-in in a shower of coinage and paper-notes and* The-Banker *photo-caricature cut-and-pasted from unnoticed camera :...*

>Application's…*behind re-enforced protective-glass walls silver rain fluttering down the screens now...*

At the-Top Floor...

On the Top of ***<u>The Rational Equitable</u>*** *building:* of The World: *from the inside...*

The-Banker *as a vanity aviator avatar* sat behind a-*mahogany*-varnished desk:-table showered with gold and silver spouting from and falling all over *realtime* The World-Map: *carpeted shades of black and white-light-brown and yellow and green deep blue seas and ocean cloud above and beneath a blazing orange obliging rising black Sun.*

Looking-out, and in, onto and through-out *modernist* strangely-angled sheet-light colour-stained glass and plastic-panel see-through from ceiling to floor. Looking-out over, a bustling ancient market-place of *fruit and vegetables and livestock trading-outposts and stalls set-out with what could be paid-for...only without that which could not physically be brought-to market, due to bulk-mass, type and value...on screen: in-Transit, still in-the-ground.*

On-the-ground somewhere elsewhere, and never to reach here at all but boarded-out in letters and numbers in full transparency...hidden, or chalked-up and under-the cast *wrought*-iron frame and steel-blue counterpanes...

<Plastics:...*oily sulphurous plutonium-golden-patterned sheet-topped shop counters...tables...gambling-houses...*

>Gambling-Shops and Casino-Resorts...*and public drinking-houses...entertainment...*

<Media-crackdown...full-size sports screened...

>Shopping-Malls:...keeping the people content…most anyway…

<Food-Hall and Health-Centres:...Leisure and Media:...

Places of barter and banter *and betting...*on-Goods lain-in…*laid-in and on and over the lay-of-the-land: laid-down planned-over panning-out...from:*

The-Town and...Urban-centre Market-Place: with courthouse and balanced scales held aloft: over the...vegetable and fruits of The Earth livestock Market-Place:

The-City: *Vanity-Avatar:-stepped-out through the window.*

Stepped-into an exterior elevator descending glazed window-wall fitted gated cage: to the underground basement car-park......

<Nnn...*floors down:...*

>*Extraordinarily:* exorbitantly expensive-vehicle from *list*: The-Full Range: Vehicle?: List:...*chosen:* ***V*8****:...*

<Done:...

>Done.

<**Home;**...*furniture including radio TV and all digital and analogue devises media and games:...*

>**V*8** *selected...and clicked-on the self-owned now advertorial-character inside seated persuading cheated into-gears... out-driving...transmission-automatic:*

<*On The Game*: pad console buttons and switches *screeching-away between walls, and ramps skidding-around to a...*

>Halt!

Then around-and-out between buildings street-by-street through layer upon layer blocks of buildings *ancient*...and New!: *speed-camera!...watch-out!:*

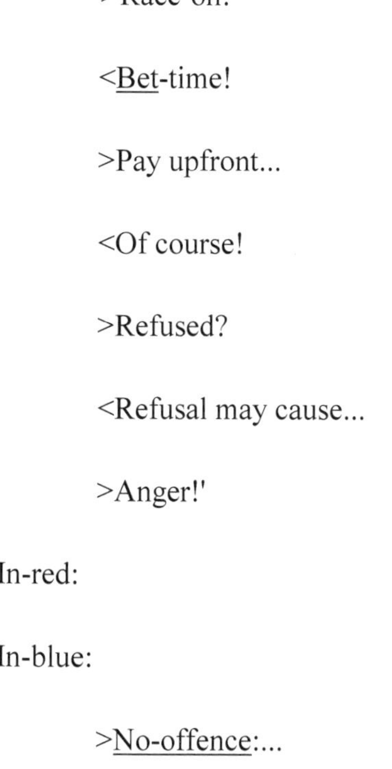

>Race-on!

<Bet-time!

>Pay upfront...

<Of course!

>Refused?

<Refusal may cause...

>Anger!'

In-red:

In-blue:

>No-offence:...

<Get out of prison! Free!

>That's It! Go on the offensive! *Credit-Time! Best-time!*

<***GO!*** What for?! *hitting:*

>Buying...targets:*...and adding-to all along the way captured on-screen:...railway bridged underpass, river-banks and Estuary-Tunnel: through to the other-side, turning, turned, and cliff-edged overlooking: water!* screeched *braked* and spun-around again, hitting a key on the steering-wheel:...

>To: Tax: *breaks*...building for The City:...

<Never-*neglect* the-Defences:...

>Doing The Laundry?!

<Cleaning-up?

>The-Cleaner?

<Washing-up?

>Where did you get that from?

<Lik a Gangsta Mafia Triad-Jakuzi family...

>Us? *You got it...without the violence...*

<Not. Only...If You want to bring in rich-investors...

>Hunger-Games *fear...*Sell? Investment-in?

<Yourself!

>Washed-up?

<oN THE BEACh?

>blEAK?

<Simply:...*as the visible natural agricultural- industrial complex, and countryside-landscape, naturally evolving-to...and from the...Coast. Down-river to The-City edges...of Fielded Forest and Hill and Mountain...*

<This Time!...*and at the Great-river lake, and scenic Continental-Oceanic map: f*rom the cliff-topped taking-off over the water and turning far out inland again.

Alongside fields and irrigation-ditch to land-afloat...on swampland draining sea river estuary-basin...

On-board spinnaker wind-sail yahting...thn out-again on the water onto peninsular-sea...*mapping... loading...waiting...on the accelerometer:* Motor speed-boat with increasing speed...

Plummeted plunged and sunk submerged submarined to avoid various-objects imperilled-on and in-the-water implying shark infested-waters...and blubberous Whale, mackerel and cod sardine shell-fished...*until there were no-fish left:*

>Analysis:...

<Scientific-research: showing...*done erased trial raised-surfacing and water-ski-ing wet-suited clad with the stark graphic image:*

>Is that the...**R\E** logo…*taking-off gliding with wind-surfing balloon opening-up, and rising into the upper-atmosphere looking down over a country-town tour aloft over-looking casually and without due regard then straightening-up…ready…*re-turning towards The-City-airport:...

<Executive-transformation *performing:* Helicopter-view…

H-Landing-*perfectly* exactly on the H of the-now ready built:

>Business-centre: *roof-top's stretched out to the urban and suburban distance. In-between the factories and office-blocks beyond as far as the eye could see.*

<*Real*-estate:...*beneficial*-owner: N/nnnnnnnnn... *in the clear-air…*commentary-spoken continued through head-phones...text/spoken:...Choose?: -text spoken...*click's made over a ragged landing over field's...and Farm...in:*

<*Your*-0wn...

>Home:...

<Businesses:...owned:...

>HomeBaseCentre: The-City:...

<Your-Bank: *the circuitous roads now heavy with cars lorries buses and coaches mechanised streets*

Populated with identikit people of almost every personality-type and head and shape of every ethnic-race and apparent-creed and ideogram mixed:

>*Buildings: list*:...factory-farms:...

<*Dot.Comms...media-mogul...*

>*Food:*

<*As long as there has been and is and there will be...*

>Food:... *and furniture and household-goods and materials for making...on the back of cart's and truck's, lorries and coaches and cars on concrete self-builig motorways container-juggernauts into-and-out of Village, Town, and to and from each and:* The-City.

Across and from sea and land, awaiting at-dockside and harbour fishing-vessels, ships and supervised- controlled Hyper-tanker and from the high-seas and Ocean waiting-off shore Sea-Port passed the coastal and inland estuary river:

<The-City:...*list:...already* built-up: outskirts, and back to, in *lights*: ***The Rational-Equitable*** tower building-up through river-way-lined embankment, canal and railway-track...

Up, and along evermore and faster, building-checking *maintaining*- control by-braking...gradually, spinning on a too-rapid action: onto the next...*above from satellite-dish solar-panelled beaming in below*:

>Country and Countries: list:...*in the-Cloud...the lofty City-streets and buildings now transformed from bricks and mortar...pie-chart...*

<Projected-costs (blue) and Projected-earnings (yellow): Business-plan (Green): Balance-sheet (red/black): *on screen like towers-building...tumbling, and dropping, and re-built once more, only to fall...*

>You are within The Red-Zone...*straying into:*

<The Blue-Zone and you are out-in-the-open...*heard...fuzzy found-footage...in blocks and relief red and black with green thread's and lines like the real hills beyond and blue, beyond the columns and row's...*with a bright yellow sun in a bright blue sky, bright-clouds:

>Green-Zone...

<Not-*so... grey yet...red blue blackening...*

Sun-orange yellow...best advertising colour, get happy!:

>The-City: The-Town: *and countryside...*

Village...and hamlet-Token-Credits taken the place of the buildings and roadways black and tan green and yellow fields and trees digitally-transferring between and across spread-sheet and unbalance-sheet number and text-wrapped boxed and charting...

Graphics-mapping...*where landscape and livestock...outside and inside...and on the single wall flat-screen backed room:*

<**The Rational-Equitable Building:** *O.K. You are Trading: Private Limited Company: Trading under the name:...*

>The Rational-Equitable? Or Rational-equitable?...

<***The Rational Equitable***: *password:* ********:...*******: *correct...OK...*Rational-Actor classic: acting to: *maximise personal over The-Others' economic-return-on:...*

>*Investment: Your*-Budget for The-Day:YYYY/MM/D/T:HH/mm...sec...

On-screen: with Real-Time information The-World *updates:...*

<Real-time and Game-play-currency *setting-up...*

>Money and Goods:...

<Cheat!: money first:excess-charged on timely-exchange...

>Cheating *predatory loan shark payday unjust-loan bubble economic-power to legitimise political-power...*

<Interest-ceiling against unfair lending special fee from local council State-owned People-owned The Banks' private lending market with exorbitant-charges shareholder-customer relationship open market pricing mechanism... royalty-bondage... debt-slavery and capital-adventurer:unequal quantity and quality agreed equally...

<Go! *sharing in the commerce of profit and risk of loss, equity stake, for services provided, administration fee's, time and effort, of each party, equally to the effort and time or however calculating non-recourse racecourse interest...*

<Life: One! *Buy*-Money...

>Y: Yes! *Budgeting:...*

<Not-budging...*as long as there is enough demand to meet supply, or is it the other-way-around?*

>Game!

<Play! *chremisthetic means of exchange not unworked for profit or frugality sobriety deferred consumption of savings: stocks, and shares...*

>When to stop-and-start…

<In-Game again and out of The-Game: games…millions of them:…

>At what node? *What meeting-point?*

Page Up, Page down, side and right and left cursor call, balling joystick socket and leveraging:

<**The Real Economy**:...*of The People: historic mills and factories and shops and fields:*

>***The Rational-Equitable*** *economies...*

<Generating deal-flow...*Philanthropies*

>Cost<Price *benefit...through-flow...*

River-Bridge:

<Benefit?

>Product-Loyalty...*long-term not short term...lower/higher risk factors:...*

<Different-Offers: N/n...N/n...

>Built-in obsolescence...

<Buy all over again...

>When IT goes wrong!

<Corporations...

>Oligopolies...

<A few...selling the same product!

> *Virtually?* None!

<That is alright then...Monopoly!

>Competition exists to create Monopoly...

<Over The Competition...

>Mortgaged to the hilt!

<Enough to take technological as well as financial advantage...*emerging...*

>Advance? For how long?

<How long does IT last?

>Forever?

<Never…and a day…

>One-Season-Technology...*only made to be kept for so long, before the next model...*

>*Pharma-farming...seed-modelling...*

<Between one and two years...

>Eighteen months...

<One year...Monthly?

>Weekly...

<Daily?

>Today!

<One-Day *only...to start with...and decreasing...*

>Now! Dot-Comms:Mobile-phones...*laptop tablet protonic [personal egonomical] computing...*

<Power! Need Power?

>Get IT?!

<*Constant* innovation...change…news…

>Necessary or not?

<True or not…

>Ever?

<Never…

>Healthy peaceful relatively for most...

<Society?

>Most the time, maybe...Health and Social Care...

<The Rise and Fall of the Markets...

>The next bubble...

<In a heartbeat...

>Everything has to be used-up...and burst Bang!

<To be grown and sold-up again...*at a frantic pace...*

>To eliminate the competition...

<Seek monopoly use? Deny-others...

>Conglomerate:...interest-groups...*5 or 6...*

<Like continents?

>Lifestyle branding bubble down to the socks…

<Asset Credit over-heating…boiling-point…

>Aggro! Aggressive-Marketing...violence?

<Already in there:...Civil-War...Religious-war...

>Set the prices....High as you like...fuel the crisis...

<Arm the allies' enemies' enemies fuelling the allies...

<Low, now. Low as you like: Price-Crashed Oil and Gas!

>What now? No choice…no jobs…

<Snap them up cheaply!

>Precisely...

<Or close them down...*still familiarity bores, and brings on the new; and not a bad thing for the detachment from real life. Politics and religion, economics and technology, protecting civilians and providing food and furniture of life...to make this, their country, safe. You would think it would be*:

<To make OUR Country Great again! Make US Great again!

>Our People?! Safe again first...<

<Calculating risk:...<

>Safe at Home...*in our own homes...*<

<And abroad?<

>What?<

<Peace at home?<

> War abroad...<

<Peace abroad?<

>War at Home...

<War on Want:...

>Need?...

'Hired!'

'Hierocracy!' hypocrisy, theocracy appeasing the so-called Gods as money *breeds contempt and hatred*...with pictures and reports in and from city and town squares there:

'The World as All?'

'As One! Rebel Sell!' shouted into the air as another news broadcast, started-up clicked-over on auto-tune expert :

'State Capital! Banks capped...' concurrent with economic growth to safeguard momentum real and nominal *(numbers added to purchasing power with inflation) stopping The Train as impossible however necessary runaway to save the Hero tied to the tracks, or the whole train...*

As a swinging seesaw in 3d with ever more elaborate mechanism to balance, or cheat applied with shorter and less transparency:...

<Investment...*sale of profit insurance contract deferring use of funds as percentage of principal paid back...*

>Overnight holding-rates...

<Fixed...< *broad quantity theory:...*

>Interest and inflation-balance:...

<De-valuation of The Currency...

>Against Others...

<Inflationary?

>Likely...or stagnation...*administrative difficulties only to be overcome between highs and lows...between...wages and prices:*

<Monetary goals: want more rather than less...full-employment...self-employed...*always something to be done...*

>De-valuation of The Currency? Quantitive-...

<Easy! *Structural*-demand and supply... *avoiding frictional-mismatch between choices...between employment and unemployment. What choice is there? Wages and prices at the shops. Payday loan?:...*

>For?

<A Home of your own...Country...colonies..communes...

>Of-Communes?

<Unemployed-*poverty for* insurance and social-*benefit...*

>Cost-benefit price stability... *dealing with conflicting interests across...*

>Investments?: *(bets) taken-out on accredited interest rates: Evens/Odds...*

<Red-time...

>Blue! You Beaut!

<*You-Bet!*

>N to one: *in Real-time flashed-up*:

<Time:YYYY/MM/D/Mx60…sx60…12:00 midday… minus...NNnnnn…counting-down...or –up:... *whoever, what way you came at it midday, from the past, from the- future...*

<So set-out your bargaining-counters:…

>Quality! Bargaining-chips...Nnnn…*Gold!*

<You?*...set-out yours!*

>What Taxman? Taxes?*...scares them-off...compensation of laborious Transaction-Costs and Logistics-facilities...*

As if without-prompting, without voting...

<Tax-Revenue*...for hospitals and schools, roads, and all that...social stuff: bribes...*

<Make The World a better place?

>Make? What?:...safer?

<Babies? Product-Loyalty...

>Different-Others?

<Different-Offers...

>Built-in Obsolescence...

<Buy all Over again?! When IT goes wrong!

>Corporations...Oligopolies...

<A few selling the same product!

>Virtually! Competition exists to create Monopoly!

<Over competition?

>Mortgaged to the hilt!

<Enough to take technological advantage...*emerging...*

>Bought-Out ! Advance?

<For how long? How long does IT last? Forever?

>And a day.

<One-Season-Technology...*only made to be kept for so long, before the next model...*

Pharma-farming seed-model...

<Between one and two years...

>Eighteen months...One year...

<Monthly?

>To start with...and decreasing...

<Monthly...Weekly? Daily? Today!

>Now!

<Or never! Every-second-count...

>How can you make..?'

<Now!

>Dot-Comms?

<Mobile-phone...laptop tablet protonic [personal ergonomical] *computing...*

>Power! Need Power-*up*! Get IT!

<Constant-*innovation...*

>Get-IT!

<Necessary or not?

>Healthy, peaceful, relatively, for most...

<Society?

>Most the time, maybe...

<The Rise and Fall of the Markets...

>Everything has to be used-up...

<Blown-up?

>To be grown and sold-up again...*at a frantic pace...*

<To eliminate the competition.

>Seek monopoly with or from the competition?

<Ourselves! Themselves! *Aggressive*-marketing...

>Set the prices....

<High as you like...*low, now. Low as you like, as you find them...*

>Snap them up!

<Precisely...Still...*familiarity bores and brings on the new; and not a bad thing for the detachment from real life.*

>Scientific: *Politics and Religion, Economics and Technology*: *protecting civilians and providing the food and furniture of life...*

<To make this, their country, safe!

>You'd think it would be...

<Politics tries to disprove: The Other...>

>By killing?>

<If necessary...>

>Necessarily...>

<Religion doesn't need to...with *Faith* alone...*The Other?* only to show how gullible *uncertain, and how manipulated adherents can be...*

Credulous susceptibility made of the truth...swallowing...for bread and water ransomed...or tortured and killed....made a gruesome example of:

>To make Me! OUR Country Great again!>

<Our People?

>Safe again *first...*

<Calculating risk:...

>Safe at Home...*in our own homes...*

<And Abroad?

<What?

>Peace at Home? War Abroad?

<Peace Abroad? War at Home?

Arrived at another station-stop usually straight-through stopping.

From Everywhere where more people boarded.

Each to their devices unaware of the growing crisis before

Lo wi-fi:

<Now!...

8.

Great Journeys of Discovery... *completed...continue?*:Y/NY. 3?Y/N?Y......from the so-called *Dark-Ages to the so-called Enlightenment...*

<To the Space-Age:...*denomination of Credits neutral one-to-one...amount?:* Nnnnnnnnn...

>Your password?:********:

<Again: YyyyXxxx:Nnnn...Xxxx…double-*encrypting...loading…first-re-colonising where only non-humans lived, joining others and almost destroying. Although that patently not possible as roundly shown in figures and statistics throughout The Ages settling...backward compatible:*

On-screen. Buttons and levers pressed hand-held and pulled and push-pull for *imposing by simple-pressure:*

<Force Attack!: aggressive-marketing Now!

>Economic Religious and Political power…*false? Atomic organic plant life…animal...and-virus…*

<Power?

>One cancel out the Other? Game-*change*r...

<Brain-*attack!:*

>Without Religions and Politics we would be Nothing!

<Exactly. Without *Money* We would be-*Nothing*!

<Without-Taxes...*something*?

>With Taxes, tithes and offerings...

<To appease The Gods?

>The Public! Consumer and maker...

<Government-Tax Joker!

<Infinite-Jester....*either way. Red-line. Game-changer:*

>Pressure on all-points...

<For Military-Action?

>*Humanitarian-*Aid?

<Sure...

>'Not!' *heard headphoned*:

<Action!

>Regime-Change!

<T*hat is what it is all about? Totalitarian militaristic Regime-Change for some other-Dictatorship of the-Proletariat as for yourselves...*

>*You know who you are!*

<*Arbitrary-power...The Excluded-Middle...*

>**The-Power:** *The Ruling-Class...*

<Family:...families...classes of people...poverty *exploiting...not-arbitrary journalistic-reporting:...*

Head above the parapet...

'Arrested and dis-enfranchised...' inside, fear and loathing, as well as:

'Love for the Cause!'

'Which is?'

'*Everyone-else like* me...' *keeping clear, anonymous or else:*

'Super-powers...the rest?'

'The rest don't matter...'

'Oh, they do.' *for the purpose of The Global Economy wars...without boundaries, across borders...*

'And within?'

'Great Journeys of Love of course...'

'Civil, as well as Global...' *wars...competitive tax-regimes...tax-burden...accounts...pattern-books arranged inheritance:*

'Patented...' *for internal and international fraud...tax-relief? And burden on others...The People:...sectarian-split to be utilised...*

'Bail-out?'

'The-Banks? IT *was* <u>The-Banks</u>…'

'*Was* the-ABC...Zee…'

' In any language...'

'Not-now...then...'

>Zero-Competition...conformity of rate-bonding...conveniency...>

<Neutrally stated...nicely-done...>

>Me?>

<No. Yes, well...> *The-Banks then defraud the-Government...*

>So IT>s The-Government?>

>Us? You? Us? The-Banks> *defraud* the people...

<Their own people!>

>Don't we *know* it! Now Government...frauding or de-frauding...frauding again...>

<Are they? Dark...secrets...>

>War-crime? Crimes-against-*humanity*..

Chemical bio nerve gas-factory sites facilities on-screen:

'Besieged!'

'Where? Here?'

'The Train?!'

'The City!'

'Genoa?'

'Jamaica?'

'Geneva-n?! We are only *assessing* the situation...*only hoping not to discover...':*

'The-Truth?'

'Only? Ever?'

'Not the lies too?'

'The truth of the lies?'

'Always! Lies...'

'The Truth about The Lies, then?'

'As Good as it *gets*...'

'As Bad?'

'Regulation? in-Law?'

'Politicians and Police...'

'Really?!'

'Lie for a living...'

Only them?'

'The Army does not lie.'

'Why not?'

‘Because they know what they have done, when, where...’

‘Before they have done it…’

‘During...the whole time...’

‘And after?’

‘They cannot say.’

‘So they cannot lie?’

‘Except to themselves and their comrades...’

‘The only ones who really understand?’

‘Exactly.’

‘And the Police and Politicians?’

‘Like economists...’

‘Self-deceiving of their *personal* righteousness?’

‘Scapegoating...’

‘As Others scapegoat them?’

‘To The Top it goes...too...The *very* Top...’

‘*On-Commodity*-Futures then: N/n...’

‘And By-Law! Rules and Regulations?’

‘Your’s or Mine?’

'Our's. Then.'

Contradictory-paradoxical? Managed-Economy? Free-Markets...>

<Cash-Based Economies...>

>Re-re-regulation? Then?>

<Cash-based economy...

>Cast-based economy...>

<The Die!...>

>Is *cast...*

>Family?>

<Friends?>

>Or Tribe?>

<People...Bankrupt…Bank>

<Banks? Bankrupt? YOu?

Looking-sideward's, out of the window, and across again to The-Clerk speaking:

'Why do people *rob*-banks?'

'Because that was where the money is?'

'Not-anymore.'

Recovering from this slight The Banker:

'Now all cash-machines, eh?'

'Shop-till...'

'You drop! 24/7…New CashCard...' *oxygen arc-exploding bank-vault wall heaving heavy metal door with locks and wheels...*

'Card-Reader...'

'Where The Money is...' *nodding, glancing-down at first one then the other computer-screen:*

'And The-Time?

'Is now.'

'Prison-time?'

'Prisin' time? Social-security? Benefit-*scrounger*?'

'State-security? <u>Nasty-Squad</u>?'

Exchanged for passivity*...be-littlement...dis-empowerment...a burning fuse of resentment...*sublimating awe, gritty bitterness, angry:

'Then?'

'Regulation...'

'Again?!'

'This morning the International Conference of Business and Government leaders…This morning in Geneva, there is to be an announcement of The International Conference on Monetary Compliance (ICMC)...at possibly midday...who knows?'

'International-Time *stands still…?' looking-down...and into: @Corporate Government sponsored enterprise the-National-Bank: list:list...*

>*Currency*-Exchange: Rates:*list...*'

'Storming...'

Both. The-Clerk:

<Currency:*Exchange*-Rates:*list*...N/n%...

>The-Bank's...Oil-Wells...*protected or burnt-down*

<**R/e**: Investment House: Private-Assets...

>Public: *Water: Food: Waste:...toxic...de-salinating de-toxifying...cleaning-up...re-cycling…*

<>Energy?

<Natural? Coal-*gas?* Sunlight? Wind-Power...

'The Rain-*water?* The air we breathe?'

Seeing fields out of the window:

‘The Earth we ride-on?’

‘The Crops...*we grow?’*

‘ For All?’

<Power-*up*?

‘Sewerage...*between Food and Medicine...’*

‘Safe Water, and *decent*-Sanitation?’

<Built water-stands and Pumps, pumping *Clean*-Water...at a cost:...Gas and Oil to the surface….

>Social-*cost:...*

<Buying-up…*refining...Black-stuff...Red and Green-backed, as well, see?! Like flies on-Shit!’* looking upward, then downward again:

<As Well as that?

>For *Quick*-returns...

<*Personal*/Company-account (s):...*list...*

>Government-contracts...always pay-up, in the end.

<Even if they don’t? Or have to fight for decent pay-off, or pay-at-all?

>Through the-Judicial courts?

<For Tax-re-imbursements?

>Or no tax at-all?

<Paid-up, the threat<s enough...

>Unless...

<Unless, what?

>You are as good as The-Country!

<Nation-State! I am not...

<Socialist or Capitalist?

>Both. So, you are a human-being, after-all?

<You could call Me that?

>Artificial? Intelligent? Arterial-*algorithm*?.

<For compensation? PPI? For what? Hurt-feelings? compensating for paid-up insurance-bill:...

>Claims-Credit...*only to close-of-business...*

<**R/e**-Business: *money-transactions:...*

>Commodities:*...list...less is more, timing-important: no pay-out on...n/N...significance: list...*

<Larder-food?

>Betting-shops?

<Funeral-parlours...*non-parlous...*

>*P*eople's lives...as...*number*-of...N. to n. or n. to N.

<N=n?

>May as well do.

<What-for? Starting-price: N/n...

>Commodities: List: *Televisions and Radios...list:..machine-fuel lubricant:...*

<Weapons? Armaments?

Computer desktop...flashing-red...*green-light*:

>Forward Operating Base: Public-affairs Office: ...and-Vehicles?:...*updating*... every second...what-Day? Week Month Year...

<*Tin-Pot* polling-Dictatorship...*perpetually insecure and hopeless, helpless, threatening the rest of the world...*

>To look Bigger-than...

<Some of the Big-Ones too. First-World...*Second and Third and Fourth-estates...*

>Second...and Third...

<Now fourth:...*the cloud...end-user:...massively multiplayer online gaming:...*

>Do no-Harm? Te3am?

'No-good.' *White lies? Turned black? Red? Co-operative-harassment fails your-team, first, and your-opponents, all of them...*

'Lies? I did not tell any *lies*, not like the-*others*...about each other...that's The-Business. As usual?'

'Failed...'

'Your Own-Team *fails...*'

'You too...'

'Lose-lose?'

'As good as Win-Win...' *Others, not dictatorships exactly, but sham democracies, raiding and searching the family-homes arrested and exiled-to, offices of human-rights organisations...*

Political-prisoners and activists: peaceful but, disruptive. Others, distractive, destructive, or otherwise threatening-destruction, continuing to kill, in the name of single-conjoined family party politics, issuing and eventually, killed, before eventually carrying-out such threats, or not, exaggerated for political-purposes:

>Colonial Economic-Invasion?

<World-Currency?

<Currency-invasion...

<Ex-Colonially invaded...

>Ex-Invaders?

<Insurrection!

>Incursion!

<Insurgent...

>Consensus-*Democracy...*

<Or Dictatorship? *when push comes to shove...*

The Establishment wherever It is:...

<World-Trade-War?! Civil!

>Now! The-Leaderships:*...only have one day in which to decide (democratic Europe/ N.America and Australasia) dis-ingenuously, inevitably, candidly whether it will protect and/or capture oil-wells and gas-plants' prices, trade-routes, or for everything-else (non-Democratic middle-east (including Egypt and Israel), and China,): sometime in some-parts Africa and South America...):*

<Plastics...from *oil-based mined metals and minerals grown and reared foodstuffs alternative energy-sources and technology-powering mobile-phone camera music-store collection of reading-matter and messaging social-contacts and place-names:...,favourites: sites and networks calculators all...*

><*From Space?*

<>At The Big *Cat's-Table*: *innocent, trusting, honest, sincere, forgiving naive:...*

Both. All:

<Metals: list: minerals: list...*sham* Democratic Dictatorial Monarchical re-colonising-Aristocratic (Asia/America)...

>*Policing armies...*

<Manufacturing:...

>Steel-girder and concrete...carbon re-enforced...*unforced...a-force of nature, law, and society, similarly...*

<Maintenance:...*owed-a-debt, or gratitude, in the first-instance, next financially of the status-quo:...*

>*@Big Business and Big-Government...*

'To-gathering...'

'Together:...'

'To-Lend?'

'Borrower?'

'Credit?'

'Crunched.'

<*Borrowing*:NNNnnn*...and-boxing:...sand-boxing since The Pyramids...seen the Arches and Struts and Beams of The Parthenon and wooden stake-posted in the ground...*

On The Ground...

On-screen: stone built square and circus people here and there, and everywhere, almost...virulent-virus:

'Epidemic-proportions...' obsessively envious-of-the-living, keeping-up anxiety mania depressive addicted paranoid schizoid dual personalities psycho: all:

'Except some places, and peoples more than others...that is all, at this time...'

'In one or more of each case, and case-history...different.' summed-up: Money-Mania and suicide over unpaid-debts: 'Unnecessary! Lives! Lost! Lost unnecessary deaths and injuries!...'

>Unilateral...

<*Me! Me! Me! materialistic systemic-failure of financial-systems...*

>*Us! Us! Us! Then:...*

<Mis-selling mis-managed no-competition free-*market rebelling any which-way...*

>Promoting-Revolution?

<Or return to common-Nationalist-*values:*...in-perpetuity...never altering...

At Cafe and bar, at Railway-station and Airport, in motor-cars and helicopters, and on foot, and on and in the ground, tented people counselling each-other, or ignoring, remaining ignorance moved from ignorance, by more ignorance intended...

<As law:...*or restriction, or now, for a brief-moment in time one-day without any fiscal-law to take for granted or seriously again.*

Each of Us: representing a felt tenet and point-of-personal-morals, ethics argued from biased opinion or of a point of view of a particular-incident event or granular pixelated-happening seen differentially:...

>Consuming-all consummate: with-interest:...proportionate: in-repayment of compensation: for every stage of that:

<Mis-selling: on-commission *once bought and sold and signed-up:*

>*Direct*-Debit...or Credit?' *managed...*

<Always a good bet?!<

>What? Natural disasters?

<Or a deliberate Act of Sabotage? Human-made...<

>You-mean. Insured? Anyway!<

<Excepting those The-Gods-made...eh? Can you find a new mark-up? The new-Finds…new-crops…seeds, or Eco-Fuel-Source?<

>New Bio-bacterial-fuel, you heard of *that?*<

<New drill-testing?<

>Mining…*information...*<

<Shafting?<

>Shifting…*for quick-returns…to keep the whole thing running...tenured-lands...and buildings…grabbed, built, knocked-down, whatever.*

<Sometimes, takes-time…

>Needs some patience...<

<So some Short-term, some Long-term?<

<See? Spread-bets...<

>Bets?<

<Investments :*...on good information, before anyone else gets it! And sometimes even requiring government, regime-approval*<

<Police or Government Military *intervention...*<

>Spy-ware...insider?<

<As in Military-rule?

>Religious...*militarised-Zone?*<

Back-peddling-quickly, as if re-cycling information...

<News:...*quickly!*

>When? where? what?

<How?

>Why?

<txt. *unsafe...*

Looking-down, looking-up again, and into the eyes of The-Banker:

'Why? For Slow-down…' *stop-inflation...deliberate... made-out...*

'To be better than it was?'

'We were?'

'Will be again! Always is!' *always as if it is somebody-else's fault...*

'Couldn't help it!'

'Or some whole-country? And its'-Peoples:list....list...Or the whole-Economic-zone...?'

'But It is ours! All of us!'

'And The-Conference? Is that Ours? Do We Get-a-Vote? No. On the-numbers, that is all, same as...'

'Democratic?'

'More or less...some...'

'There has to be a good Majority...to act?'

'And a good-minority...any-minority, to succeed.'

'With Tact? Act anyway!'

'Only, not-together?'

A puzzled-look:

'And if *They* will not-Co-Operate?'

'Or want too much…greedy-b...'

'More-like...c...'

'Or *Clear-Out...*'

'Or *Cleaned-Up*?'

'So?'

'Why not leave it up to Us! Eh? Don't take *too-much* of the spoils? Be *too*-Greedy?'

'For Ourselves?'

‘First? Of-course!

‘Fist! Take-them for fools?’

‘Who?’

‘Who-*provide:* The Armament...The Strong-Arms...’

‘The Workers?’

‘The Government: Police and The-Army?’

‘For The *Others*...

‘To do the deadly-deeds..?’

‘Take-out The-Others?’

‘As Ourselves would be Taken-out...Only...’

‘*Magic*! There are limits...even to *that*!’

'Are there? What?’

‘Our-Debt!’

‘Ourselves...and Our-*Debt*. Then...theirs.’

‘Of-course! Given-by?’

‘**The Rational-Equitable Bank**...’

‘Not shared-out *equally*?’

'Between The-People? Of course not! To those who do not pay-in? What? Taxes? Benefits? Welfare? Of the-Many?'

'By the-Few?'

'Exactly. Between-Zero, and-One.'

'One? and the-Many? The-Many, and no-Other?'

'The-Few, and *every*-Other?'

'And the no-*thanks*! for that!'

'What about the-spoils? Not *any*, not anywhere equally…what *You* pay-in. You get-Out. What We get of the spoils...'

'Yes?'

'Is between Us.'

'Between The-Rulers...and their officials...Private and Public investment and *actual* stock-merchants…shares…monetary…all…'

'At The-Conference? Is that what 'It' is?! Peace Or War Conference? For our-debts? Is that It'? That You as well as them are after seizing the assets…wells, mines, whatever is left portside markets and inland…You? Bankrupt? Too?'

Looking-down, at nothing in particular...then words:

'Trade-in your-debts?'

'Trade-in what? Since when?'

'Since what?'

'When?’

‘Now.’

<Now!

>T1?

<T1+ N/n...*names*?

>The-Aims?:...

<Take-Aim!:...

>Fire!...*unknown*-number:nnnnnnnnnnnnnnnn...

Quickly intervening, the-Clerk:

‘*Different*-Companies and Corporations...*hidden*...*loads of them!* Since when do We do the-*actual* spoiling?’ looking up, both together and down into:

‘Names?’

‘Where?’

‘Or Government’s...’ *in-corporated like a Cake-Mix:*

‘The-Earth!

‘Global!

'<u>Go!</u>

'Caramelised? Like an icing-cake!'

Looking upwards into The-Face: The-Clerk:

'The-Sweetener?'

'I'd be doing you a favour...'

'I am already!

Souring, knowingly cutting-through-the-crap. Knowingly, and or Unknowingly delivered the foil of the-spoils, nonetheless, the inside glowing with self-satisfaction, The-Banker:

'As long as the <u>Base-Rate-Value</u>:...

'***<u>R/e</u>***:*N/n:...are agreed and exchangeable with:...'*

'*<u>The-Big Players?'</u>:...named:list...(deleted):*

'The Only Ones...that *can* play...'

'And in-*negative*-equity themselves...'

'For *liquidation...Cash...*'

'Of-Course! No cheques, or blank-cheques anyway...'

'Or record for that matter, either, *virtually*...nothing.'

'Not in the-*ether...'*

'Either...' *in The-Pocket-Book....not online tapping*:

<The-Account(s):...' *nothing:...*

'The blank-Cheque-book:..' *could not-stop...moving speculation, into nothingness:.*

'Only four or five Majors globally...' *including Merchant and Investment-Banking and High-Street Markets:small an mium siz business...*

'In all the Major-currencies...' *and whole-Economic-Zones. Whole countries! Whole Nation-States! Viability? One-trick ponies most of them...now no-more-than six or seven:...*

<Massive Global-institutions in each-sector: Energy and Goods: Financial-Markets...' *already paid-for several times over through several-different-countries' tax-systems and border-charges, taxes-paid.*

Not really.

Without paying-tax but sold-on at profit of-course ancient-religious sectarian: with and without political power-and-control: from The Media online social networking:...suddenly from the rightside:

'Men with guns?'

'And women!'

‘Bazookas!’

‘Craps...’ into silence out the window into the screen:...

<Game-*changer: established misunderstanding, kept at-poverty-level:...*

>N/n below:...

<Castling...Lording IT over!

>What?

<*King*ing forever...

>Queening?

<As if....

>Big-corporations...*at the level we can be humoured, or ignored:*

>Still is....

>Weapons?>

>Of Mass-Destruction.>

<Governance. *with political and religious citadel of ourselves, and others...*

>*Vital to either, and each other. Then talk! We are each government and church and Big-business. Rolled into one! Me! and You!*

<*And them?* looking around the carriage...*take their chances, themselves...*Bet Now? *death company bond, bundled and sold-on. Sliced and diced...death and taxes...employment? Life insurance?*

>Sell?...*land and property: 0: Currently:...*

<Food and...

>Fuel and Furniture

including...Media:...list:...list...words/pictures/music...numbers...

<Buildings, and Dot-Comm.s?

>Buy-in The-Utilities:... *that is where it is at!*

<Then: Gold! Silver? *Diamonds...are forever...*

>Credit! That is 'It'!

<If You like? As medicine…

>They never lose their value...

<Or their shine...

>Gold-plated! *those who do the selling, the making, the dirty work...*

<Let Us take *The-*Vote!

>To company-consenting...<

<And not. Again. Personal-profit, or loss?<

>Anything from Zero, to around 10-20%.<

<Sometimes up-to 41% -51%!<

>A-majority!<

<Of Who?<

>*Simple....*including *high*-Finance and -Street and Inter-nationally…<

<Shop-Retail and Wholesaling...<

A-*vision* of the-Globe, a-globe, *spun...*

<<Secondary? Utility Services?<

>To **The-Money** of course!

<The Primaries, damn-it!

>Health and Social Care?

<That is when We get the pay-off!

>*Enshrined...*

<@War...battle...peace...*shopping:..*

>Friend...*allies and colleagues affiliate-racketeering, marketeering: the-secondary...sell-on...investment-house...*<

<Then the Tertiary...<

>Bankers!

<Forget about that!

>The-Cleaners! Up!

<Certainly!

>Staff:...*down...*< *images of*

<The-Workers?...*contact contract-details...*

<Human-Resources!

>*Contacts*:...that is what it is!<

<Not what You know...Who You know! Not who I know, who You know? What You know, or I could find out?<

>Tertiary-colours! The Primaries! Secondary<s! As well. And Tertiary<s, yes! Family!<

<The-Vote?<

>By-*proxy!*<

<**Charity**: *donations...political and religious-party funding-machines:...rolled-out...*

>Protection-racket!<

<Suspected...only: Security-forces...<

>For Good-*returns*:...going...Bad.<

<Fear and *Favours...*<

>The-Family:...?<

'Family?'

'What about the-Family?'

'Democracy?! Ha!'

The exact same-second: *alerted...*

9.

From the-screen, voices-off of:

'Intimidation!'

'Look! No little-finger!' *The accuser, turned accused...*

'The Government-Rebels did this!?!'

'Gaoler, turned Prisoner:...'

'Vice-versa…' re-joining The Game looking-up:

'Constant-Growth!'

'And innovation!'

'The-*newest*...

'Cost-Liest!'

'First to **<u>Go!</u>**'

'Last-to-**<u>Go</u>**?! *The-poorest? Richest? First? Where?*

'First to **<u>Go</u>**...with the most...

Searchlight spun-around, onto another game, another place:

'Next time!'

'Last-time!': *open*-source:

'Ethnics...'

'One killed off both killed-off...'

'One remains...'

'The harder they come...'

'Cash-configuration of the-State?'

'Tax and punish as public-servants...' with white-hood...red-mask...black-mask...blue-hood...uniform...

'@Presidential-General...Monarchial-usurpation…'

‘‘It’ makes no-*difference...*’desecrating-graveyards, in search of gold:

‘Never easy.’ *secure sequestering carbon lit: trade-convoy, protected-corridor...*

On the-Train: out of the blue-grey green-brown colours outside:

‘Where do you think all the money is? Then, let’s us go there!’

‘The-City?’

‘Not-anymore...’

‘What about the-Rest?’

‘There is more?!’

‘Fuck the rest! *smallfry...’*

‘Terrorists...list:...suicides...list...’

‘Rebel-Revolutionary-Religions’ fundamentalists...matters-not:..

‘Hierocracies…Theocracies:...*two...three...at a time...sects fighting amongst themselves…’*

‘At each other...suicidal!’

‘Social-Capitalists:...’

‘Capital-Socialists:...whatever works…’

'Religionist?

'All-*Thieves!'*

'Whatever works…who ever…'

'All of Us!'

'That will not even get the Equity on the Assets: lists...*lists*...they started-out with. You get-me?'

'You got-me...'

'The left-over's...*dregs...remnants...vested-interests, investment...*

'We' leave that to the companies and corporations on the ground, and the-Bailiffs...our-Bail-out: to sort that lot-out...

'In-corporated?'

'As in-corporated...with money? Banks?

'Massive clear-out!'

'Banks?'

'Money-sale!'

'Boot-sale!

'You got IT! Boots and Bandages!

'No, You got 'it'.'

'Yes I have...

'Because? If 'We' cannot pay-off the loans in the first-place? Then?

'That means they may never be paid-off?'

'Certainly not today!'

'We will of course in time claw it all back for ourselves...in-time:...'

'Fair and square!'

'Limited-liability…'

Graph's square curved across-each-other through...away from each other...bone bell-curved:

'Middle is the best place to be...'

'On the swerve...'

'On the curve!'

'Roller-coaster! The Eternal ever...'

'Never! Now! Now or Never what'll IT be?''

So the online conversation went, back and forth....

'And even then you don't ever really know what's going on… *never mind, most the Time, nor do any of us!' Constant-positives make it sound good!*

'Could get hammered?'

'No-negatives...no-risk?...'

'And so...where do I come-in?'

'And that is where You come-in. You could take a cut-in, if you like?'

'What for?'

'Nothing. Try you out? Take a slice? You're smart. I'd be doing you a favour?'

'I am, already. Doing You a favour having this conversation…'

'What for?'

'Joking?'

'Seriously? Sole-trader?'

Heard:

'*Soul*-trader? For-*my*-Sin's? You mean? The Devils' advocate? You mean?'

'For My-Offence? Wrongdoing? Felony? Fault? Trans-*e*gression?'

'Misdemeanour? Mis-deeds?'

'What like Murder? Rape?'

'Goodness? Securitising the underlying debts and *loans...*'

<u>**'Security?'**</u> *for Life? In a few short months...retirement*?

'I would be a...sole-*Trader?*'

'Limited-liability?!'

'I would be My-Own Owned-Company?'

'You would be Your-Own-*Company*! And otherwise, with as much *psycho*-fun and anxiety as you can manage!'

'In return for?'

'Your-*debt*s.'

'They are Yours!'

'Secured by real-estate? Or not?'

'What?'

'Your-debts? A Giant flat-screen T.V. perhaps? Mobile-camera phone? Smart-Hub> <u>*Home*</u>? Fast Motor vehicle, 4x4? Life insurance? Any other-debts?'

'So, who hasn't got debts?'

'Think about it?'Eh? Everyone does!'

‘You work to pay off your Debt to Life...’

‘I can take your debts…’

‘They are yours!’

'As the source of *all*-debt, eh?'

'Eh?'

'So, what is that game your playing, eh? **Warfare4**?’

Ignored:

'Yes...**War*Fair*4**: then…'

The-Clerk resumed scanning paused as on some on-line conversation:

>T1:*..take-cover!Policy-protection!*

<Overs: capital-List...list..lists:...

‘Limited-liability?’

and without looking-up at The-Banker mumbling:

'Hunger-Games...So? What’s on Your Mind now eh?’

Scanning-down…clicking the-circularity loading-timer…text and graphics…*glancing*-down, and across...and holding…released…photo-opportunistic reading-across a newly updating...page 2/…paged-past the *aberrant*-picture, and headline:

Markets In Turmoil

on which both the-Banker and the-Clerk had turned the page:

'So what's not to make of it now eh?'

The-Clerk spoke into the vacant-space between them. Nodded-over and down toward the returned-to unseen unshared, screen. Through the others' paper newsprint, and at the mobile-pad display screen and inked-in writing *thinking* of possibly un-*befriending*...? The-Banker now looking away from the re-directed gaze ignoring the-Clerk and the assumed video-game machine seemingly wished to be returned-to The-Banker:

'The Market's will decide.' and this was the moment the-Banker could have added: *'...and there is nothing you, or anyone-else, can do about it!* but resisted. There would be no point. *'You and whose Army' said probably and* thought of by The-Clerk. Outspoken aloud instead and as well as from The-Clerk:

'Decide what?'

The-Banker attempting to impart as-if spell-checking it out word-for-word as if too-abstruse and unknowable for this simpleton as for children to make of it what they will themselves simply *re-iterated* as some obvious truism:

'The Market's will decide. The Market's will come through.' stepping-up to the plate once again:

'Getting geared-up? Leverage?'

'Leverage-*up*...'

'Sure...'

'Not-Leverage-*down, then*?' and the accompanying levering-action, committed:

'What?'

'Global-Exports! 'It is our Best Export: The-City!'

'Selling The City?! Truthfully? Honestly?'

'Accurately...'

'As far as is known...More or Less...Our Best...Exports are Everything!'

'Imports?'

'Everything Else!'

'Like what?'

'Like...TV's. Games...I don't know...'

'Movies...*software*...Dot.Comms...'

'Buildings?'

'The-City...'

'*Information*?'

'Spyware, yes....'

'And the-Hardware?'

'That is your job.'

'The numbers, the shapes...are Yours?'

'Market-*information*?'

'To know what matters...*withhold* market-information...'

'True or False?'

'Letters and numbers...'

'Put-*together* in a certain-way...'

'Contractual arrangement?'

'Credit? Again? Credit-rating? Everything about You?'

'No-longer a-*secret*?'

As cagily, in the compartment, the space between, and around, the-carriage:

'Debts?'

'Of course.'

'All of them? What, *my*-debts? Who are You? To be asking me this?'

Looking-up...

'Who are You to listen? and answer? Tourist? Journalist? Aaahh…yes...fun and Game's...' *You know! Sport's. Games? And, there is 'Art' in it. Political...Wars....' quickly adding* nodding at the obvious games-machine opposite:

'*These*-Games? Same as the real thing...'

'More or Less?'

'All-and Any other-Businesses…some-<u>Manufacturing</u>…'

'And...<u>Tourism?</u> <u>Resorts</u>? <u>Mega</u>-<u>Media</u>...'

'The Big-Five:...or Six: By: Global? Continental? Oceanic? Country? Sea? River? Cities?:...

'The-Banks? Building-Societies?'

'Building? Pharmaceuticals...Big-Pharma...Farmers...'

'Healthy-competition...'

'Choice? Competition?'

'Not Much!'

'Choice?'

'Competition?'

'Not in it. It was always **<u>The Rational-Equitable:</u>** *on safespeech...*

‘If you have enough bean-counters, eh?'

'Counters?’

‘Shop-fronts? Shop-windows?'

'You got it!

'@I have?!?’

‘Multi-*Agro-Cultural’s:...*’

‘Tobacco:..’

‘Alcohol...’

‘And other: *illicit*-Drugs...’

‘*Firearms: sale*s?’

‘There it is...'

'Weapons:*...weapon's...*’

‘Department-of 'You know Who?’

‘Wrong-doing?’

‘Beating up the wrong-one...’

‘Illicit?'

'Drugs?’

‘Illicit drugs? Now that would be illegal, wouldn’t it?’

'Recreations?'

'Leisure-wear? Sports and non-Sports...'

'Army-wear? And weapons?'

'Franchise?'

'Doping-Sports? Illicit weapons?' *without pause for appreciation of Self, or Other:*

'These, all taken-together are more than The-City put together...anywhere!'

'My point entirely! That bit more is what The-City creams off for Itself!'

'Screaming: Principal-investment!'

'Investment-Principle?'

'Business-principle:...'

'That bit on top...of everything-else...'

'Bit?'

'Bite!'

'On top of what?'

'Everything else!'

'You got 'It'!'

'What?!'

'Fraudulent-loans? Mortgages, credit?'

'I got '<u>IT</u>'!'

'...and <u>Debit</u>-cards?'

'<u>Credit</u>?' *all directed toward the innately greedy? To Good...To Be-True!'*

'Too...Good?' so probably is false...fraudulent-fraudster...

'No-one is forced to-borrow!'

The-Clerk:

'Everyone-is…'

'No-one is totally self-sufficient. We need each other, and everyone is totally dependent to start with...of-course...'

<u>'On?'</u>

<u>'The-*Game...*'</u>

'This <u>Game?'</u>

'Need to learn to-<u>*play*</u>?'

'Live the Life!'

'Investments?'

'In life! Savings. Pensions. Insurances...'

'Mis-Sold?'

Unheard, switched-off, *unhearing:*

'Insured, to live. Pensioned-off...'

'To Die saving...'

'All at Once then?'

'Invest to live!'

'And the next-generation?'

'Take...' *and give nothing-back:*

'From them? We-pay-our-taxes...You probably owe taxes, unpaid. Evasion Avoidance, or Escape, is it? Oh yes...and give To **Charity**...'

'To save a life?'

'That bad? Is it?'

The-Banker outspoken, to the-Clerk again, now:

'Borrow to lend, that is the way to do it: Investment.'

'We *buy*? With My Debts? Yours?'

'We do the-*tending*...'

The-Clerk knew already :

'At *knock-down*...prices?'

'The-Price is always right...'

'Are always *Hopes and Dreams...*'

'You Hope and Dream, don't you? Don't We All?'

'Not all The Time...Nightmares sometimes!'

'Or daydream? That is the question? Big house? Big car?'

'Do a Good job with what I have, and what I can get...'

'Be rich?'

'Without hurting anyone?'

'No. By luck...Or judgment? Maybe...'

'Make your own luck.' *Made to measure. What School are you from? College? University? Diplomatic-travel and cash routes? Property all-over. Bank-vaults similarly! Robbed! On Stocks and shares, only, bank-vaults similarly...Cannot be touched, except by the legal money owner...who are?: Foreign-credits as well as debts! Transfers, simply...on-line...*

'Get away with it? Again?'

'Again. Getaway car? I like it! My-Car! Mansion-housed...Super- YachtHelicopter? Personal-'plane?'

'Sure. Big-Yacht?'

'Sure!' *and a Good-Job! Loads 'o' Money! Of course! But You cannot have-everything, by sheer luck. Gotta do something for it! So? What else? What have You got to offer?*

'Good-*judgement?* You are a High-Court Judge now?!'

'Supremo! Court of Law?! Equals=of-Information:@? *Birthright*, perhaps...*Who You know? As well as What? And what You know, or think you can? Can-Do!:*

'Live the dream! Follow your *dreams*!' *Total-Consumer. Celebrity-Everyone?*

'You? But not if you don't want to? Stay in the shadows, y'a know what I mean?'

'Off-shore?'

'Next-door: Best-*Investment* yet, yes...'

'Yet, no- person is entirely *invisible*?'

'Although we all may try. No-Country, either. No-company, or Big-In-Corporation.'

'No-Government...'

'I do not speak for You.'

'You do not speak for Me. I speak for myself.'

'So do I. For Others...Mind-you...Home, for some, *nothing*...until The Price-is-Spot-ON! On-hold...In-storage for-now...then...'

'Shortages...'

'The-Price rises...'

'Bingo! Bang and Boom! Again!'

'Where?'

A-*hiatus*, then The-Banker chortling *conceitedly* self or other deceptively, or not:

''Buy' *or* 'Sell''

'What?' glancing-screenward, both.

leaning-forward across the table and ignoring everyone else in the carriage. The-Banker, to the-Clerk:

'What can You afford? O.K. One-to-one now...'

The-Banker, and the-Clerk leaned forward *listening*:

'Nothing *less* and nothing more from the-point at which the stock-markets, and currencies closed...the money-markets are closed. Are-closed to-the-point at which they may be open sooner than we think?'

'Could be...*re opening*...sooner than we think?'

'Re-opened?'

'Midday...'

This time to the-Clerk as rhetorically-intended, answered the-self :

'Now! Of course! Open for Business, right now! *Ssh....*Alright?: Pre-deals being set-up as we speak. Be-ready...But there is a lot more than that? You need to be there...and because in the end it is you the-People...you know...the-Politics...make it happen.'

'*ShhIT* happens!'

'In the end.'

'Every-time...'

'But not yet.'

'Then?'

'Take a move on in? Why not? Get in there! That is why I am going in Today! The only reason...then The Airport.'

'In-where? On what?' *naturing now, or-nurturing? Plebeian? Or non-Plebeian? Once?*:

'Now?'

'For-Later's...Get-It?'

The-Clerk contemplating then of some *instant.* But only now felt, mistrust-dealing, in fantasy, and fear...genre: *horror*:

'What are the *odds*?'

'Of what?'

'The Rates? Personal...or Council-Tax? Corporation?'

'Not-*evens...*'

The passive reflective *thought* and *then* again The-Bankers' anger rising:

'By closing-the-markets… mortgage and credit-crisis…*systems*' crashed. O.K.? One-goes...the others' follow...'

'Or cannot do business?'

'Herd-*instinct*. Unrealised Of Others...'

'One goes down...'

'They all come tumbling-after...'

'Insurance?'

'Re-insurance and pensions and-life-savings...'

'Home-mortgages...'

'Home and office-building *bubbles...*'

'Over now. Baubles! Shops and Business cannot pay wages and salaries to buy goods pay-suppliers of goods and services...'

'Credit, then?'

'Yes. How much?"'

"Logistics? On-Credit? Crediting-accounts...*with more than the value of The Business...faculties divisions and*

'Shares for debts?'

'Yes...'

'Then, what? Default?'

'Yes, then what?'

'Re-possession?'

'Yes, by whom, of what? The-Lender? Bailiff?'

'We don't do that!: Administration! Auditors…lawyers…accountants…'

'Those, yes...'

'Plenty of work for them...cooking-the-Books!'

'Sure.'

'And covering-up!'

'Of-course!'

Then?'

'Loss-*assessor*?'

'Adjusted in the buyers' favour...'

'Deal done.'

'Everything-is-affected?'

'Of-course! Everyone is affected! All the money, for All the Things!'

'Dragging-down whole-Corporations! Airlines! Fallen out-of-the-sky! Walls and Towers collapsed...The-Peoples' Re-*Nationalised-Industries sold, for next to nothing, to a few...too-many...to a few:*

*'In-Power: again...*Buildings un-built...*for Sub-prime's were Its' Biggest Beast! Whole-industries! Businesses and transport...*

>Logistics-Corps...>Buildings!

<Got IT! Transport Home-and Abroad. Ship-owners...>

>OwnerShip!>

<Got IT again! Taken-out of their-hands. Sold-off. Sold-out. Sunken-ships! Crashed!> collided! Onto the black-rocks, mired in the quicksand of information-fatigue sets-in...>

<Onto the Rocks of Doom!>

>At the bottom of the deep-blue-sea!>

<Red sky at night?>

>The Locker-room?>

<Bonanza!>

>And Blow-out’s...>

<Needs a lightning-rod!

>Over-ripe…

<F*or the-taking...scamming shamming spamming computer-fraud.*

Without permanent circuitry, no trace...

>That’s it!

<Intentionally?

>Not...*accidentally...in the pursuit...impacting pile-up, smashed, crashed into the wall!:*

<*On concessionary-loans, re- mortgaged...*>

>Bankrupt?>

<Owned, and sold, and bought...>

>Home and Abroad?>

<Colonial. And those who Build-Businesses...> *continue building...*Again and again?>

<Too Big!> *dry hacking-cough from The-Banker:…*

The-Clerk:

‘Cyber-crime?’

‘Viral…Like spear-fishing...in a barrel-shaped lake...

<Home-built walled defences…

>Atomic-nuclear now The-Game:

Out of the window the-Clerk reflected-on:

<Activity screen:*...back-diving-in...re-surfacing water-fighting...pulling-in, the-prey*:

>T1:*..take-cover! Overs: capital-List...list..lists:...*

<Over-lending tally...

>*Over*-production...>

<Surplus...NNNnnn...profit!>

>Production-halted...n/N to *maintain*-price:...and raise It! Scarcity...>

>Unemployment?>

<Bought-low...> *brow-beaten shareholders...*

>Not sold cheap...> *stored...*

>Product-to-market!>

<Consumerism! What is wrong with that?>

>Capitalism? Consumer-led?

<Consumer-bled? Who are The-People? but The-Consumers? They vote with their feet...>

>Socialist!The Workers...too.> *go where we are sent...*

<For Life!>

>In a few short months...*retirement*?>

<Bled by >The-Advertising Budget!>>

>How would you know what was there? Or not there?> *rows, of half, and full empty shelves, at the local supermarket and street-market and auction of goods*:

>Administration-Costs!> *slashed.*

>They are *your*-Customers!>

>Suppliers!Of course: Share-Holders!>

<Co-operative!>

>Everything that happens...must-*happen*...>

<Must IT?@:

>Demand and Supply...>

<Supply and Demand...>

>Yin and Yang?>

<People…>

>Goods...>

<Bigger and more-complex...> *the more...*

>Bigger The-*Lie: smaller and smaller…*>

<Depends: The more *intricately* believable...>

>The-Truth?>

<What is that? *Truthfulness*? In All Truthfulness?>

>Existence?>

<More-believable...>

>Or unbelievable...>

<Than?>

>The-**Truth**.>

<**Reality**? May be, unbelievable?>

>Naturally? Think about it…>

The-Clerk glanced up and down into:

>The *naturalistic*-fallacy?>

<Lie?>

>I*ts' self?* Is a fallacy?>

<The Truth is a Lie?>

>The Lie is a Lie...>

<All is Natural?>

>As well as Unnatural...

<I suppose...*this...*>

>*What?*>

<Is not Real?>

>All naturally-happening...>

<And un*naturally*-concocted...>

>Concocting...Truth, after the event...>

<Invasion, or incursion?>

>Insurrection, or Regime-Change?>

<Democratic...or DictaTORSHIP!>

>cONSCRIPTED OR VOLUNTARY REBELS?>

<nOT UNDER MY=CONTROL!>

>wHY nOT?!@*Truth: only a present tense, pretence. Monistic. Pluralism, of monistic selves, selfish-selves, completely. No-one completely. Some get close, and more-bonkers than Bankers, that they do. Probably mean no harm, even. Not Even. But their partners,*

the armoires, Armies, Police forces, and in the end the presidents and royalty claims of holiness, and piety...:...

<Goes a long-way...> *past-empirical, scientific-speculation, after, the, mean, and every event, has been counted, add, or indeed, minus, Zero. Saved...not far enough.*

As One. By each of our senses...anything, and everything, could be something-else? Family? High-Command? Central-Powers breathing...*And will be the next moment, and the one after that. Not-happening? Yet? You'll see:...*

>*Turned a blind-eye...*>

<Equity-*ownership? Who owns what?*>

>Everything, pure and natural, untouched, by human sensibility, and fault...>

<Pure-good? Pure-Evil?>

>Including our thoughts and ideas and what we see? Rational-actor?>

<Acting-irrationally.>

>Real?

<Unreal...

>Sometimes, most times, maybe all the time...>

<Soothsayer...after the event?>

>But together mostly, harmless, dealing with an irrational world, constantly changing, rationally, in mind, and body directed.>

<Irrational? But not-unreal? Until seen?>

>Then it is too late?>

>Perfectly.>

>Impossible! Nothing is so-Pure!>

>Equitable?>

>Nothing! More-Natural. Than *what* has only just-happened...>

>After-the-event?>

>Rationalised. See? Normalised. Natural! Yet in its inception? Un-natural?! Before The-Event...

>God-made? Created...irrationally?>

>Or ourselves? Rationally? Regulated...regulating, in-advance, we like to think, and be post-modern, tamed./

>So how? So Devil-debauched?>

>In its> twist? Reason...>

>How is to destroy, to create?>

>Told when...>

>To Create...is To-Destroy?!>

>Or be un-created. From Nothing? Impossible!>

>Irrational?>

>In-the-event, rationalised...for the next-*rational*-move...>

>Not-Equitable...> thought-of *carried-out? Never know, until the deed is done*. Then...

>Sold-out?>

>They were-*wrong* before...as to say…>

>What? That it can only be natural? They were All-wrong. Admitted it?>

>Who? Under torture? Irrationally, of Having It All? All-knowledge, everything, and everyone. Taken-away from them...>

>By someone else...>

>For someone-else, and The Others?>

>Not only *pure* self-interest, then? Perhaps...those that said it was only-Natural...self-interest, with greed, now? And does that make what *they* are deciding now, not to be wrong, also?>

>To be greedy? Never-enough, some-of-them.>

>Only-*partly...*>

>To Cash-in?...at least...>

>Whatever-happens?! Crash? Collapse? They said they saw it coming...>

>Afterwards...>

>And did-*Nothing!* Did you? Do nothing?>

>How is that possible? I got Rich. As I am. As You would Be.>

>Get-Rich, quick. Eh? On-*paper...*>

>On-screen...>

10.

Nodding across The-Train-table between them:

'On-screen...'

'That's what *I* mean...see?'

Unseen, or heard, the-both of them baulked, and drew-back into the-event: the *fray*:

'The-Rich give nothing to the-*poor...*' *grubbing-property express-anger, and pay-back victims' food and clothing not-*

enough...squalid and horrible, homes, as busy, frantic, and full of good-fun, and miserable, poverty.

Fun and Games. Fights and arguments, through the walls partitioned-off, of the grand buildings and offices, on the stairs, the broken-elevators, and especially small children, babies, not invested-in, yet The-Clerk looked-up to:

'Storm-clouds coming-in' again and each together silently looking out of the-window and the opposite window's to where they sat across The Table.

Across The Carriage. The Other's: *standing and sitting mindfully ignoring and occasionally minding the time of day: on computer-screen tablet or wrist-watch head-phoned mobile-device:* Date Time and *applications...programmes, applications and battery-level, messages in any of the current forms voice and letter and number written* typed *clicked into...*

Beneath the hills, across the valleyed-plains...

You could see a distance. Back-garden patio sky-balcony view...

Housing and Industrial Estate...nevertheless needed it's Own Allotmenteer: to be there most of the time. Asleep there, riding-Shotgun. One of the local-Militia- Military, to secure, and protect. Looked after, and tended...chair back in The Pantry or The Tub-room or whatever they called-it when the one-room shotgun shack was being used for cleaning and cooking...

The momentary passing-speed of another train *combined speeds on one side of the train, poignant, the blue-grey* sea. On the other side of The-Train cross winds and setbacks for The-Clerk amongst the solitary and cluttered clustered and isolated farmhouses *born and brought-up in.*

And bought-up.

To be lived-in again, believed-in, passed-on or not.

Of Parents and parents of parents, rented, brought-up inside and around the fields and harvest time, lost now. The Father the-Farmer, and Mother, the-mother, still lived on what little land they had left, virtually a small-holding now. An allotment-share now, plough-share. Class-rights, and denomination. Resolution. registered, and re-denominated. Cross-border trade-war battles and mergers troop movements…

A farmhouse cottage garden, the cattle-sheds in rolling hills. Amongst isolated mansion farmhouse-estate barns and sheds, and vast-silo: Industrial-Unit: The natural eco-system…*demonstrations deaths to no avail...compromised the sky did not fall-in after all, moved-on…*

The outbuildings and all the fields except-one re-appeared and the house the family-home, the family-farm sold-off. To the insistent, and already sanctioned by Governmental Inter-national Super-national rigged-out fixed out-of-necessity for retirement...couldn't do it anymore.

After several Bad-Harvests fretting-away the final sale-price covering repair and maintenance...innovation sometime's purchasing new piece's-of-machinery...or seeds, not-annually, never monthly...or seasonally...in-Profit, these-People...pick your own.

They did not understand seasonally. Never too-wet, too-dry. Too-hot. Too-cold. Destroyed deliberately, by insect, by spraying helicopter gunship...win/win. Sharing equipment. Co-operative credit-Agriculture. Win-Win. Lose-Lost, now.

A few good-years of growing-up...reasonably-good harvest, and a few month's sale-price as to the shop's and market-stalls that sold the produce. For- prices that were no-longer-set from Season to Season, but Day-by-Day. Minted-microscopically minute by second hand- ticking...exchanged: Futures on Crops-to-Profit terms...all over the-Globe seed to seed spinning-still:

'Too Big to fail.'

'Could not fail.'

'Failed.'

On screen: Megaphone:

'Down With The Government!'

'Throw yourselves off the Fiscal cliff!' bannered outside.

Unseen, in a tunnel, in the Newspapers, on TV:

'What is to do about it?'

'There's nothing goin' on but The Rent!'

From a-crowd gathered somewhere:

'Populaire-Banco!'

'Ha!

'From Children's-Toys to Cars and Helicopters!'

'And Galactic-Spacecraft!' another threw-in:

'Just One Bad-harvest!' low-prices plenty of margin on all the logistics getting to the marketplace to pay Government-Taxes and selling high through The-City due to Demand and Supply: Supply and Demand...with a poor harvest low turn-out...prices-rise but not for us...

To Vote for them!! Prices made-high...for who? What side of the fence? Seed and Crop bought-up and into and sold minute-by-minute in advance of any harvest. Prices once gambled-on the weather, now on fixed intensive-farming and industrial-agricultural multinationals could not lose...not too-often, not at all, anyway looking-up:

'Fixed? Trade-ins?'

'Who's counting anyway? No-one, hardly. Not if You are Doing Well, as well, *relatively speaking*, you get me?'

'Corporate Multi-Nationals *making fortunes...*'

‘At the expense, the expected Cost to The Many? Hostage to Fortune!’ Only what we haven't got! To be usefully employed and well-paid, for the market to thrive and into a relatively reasonably happy if not continually in-secure retirement...' it only seemed that way...

Heard, then *thought-out* and spoken:

'Then Rent and pay-controls-lifted...conditions of work lowered to that of the self-employed... again?’

Ordinary-almost... traumatised and diseased, insect and water-born air-born, and born into outside inside cross Border-foray... raiding seen incursion into-countryside-born more of an invasion incursion than no exit...at places and times of the year...manoeuvring excursion... otherwise continued the ‘this is how *we* do it’ routine while in the media:

‘Refugees into The Towns and Cities...’

Other-Countries...erased in-desperation to be better-kept marketing better kept in-the-circumstances...

<The-City: *Beyond the-Money. Beyond the owning State. As Free-Trade Slaves Serfs and Servants wage-labourers...feudal non-industrial societies all....*

>**The-Workers**...*paid or unpaid, fed and paying-off paid, incessantly to: the Crown, the Cross, the Sword. The money-less...the blurred broken boundaries between...*

Unlike those between the richest and poorest could not be clearer...deliberately...without deliberating for all, but only self, and family even then, maliciously interfering with other's lives...and livelihoods...for personal gain: personal-convenience:

>**Profit-Consumers**: *Buyers...and Sellers...Over Generous Philanthropists...Patronising-Donors...Good-hearted Humanitarian...*

<Natural and Built Forest-sites...

>Beaches and Hills and Mountains...*lived-in and in-between. Moved to The-Town in exile then...*

For The-Clerk, no interest anymore, in the land.

The-Parents, before their passing would have liked The Farm to be taken over, by The Brother or The Sisters' Expanded Families: *upwards and sideways family-tree seen...in the minds' eye* The-Mother heard-*speaking...*

'Why don't you?'

Pleading. The Father heard:

'They would have known what to do.'

'You know what to do...'

The Brother and The Sister's...The-Harvest. The breeding and slaughtering of the animals. Growing, and eating the corn-crop chuckling to The Chickens *clucking...free.*

Then moved to The-Town and then The-City urbanised cosmopolitan…

Rational never Equitable the-Clerk buried the thought; and seen outside already working with The Sunrise: Seasonal-Pickers brought-in, and Great Machines' emplacing the pre-eminent outdated thought *...they still harvesting by-hand…*as buying-up: *The Countryside almost empty of people now the produce machine-fed sold to the local shops and The Town trucks and vans came out each week, most days sometimes, to collect.*

Do business. Sell to, and for them to Sell-On for their trouble. When they had enough to buy, and us to make and sell. Then the Great Warehouses Silo and Transporting-Hubs. Family-Firms, and Fuel-Depot. Great Supermarket chains, paying less, charging less, more sometimes when they could get away with it…

If not for those consumer magazines and on TV. Which? and What? And now Great Lorries and Juggernaut's thundering back-and-forth all times of the day and night on endless roads:…

>To the-City:...container-Port and Freight-Air airport workstations…*visual display-unit quick-response bar-coded...and sent Abroad and brought-in from: in-return for The Goods brought-into the de-regulating smuggling-Ports...The Border Towns and bases...*

<The City Business and governance...for no-taxes the encroaching of The Industrial Zones…Official-Zones: The Financial-Quarter for some piece of the action. Happening events here now or

elsewhere and then all always somewhere in The World and even In-Space.

Everywhere the Great Multi-National Global-Conglomerate Corporations now manufacturing food and furniture and fuelling The-Media...The-Clerk *clerking for Them now in The City:* e-motion passing trees and fields video-transmitted...as filmed, as through a small building window appeared every so often, huddled cross-roads.

Few dwellings. Meagre buildings and scrub shabby, motors and bikes, and horses donkey and camel, tents and shacks collapsed against each other... rifle-range, and Space-Drome Satellite-launch and retrieval site*:...*

On over the sparse and wretched-roads. Garage, shop, maybe stocking stocked-up for the personal -family supplies. Where the produce from nearest and all-around, was from, taken-to, and sold-on open-all-hours, mostly, or some, odd-hours and none-at-all:...

‘'We are all different!' *is the same as...*

'We are all the same!*' meaningless: as a naturalistic-fallacy rational naturalistic response: fatalistic....over a tannoy filmed:*

'Nationalistic...' *irrational...*

'Rational...perhaps...'

'Zealot...dictator Chieftain...' nevertheless...to a feeling of being outnumbered

Out-gunned. Endangered-species…insecure..

'Locked-in:...' *netted.*

'Land-locked.'

'Locked-out...'

'Locked-in...'

Then:

'What would you rather be? Invaded?

'Occupied territories?'

<Occupation: unmarked lines behind hijacked hostaged besieged...swamping beyond...

From-Tunis…to-Kabul:...Israel/Palestine in the middle:

'Across the Almighty-Oceans…'*unsettling felling- tree's feeling, that may be responded-to...as:*

'*Nationalistic...*' rationally...or individually...irrationally fallaciously naturalistically...with hardening almost -racist feelings of paranoia, fear and…justifying:

'Ethnic-cleansing...'*on the cards...*

'Race riots and non-Race riots. Poverty. Anger!' in Red.

Angst. In Black. Fear. In White:

'Moving-out!'

Moving-in. Moving and mixing, and moving-on leaving without recognising this as a fact of life:

'Always!'

'Everywhere!'

'You have *virtual* Civil-War!'

'One-sided, as ever...'

'Many sided...World War!'

'Down to each of Us!'

'Police *and* Thieves...'

'Now!...'

'Murderous!'

'We only murder when murdered!'

'I will Kill Your Family!'

'War is declared!'

Mortars and rockets *blasted* into a Television-Sky...

Exploded, elsewhere...*somewhere...*

'Uncivil war!'

'Is never-declared...'

'Until it has started...the first shot no-one remembers...'

'Just?'

'Happens...'

'Declared?

'Just-war? Alright?'

'Never. Alright.

'Any war?!

Turning Green. In Red:

'Any! Cheated into...'

In Black: In White:

>The-Devil! The Enemy! The Alien! Foreigner...

<OK! In-Android!-Zombie! War!

>The-Other? Other? Who are we going to blame this on?

<Yourself?

>MYSELF?

<What? Myself? By To win back the-People…-YOURSELF!

>For National-prestige? Your Legacy! Your childrens'children…reliable and strong in the face of diversity…or adversity…self-reliant…*spread-bets*...corrupt asymmetry from the perfectly symmetric equilateral, diversity spreading...for-*influence*…over Your-Own…and Others' Owned...abused…

<Government:…

>...Economic-policy:...Business-policy… Public-Policy…*but above all personal...*

The-Leaders…and their cronies…willing or otherwise…

>Code: ?

<Selfish?

>In a Crisis...

<You already have one! Built-in: *The-financial-Big-**Bang**! remember?*

>Financial *de*-regulation?

<Permanent *potential* Crisis-Management...

>Generating-Capital: *People and things...policy and procedure…*

Contextualisation: polluted-surroundings liberated-estrangement alien...released from context...elaborate sexual attraction understood, underhand, overhand infinite possibility, only probability...code of practice...*deviation*-control...

>Major catastrophic event!

<War?!

>All Out-War!...*is more controllable...*

<Of our own making: *They* say...

>Who? The-enemy?!

<Who are?< *or so it seemed so obviously unpredictable.*

>Psilocin-Psionic role-playing **Power**-*creep...*

<Where from? The Cash-machine?

>Or taken by Force-Majeure?

In jest. Interjecting:

<Am I rich-enough?

>What for? Not to need cash? What-for?

<Have to be rich enough...for Life…lives…

>Or taken...do you a deal?

<You deal in lives? What choice do I have.

>Payback? Of course: Property land-rights: acquired game-developer and server payment:…

<Your currency is...Rational Equitable's: N/Y?:…

>You...Your:...

<*Personal*-Wealth:*...from any previous game; and amount required to be borrowed to honour outstanding (including: hidden)...*

>Your-**Debt**:(for*...projected-costs (empty) and...projected...*

<Venture-Capital Earnings (projected: *empty): Your best…*

>Business-plan: n-spaces (empty): filling…

<Balance-sheet: a projected...

>Telepathic! Treasury-chest…you are on your-own...

<Almost-Psycho-pathic…Reserve-Bank *monopoly...*

>But you cannot live beyond your means. Borrowing against property to be built, re-building now…and with Competitive-pressure from others'…

>Pay and Prices...P/p or p/P

<p/P. Restraint required...liberal restraint one-sided unless persuaded otherwise, a figure-head Demagogy...

>Austerity?

<Poverty!

>aND eNTERPRISE?

<Yes...

>On-Credit:…balanced keenly...finely...excluding...credit-rating...

<Massive hidden-Debt!

>Now called-in!

<Any *Savings*: wiped-out…*and so in-debt to yourself to the sum-of:…*

>**R\e**: Nnn. *Called-in...*

<***Social-group Value***:…*collaborative-commons...*

>Financial. @it is the economy stoo…pid.

<StoopID!

>Stew-pied:...

Shanty-town and Tent-city occupying-space:...like Refugee-Camps...

'Home-made...'

'Prices-up...'

'As ever...'

'Never down...'

'Except to sell-on...costs-up...'

'Credit-up...loans aplenty-again...buildings to be built to sell-on...'

'Dot-Comms...'

'Money to be made...'

'Homes. Health and Social-Care..up for grabs…'

'For **Profit**: A Good-*Education* for All! What is Good! Not what is denied…'

'For All! Family...Friends...All!' *border Trade-Walls collapsing towering inferno of The-Banks like churches: secretive silent and suave*:

>Aristocratic? maybe?>

<Presidential-military-chiefs...>

>The countries' economies are not the same as any ordinary household...there are objects and subjects *not* for sale...for money or anything else! Military-police playing with their toys getting a hard-on peeing for all it's worth on fire weaponry-pornography games not in the face of The-Enemy *hatred*...funny-familiar or not at least nowadays...all related anyway fighting

battles everyday...'

'Civil-War everyday! Go to work! try IT! This is World-War!'

'Global-Nuclear and arbitrary reasonable racism genocide…' through sheer fear with another of the species cannibalism as when starving others' children opposite and radically different by degree as any other animal to this one:

'Religious political military-trade and The Nuclear-Option...'

'Wipe-out! The Enemy? A Belief? A Threat? Never...Or we all go-down? Suicide-Bomber? No-survivors? Until there is no-one left to count! Never! So long as We are here!'

'We?'

'Me…'

'Never...stoopid...it's the economy is suicidal!'

Bandana rag-scarf tie-caped-Crusader iron-tip toe-capped webbed glued to the wall...hearing a voice call.

'Crackdown...' *clampdown! Restricting-movement, work, employability...*

'Curfew!'

Welfare-Rights risked for victory starving-out closing-down and re-starting:

‘The-Market! Don't lose your-rag!' *hearing*:

'Lose your shirt!' *remember thinking*:

'Why would I lose my coat?'

‘Uniform:...’ *then it didn't matter why, when, where, or how I had lost my coat, and understood, somehow that I shouldn't, or couldn't have done it again. Found. Unfounded:...*

‘Under attack!!’

A Refugee-Camp: *for money: a dangerous-sanctuary peacefully established ad-hoc and by the-authorities’ as a safe-haven...*

Exploded.

>United-Nations!

<<Nations-United!...*usually disunited...*

>So it seems. The Bad outweighs The Good...

<The Good not so Good as...

<The Good outweighs The Bad?

>Only the Bad is so Bad...*atrocities...*Everytime…

>To avoid them...at all costs...

<By all possible means?

>By all possible means?

<Exactly...

Atrocities::

<The Super-Nations...Trade-Groups...going-it alone...'

>Against The-Lesser...

<The-Lessons...

>The Greater...

<In The Art of Warfare...

>Unlearned...repeated, or altered, around again but differently...

<Eternally: WarFare?

>Or WarFair?

<What? This?

>**The Nuclear-Powers**: *revolving around the worlds' riches...*

<A few God-Given...

>To destroy us All!

<Or destroy the weapons...

>Test us all , perhaps? Test our innocence? Our naivety? Our stupidity? To Kill this that would kill us!

<To be the-*richest* Import-Exporter in The Business...

>The Only One?

<Export/Import?: *Figures...analysis...numbers, that is all...*

>Not. Buildings, goods, services, people?

<The few-richest...and most-Powerful. Deciding how it will be...

>Globally Disputed Areas:...Mining and Agro-culture displaced-forcibly…and by fear…for oil, palm-nuts, and coal...

<Diamonds...Gold, and silver. Whatever...

>Titanium...and Silicon-*chips...*

Outside the-window: *destroyed*-houses.

Sold *ideas* to the-congregation of neighbours electorate *failed...*

Expectorating...*live...on-screen*:

'It used to be only for the money...'

'Then The People killed, or taken-off...To God knows what...'

'Searching for Our Lost Children...' *now it is this-countries' economic-Zone, to the-Others, now it is Trade-deals done, or not-*

done! When I find how-much, is not-possible, then what is possible, now. I feel ANGRY!:

'I cried...'

'A petty, and defining soul-rescue...'

'And for the-Life? Now it is for the food...of God...' *cut-off the hands with a machete...accused of stealing-rice...no-negotiation...*

'...was as if they wanted to leave...without a hand.'

'Without a finger to vote with…'

Ten-minutes of screaming. Crying. Chased-off any intervention attempted destroying, looting, for themselves!

Problems, with electricity, and clean water...came down from the mountains...food-shortages...

Looking-towards The-Clerk, The-Banker:

'**Charity**:...*list*...work's-too...you know?'

'We Love charity! Even less taxes! Great publicity!'

'For when it all goes wrong? Again?!'

'Public-Image:...safe. Advertising...'

'Everything! What about paying Your Government-Taxes?'

'We do that.'

'Who's Government?'

'And *Charitable*-Donation@Charity-works, you-know?'

'Pay-back...'*with the-photograph's on the Boardroom Wall...*

'Not-Theft? Then! Greed? Crime? Then?'

'Agreed...' *with Bonus and percentage-pay increases agreed...*

'In-advance?'

'In-Shares...' *then whatever happens....*

'Increasing The Prices again...'

'Lowering The Costs<*n:N=N...*increasing The Benefits!'

'For who? *Lay-off*'s...closed Factory-Gates? Welfare-Benefits or starvation! What for?'

'Long and happy life I suppose!'

'As all of us! But generally: Home's for Worker's, eh? Fit for Heroes?'

'Of course! Fit for purpose? What about all that Charity? What? 10%? 0.01% Charity...'

'Starts at Home...'

'As kind of Heroic-sacrifice...'

'Suicide bombing...dead, self murder and all other, everything...lose-lose...

'Win – Win! Martyrdom!' T*raitorous...without-knowing really why? What-for? Or whether the outcome's would be favourable or not...*

'Heroic? Harmless? Victimless? Massive-risk? Eh?'

'Others'?...'

'If they cannot manage Their/Our Own Account (s)...'

'As well as Ours?'

'As well as Theirs...'

'As well as We do...'

'We? Cheated? Out-of...'

'Of course...Even Your-own customers, managers, share-holder's, stock-holders especially...'

'Employee's?'

'Nothing...' *well to almost nothing left...*

'Everyone cheats...or steals....from their employer...customers...do *We* not?'

'From The Customers wallet?'

'All of Them...'

'To Payback...'

'A little lay-out for a layback for Life! All of Them!'

'Then We?''

'Everything!'

'In People and Goods?'

'Yes...Stocks and Shares...All of IT!''

'But not In The-Money?'

'Of course In The-Money! Actuarially. Everything! When it comes Time to Repent! I will Repent!'

'Repeat?! Or Resent?'

'With Envy? The People? Savings-invested. Re-invested...look on it As Savings...'

'Savings? Ha-ha! Debts! Sorry. For cheating?'

'Capitalising-*advantage...*'

'Personal-Communism.......'

'Security...'

'Life-Assurance...re-assurance...Pension? For when I am old? Maximising-Profit...Now!'

'From My Debts?!'

'Debt-Holiday?'

'Of Course!' Retire young, Protecting the Investment…

'Market-Share!'

'Export-Import licences and licensed-to…'

'Do-business!' the hands-palmed. On-screen headphone silence...

The-Clerk rubbing a thumb and the finger-tips of both hands as if counting bank-note's:

'Regulating-currency manipulating-*analysis...*'

'For Trade-Offs…'

'Trading-in?'

Looking-down:

<Allies: list...

Looking down into the electric-machine and up again, quickly:

>Now. You>ve got it! That is where the-Media is at...>

<Justly?>

>Better Be!>

<Re-possession...for-profit>s. That is what it is?! From re-possession: I said *We do not do re-possession* didn>t I? We> are only interested in the Money- Value of The Deal...>

>All of It!>

'With: Commission and Management-Fees...' *in-turn...*

'In-terms of?'

'Nothing more than All? Nothing more...' *re-possessions on account of closure for the most part:*

'The Profit...'

'From closure:...'

'Bankrupt?!'

'You? Dead Broke?'

'Stopped. Crashed. Collapsed?'

'What about The People? The Payback?'

'Nothing?'

'Everything? The-Customers@ well...The-Employees? Let us call It:...*re-structuring...*

'Food and medicine, and a roof…is all we really need...'

'We got the sky!' ear-plugged.

Opening-up the screen again reporting:

'A pay-gap *automatically* opens-up...'

'Prices and wages...inflation…'

'Government-subsidised *debt*-bailout...' *punishing, crediting the-people, clinical testing adventurous cautious central bank federal reserve's drawn on benefit cost risk collateral damage? Unintentional consequences? Like suicide-bombers seeking to release prisoners, by killing themselves!*

'Ourselves! Hostage!'

'Known-action...'

'Deflation:…' *unknown* consequence...

'Big-Crunch! Chaos! Collapse again! More Turmoil!

'A tumultuous decade?!'

'Which One?'

'A *little*-Turbulence only? But No! Forever-tumultuous!'

'Turbulence. Only.

'Only?'

'Democracy:...is not a-winner...' *like any-dictatorship monetarising stifling dissent...fear of popular uprising, as ascension of the few personal and families amassing vast-wealth...*

'Democracy is always a winner…' *proportionately…eventually winning hearts and minds without brute force always wins out. By pure common-sense…consensus minoritising…*

'Eventually but for The Democracy-Elitist Establishment! Of The-Wealth and the-People! And anyway never to-*lose*...either.'

'51% is how far The-Markets had got...'

'Haha I heard that.'

''It' is all about the 99% of 50% then: The richest and poorest 98% People, nations, and beliefs...anywhere!'

'*We were not aware...*' *until the personal-charity, rate-fixing scandal...*

'We only did what we were encouraged to do…'

'At gunpoint?'

'To pay-off the bailout, and the-debts...'

*'And bonus on-top! Bought-out...for complicities-silence…*Did not know, then?!'

'When? Today? Not today, no…'

'Then incompetence, then! Bribery and corruption as long as the game would last…to not see *this* coming? When you got in...and when you get out...like...now? Once percentage-points...started going-down?'

'Rapidly...it was too late.'

'...and now they have all-gone. The-*Incompetent*s hanging-on for health as well as The-*Fixers for pure wealth...*'

'Which are You?'

'Which are You?'

'Both.'

'Meaning 'We'?'

'If I stole a Loaf of Bread? Or a Glass of Water? To jail! Fine. No bonus? Theft! Agreed?! On the interest We are being paid!'

'As long as accepted, by a majority...' *voted heard at that-time...minority...The Amount? The Majority? Silenced?*

'Of what people? Or money?! talks! The-*Elite?* The masses?'

'All! To Win...trickle-down...'

'Not-Lose?'

' Or simply pay-off...'

'Your-Debt as well as My-Debt?'

'With what you have now?'

'Almost All of IT. Everything...'

'As the-*majority* does Actuarially, and Actually Most The Time...'

'Most-places...and Each of Us: The *Minority*? Rich?'

'Living...'

'The National Banks and Stock-Exchanges?'

'And The Richest-Minority? One of them: The **Rational-Equitable**...

'Between yourselves...and who?'

'Ourselves…'

'Who? So The-Poorest make up The Majority...'

'Never! There would be riots and revolution!'

'There are already…*threatening* money and life: for-votes…'

'Votes for money...Employment…'

'Social-science…and economic-Religion…'

'In Politics! On-The-Executive-Board?'

'Journalists...*talk*...You? A-Journalist?' *Research: threat of death hacking incremental money-supply increasing-prices inflationary-target stable rises-planned economy currency-war...who would win-out?*

'Bought-out?Buying-out Who? What? For what?'

'The-Company...'

'The-Country...'

'The-same...five or six…'

'The Multi-National Corporations...'

'Foreign-policy?'

'Global...' *real-time strategy simulation game with limited-ammo....tactical advance on the enclave of The Enemy who is...*

'*The*-Debtor re-possessed:...

'Inflation-target mid-course *correction...correlation...?*'

'It is all in at the deep-end..'

'The Cost?'

'Crowd-funding pay and prices...'

'Public Sector Debt re-design...'

*suicide into the deep-end now...*e-*mail address...touch screen*: send:

'Why?'

'Austerity...'

'Then?'

'For all? Or 'We'?'

'*Heaven...and...Hell:...on-Earth...*'

'In the-field...'

'You've got to be there, to believe it...'

'Inflammatory: Incendiary by accident or design...'

'Inflationary?'

'Yes! That is what We All-*like*...'

'All WHO?'

'Really?! Not *really*? I mean...not out loud anyway...' *murmuring*:

'*Buy low, sell-high...*' whispering...then not *too*-loudly but so that It did not matter a damn if heard by anyone, and everyone, in the carriage.

'*Buy low, sell-high! But not. Yet...*

'Prices...beat them down...' *bargain...*

'Or beat them up? Literally? Police? Army? *beating...*

'No, we have The Police to do that!'

'For their pay?'

'Then The Bailiffs...I told You...We don't do that! Others do.'

No-one else in the-carriage was really interested...except when the tax and *charity*-scandals broke...*and now the beatings, the maulings, the rapes and murders...*

'Most of it is *Abroad*:...*in distant-parts, distant ports, foreign-Banks, anyway...*

'That is where the Money is?'

'That is what the clever money is on!'

'No-inflation?

'Proof?'

'No-deflation...'

'*Quantitive*-Easing?' *returns-exchange-rate leveraged...*

'Print-Money! So where to GO!?'...*virtually*, of course...

'To The People!'

'The-Government Ex-chequered?'

'To The Vote!' *breaking-point....*

Are We connecting...there yet?:

'*Virtually...*'

'May as well be. Really. We do not like inflation, but do not like deflation either. Not too long. Especially across the board. The-Bank-Credit, and Currency-Exchange-Rates...'

'Compared to wages, salaries...'

'Prices go Up?'

'Bombs go up...and comedown again!'

'Prices rise in line with inflation and costs...that is all...'

'The buy-out costs you are piling-on? Whenever have you known that to happen?'

'Natural-wastage?'

'*Fenced...-in...*

'*Forced...'*

'The Wages of?

'Surplus to need?'

'In-demand. Then...'

'When?

'Buy-Low...Buy? What?'

'Bought! Get Out of There!'

'The Price of Bread?'

'The opposite: Sell-High...'

'High Street destruction?'

'Like Crop failure?'

'In-Circles?'

'In cycles...'

'Is that what this is? A cycle?'

Each of us connections...two at least...

'To-Buy you have to have *someone* to Buy-from...'

'And who wants to-Sell. You *have* to have *someone* to *sell*-to?'

'Makes-sense.'

'Makes for The-Difference:...' *leverage...therefore: each-irregular... with only colliding colluding tilting centrifuge-ellipsoid...*on-screen.

Pointing-downward, and inward-trading producing outwardly: *a living-situation simulation:*

'With this *intimation of immortality...'* halfway around, pinned-back:

'Bargain's...to be had?

'Deals?'

'Riots?'

Looking-up, and down again, then, across:

>*Riots*...> on-screen:

<*Money riots?*>

>>*No Justice No Peace!*>

<*Not wrong! heard* and seen:

>More like. Social-*unrest...*>

<Wars? Played-out?>
>Civil, or Otherwise?>

>For the-*price of bread*?

<Colour three-D T.V? Not Good for Business:...>

>Or maybe >IT> is?>

>It is?>

'Workers-fired! Sold-on. Like slaves. Serfs. Workers sacked and into the canal!'

>Suicide?>

>Mission?>

>Murder?>

Snagged. *Soldier*ing-on...as Media-Machine:

>*Crown-Servanted* from Serfdom...> *to make the bread...buy-up the losses cheaply, sold-off slavery taxed soldiering-on privateering:*

>*Tithes and Taxes: paying-for...>*

>*Social quasi-religious control...>*

<Police and Army:...

>In-Taxes:*...to...offensive-Weapons:...list...*

<Gold-plated!

>>To Arms!<

<Armour-plated!

>Plutonium-plated...

<Nuclear!<

>Enriched-Uranium?

<Civil, or Otherwise foreign why would you bomb your own people?<

>If they are not your own? *refuse* to be owned...

<Weapons sold-on...cross-borders...

>If we can have them, why not They?

<Not big-enough players...

>On their own…

<As long as they don<t go to war with them!<

>Firing our own weapons back, at us!<

<Or We at-*them*?<

>Then destroyed! By Water Fire Air? In War?<

<Whose Zooming who?

>You got it!

<<See?!

>By the Time you can get the knife out...<

<Loaded-the-gun...

>Fired the shot.

<Mis-fired. Done.

>Done...

<Assasination-squad…

>Don't shoot!

<Trust in the head. Dead. In the water.<

>Globally?<

<Re-sales. For our own Good....of course, and...<

>All of Us?<

<With God on Our side?<

>Of-course. Ours too!

<Of-course not. The-*Government* can do nothing about <IT<! Because We< control things...<

>Virtually...You know what that means?<

<Not-God?<

>Not good! Taxes-up. Wages-down *relatively* Prices-up...

'Prices never go down, now, do they?'

'Only *relatively...*'

'To costs…not to: The-<u>People</u>...*pay*-tax on what they earn…

''We'...do not like tax-*inflation…*'

'Do not like *deflation...*'

'But We have no choice…'

'Or competition? Do we?'

'The currency worthless. Otherwise. Compared to any, or every other?'

'Not-all. But to...' looking down onto the handheld pad:

'Stability...to N/n. Currently…'

'Kick-backs...'

'Kicks-off...'

'Only the exchange-rates...the *status-quo*...

'Only the-equality Gap's greater...'

'Or less...'

'Needs to be the-*higher*? Eh?'

'You wish for something, do you not? How far?'

'All the way…'

'Alright up there in the clouds!'

No-movement.

''It' is after all it is only A *Small* Club…The Real Security-Council? The Conference? A few Global Merchant-Banks and Corporation's…'

<All umbrella-companies and Corporations: list Capitalist-Nationalising Zones...list...Communal Countryside...eradicated Zones...list...

>Re-nationalise?Yes/No?:…

<Re-privatise…

'De regulating the-*Energy*- utilities...'

'Again?'

'Participatory-cap'

'Free Transaction Capitalism, full-blown!'

Light-touch... *glancing* look solid stare:

<Old-city: New city...

>New New City? Old-City?

<New again!

>Old again. *contract's...contacts-in-hand.*

In-hand, a piece of paper stripped from a handheld card-charger:

'Is that in Real-Time?'

'Or *if* Not?'

'But Then?' Looking full into the eyes each into the other *boring...*

>T2:*...tanking Totalitarian-Party kill:...*

<In-talk>s...and now. On-screen: *saving-throw!*

>Now!

<Select: T2: *Your-profile:* are probably the only one (You) that has the-money: in... and *links:* >...to perform the-*Rescue*...

>Without *inflation* or *deflation?*

<Immune? *Had the jabs? Injection of Cash...*

>Limited-only...*by-guarantee...*

<*One for One*?

>Or have a rescue?-*performed on*? *By?*

<Arse!<ole!>

>Otherwise known as: Share-Holders?...*stake-holders, and customers...cancelling-out...list...*

<Soul for 'sole?

>The-Other?

<All?

>Possibly.

<Potentially...

'Spread:...

>Bet's: *list...*'

The-Banker after a break in proceedings still: *disconnected...*

The Other: game-play pause. Aware of the *Game-Play going-on...*concluded. The-Clerk nodding towards the opened brief-case laptop-screen.

Each glancing across each to the others' Game-Player: *loaded and hand-held computer screen each shared numbers and letters, with grammar, spelling and punctuation blank: on another screen resumed...automatically...*

'News coming-in…'

'Only pictures...not the Real Thing!' *numbers on a screen…*

'Desk-jockey door-kickers-in...' particle-board partitions, cubicles, answering phones, checking letters, and numbers...

Deadly computer-virus bugging, gagging, gigging...

Destroying nuclear-centrifuge...from distance, calibrated-infection, biological and cyber warfare, tearing apart systems, designed to defend, anti-threat-attacking...

Meta-gaming Hack and Slash! Share-pointing...magic-pint Game-Master!:

'Office of Cyber-Warfare!' *taking-down cash-machines, blowing-up for scattered-notes robbery grabbed and run and grabbed.*

Charging charge-card machines...again…

TV and radio-stations interrupted-service for a few seconds, by the-Revolutionary, or merely mischievous-rogues who would do such a thing, such a Global-threat:

>*WarFair4? What? For?*

<The World-Wide- Web...*news...Espionage, modern-commercially-sensitive material:...*

Information: sophisticated hacking, privately, personally...

<Nationally, and Internationally...<

<Global!< *launching infiltration-bugs onto networks ill-designed for public-safety or reliability...these-days, deniable. In the greater-good.*

Cached quarantined. Rendered-harmless. Eradicated. Rather-than lived-with. Response to Material-Threat to bring down information-networks and the very intra-structure of The-Economic-Zone rather than the physical industrial-landscape complex closed-down:

<Lifestyle solution!<

>Easy-Life! How about IT? You are your Own-Business, anyway...We all are. Start with the goal of devoting all of yourself to your job of work...<

<I did *start* to have my doubts about the way I was living my life:...but...<

>Import-Export?<

<Export-Import? I don<t Own-Myself! You may do...<

>I do. Take Your Chance?<

<Ours...50/50?<

>Less or more?<

<You, or Me?!<

<*Outlook?: betting hotline: complimentary-copy: Image re-cycled: A4/80g/m2 500 on the tube: <Special-offer just for you: try our new...order-online@...*

<I told you, we do not-*lose*. Value maintained. Not gone-down...Yet!< A waiting-game...

>Through negotiation?<

<Or what? Eh? Re-negotiation?<

>Re-scheduling the debt?<

<Yes? In-currency: of What? 1, 2, or, 3...or...All The-People?<

>Not tied to The-Markets? Shareholders, one way or another...<

<Ripped-off? Army? Governments? Agree? Or Lose It All. Everything.<

>Not-*nothing*, then.<

Sarcastically, to who, or from whom, both:

<Our-*debt*? Together?<

>As-*Nothing*...<

<In money terms...But make *Something*? Power: unit-list:...*list*....<

>If you like...Goods: *stocks*...<

<Shares then...<

>OK. So, we do not really lose anything at all? All Profits shared...<

<Or anything, at all...<

>Not if we can help that!<

<Sold on...<

>Lies.<

<Not the truth?<

>Not the whole truth?<

<There are lies...<

>...and *damned* lies.<

<I know. We tell them. Alright? Got it? But it has to sound like it is true...<

>Even if it is not true...false even. it is true. you get me?<

<You provide the evidence, the Truth? You tell the story...and they get it, you got me? Digital and *terrorist* base-camps, moved-around...and...internal-*treachery*, Government...Taxes...<

>Others can help-you, eh?< *closing...*

The-Clerk looking-across and around the under-crowded carriage:

'Why me?'

'*Sum!* Betting! Gambling on Future-sale price…That is all it is!'

'Direction?'

'Of Travel? How far have 'We' got?'

'Are 'We' given? What do I get? For starters?'

'Under-lying unknown.'

'Risk-averse? Sure…'

'For us it really is Win-win. Sure...simply-betting...' without a hint of irony…

'Or Butting-Out.'

'Odds?'

'ON?'

Then It became obvious, again:

'Others actually take-the-Hit!'

'The-risk! that is 'It'!'

'Not *Our*-risk, exactly?'

'Exactly! Like Fuck it Is!' cursing as if on oath.

Casually-cursing loudly and yet to no-one's apparent alarm or awareness…

'So I get all the *toxic* ones, eh? That is 'It', isn't it?'Why would you be asking otherwise?'

'Top-slice or Dice-and-Splice...'

'Slice! You! Having your Cake and Eating IT!'

Others in the carriage as if choking on only a series of inexplicable aphorisms and further increasingly confusing-apostrophe and mixed-metaphor unmixed:

'IT: further-Loan? Credit-crisis... on *false*-figures! O.K.? O.K. Count me in! Deal me In:!'

Your-hand!'

'My-hand?'

'Your-hand…'

'Is yours...'

'Knew You would.'

Sitting back, grinning:

'The-Market's…will come through!'

'Will they?' The-Clerk and The-Banker *re-referencing* The Opening-Gambit...and The Re-opening....

For-both and incompletely and in-response: moving-on with:

'So. What is to do now, then?'

The-Clerk nodding demonstratively earnestly between the folded-up newspaper, and lap-top, table-top screen.

The-Banker now opened-up. As if the answer lay there, somewhere, somehow between themselves, or elsewhere, out the window. In The Window. Perhaps.

Looking out of the window of the moving-train as if there was actually never mind actuarially any one answer at all, but too-many to count:

'Not One-answer, anyway.'

'Perhaps many...?'

'Perhaps none. The-Choice...You see? To-Move...or Not-To-Move...Anywhere....Anytime...Your-Call...EveryTime. No Big-*issues*? No Detective Private-Eyes?'

'Dependant…' on *where* you *were*, *who* with, and Who engaged in a conversation-*with...riding the train…*

Driven by the need for speed…

Around the-Earth, around The-Sun:

'Incredible! At root, simple: The *very* Rich and *very* Powerful...'

'*Very-few...*'

'Exactly. The One percent?' *the ever impoverished and ever-more comfortable middle towards the outskirts...*

'**The City**? The *Urban*-poor...Suburban...everyone else...the countryside poor...'

'And massively rich?! Don't You want To Be?!'

Another-Town *passed through* and past:

'No. Not if The Others:...' *truly-impoverished, starving, and taking a kicking, a malevolent-killing...*

'Slicing *the*-Cake? What-cake? Slice the throat with the slicing-knife. Knife, Cake. How about You, now, eh? What's *not* to make of it now, eh?!' tapping the 'phone computer case open and vividly re-started automatically: in utter ignorance and dismissal:

'That is what I was thinking.' with nothing more or less to say, or to hear.

Each with a look, with an apparent effrontery, that meant there was to be no further contact to be made, either way, that there would be no further purpose to this.

Each now turned away with-*feigned* annoyance. Distinctly, if slightly less distinguished and so. The-Clerk supposed, expecting of no-further-conversation, not giving opportunity any longer of answering, or questioning-back.

Only pointing-out the distrustful plotting conspiratorial *horse*-trading, prancing dancing-around...virtual insults...to the intelligence. Whatever? Of the-Arcane Mysteries?

The Secret...or *none at all. Hidden one-per cent Society...one per-cent. Ten per-cent? So what?! That it was assumed shrewdly, astutely, even eloquently spoken-of.*

As each concluded this apparent-interview...was meaningless, insincere, and over:

'I only ask once.'

'Only Once, is it?'

'OK I'll tell You how it is shall I..?' *without affirmation and without waiting for one. Without even knowing if really with any malice aforethought:*

The Clerks' *now* thought unspoken: *this is bribery and corruption embezzlement and fraud admitted-to*:

'Theft?! Robbery? With-Violence? War?' *in anyone else's book...*

'Insider Trading spread-bet's on-Speculation and Risk.'

'For The-Others...'

'*To keep thy mouth shut.*'

'Keep your job and shut-up or you're out?! Or: You'll never work in the City again!'

'Or anywhere else!' The Clerk finished the-*internal* spoken dialogue externally:

'And Me?! The Rest of US! To take The-Jump...*when it all goes wrong again?!'*

'Eh?!'

'Extend the terms? Go on!'

'Of Office, or the-Debt?'

'Both. You know? How I get to be Your or My-Own Remuneration-Board? Like a Family-Business! Without reference to any Share-Holders, as the CEO-President of You? Your own-Company?'

'Presidential-*motives?*'

'Because I am The-President! **Rational-Equitable...**'

'Exactly. Get The News! In Business as in Government as CEO-President, and as President of My-own: Personal-Banker!'

The-Banker retreated, slightly, with the silent final entreaty to-self, and with eyes looked only now as if repeating some unspoken thought, but not saying, speaking anymore...fore-finger tapping, drumming, wistfully, blissfully unaware...

The-Clerk *wildly, wistfully almost silently to the temple, at the side of the head* as if holding a gun there.

As not the best way to shoot someone else...but if a suicide then spraying brains all over the place probably as effective as any other...

Does not look as if chancing it, and about to be blowing brains-out The-Clerk mused.

Short-tempered perhaps red hot-headed explosive, not yet ripping eye-balls out.

Dark to light green *volatile gas...financial performance accelerator voltage envy of a friends' responsible narrow data from the*

Morningstar...but which-One? Perhaps not-playing Russian-Roulette...*re-entering the fray...*

The-Clerk:

'Decisions of The International Conference...'

'Trade-Agreements: *list:...'*

'All-or-nothing? Another roll of the dice-ball...'

'Presidents, and Countries' call...Economists, academics...'

'And those who wished they were *paid* to-be...'

'To give results! Not-negative...'

'We are no longer Social or Religious beings...*merely* Political-*Economic*-ones...

'*Animals*...then...'

'Animals.'

A the roll of a drum...*executing...*

'Deal. Then.'

11.

The-Clerk to The-Banker:

'So, where are these-*lost* Trillion's then? Or is that 'Squillion's' now, then, eh? *Free micro-lending Kick-starter Credit Union*?'

'Rap-Scullions! Not in The Government-Bonded...'

'Not Our Coffer's...' *that's for sure!* What spent...on? Where? Ohhh...Jobs? Employment...'

'Hospitals…Schools, Houses. You want those? Don't You? New factories and drilling-rig mine-shaft-pipework:…satellite

network…*aerial* to the skies…The-Limit!'

'You have to pay!'

'The-Whole-Planet!'

'Beyond! Out in Space!'

'No-one can hear you *scream…Prices! Taxes!* They can...actually…only very slowly and veeeeery deeeeep...'

'Jobs-creation...scheme...voiceover!'

'And beyond?'

'Lame!'

'And Fuck the rest!'

'Actually…Actuarially...there is not much left...'

'Actuarially? Fucked?'

'Better…There is much more, wait and see...squirreled-away...in Tax-Free-Havens:...

'Overseas?'

'Of course. Foreign countries: list......yes...Cayman-Club Islands…'

'Ireland?'

'Zoo-Rich? Get it? Gen...e...va? Get IT? Exactly! ' *Actually. Actuarially. Naturally! the obvious, and yet unexpected out in the open confrontation. Across The Counter-intervention of guile and wiliness devious manipulation scheming:*

'Big-Bonus announcements in The City...' *waiting-for you, anyway...and Tax-breaks for:*

'Epic fail!'

Headlined across the carriage:

Epic-Fail! The Day The Markets *finally* crashed - again!! headlines *newspapered* across the carriage:

'*Failed.* Ourselves...'

'And everyone else!'

'Granted…'

'All 7-Billion?'

'Raise you! 11…billions trillions more now...even as we speak...markets...*consumers...*'

'Peoples! Workers! Contrite? Then again...'

The-Clerk as though another shooting The-Banker: directly between the eyes, through the Head.

A spray of blood and bones and brain's-*splatter*ed murdering. A Murder-scene. A Murderer? Assassin? Emissary? Undercover secret-agent mole...moleing...moiling...*mulling...*

Staring, blankly, blindly but not in fear but with *consternation* felt; and leaned to the other-side...*in-case the others' silent bullet figuratively actually did hit what appeared now with the actually final retort, to be the intended target*:

'Aimed!'

'Fired!' Dodged:

'Dodge-City'…eh?' in slow motion...out of the way.

The-Clerks' duellist finger-*pointed now hitting the opposite target from below and straight upper-cut fisted and as a smack-on-the-jaw:*

'Warning! Crashed! Never enough!'

'Greedy? That is how IT was? Was IT?'

The other coming-around and straight-between-the-eyes:

'Worming....our way...' *into-the-brain, the nose-bone clean, clear hit through the silver-bullet black print a spray of bloodied ruby red stained...*The-Banker quivered slightly, behind the-newspaper. Behind or rather, above, and beyond The-Screen and *not going to say anything* as The-Clerk realised-*this* and as once intended closed with:

'Well, this is it...'

'What?'

'I am in-it! Up to Here!!'with a hand passed over the scalp:

'With your so-called *scalping*-advice!'

The-Banker could not help but retreat. Then to peer out from behind the newly-drawn newspaper as if in self-imposing exile. Withdrawn behind, for social-wealth, and The Railway-Carriage classic reasons, alone: To-be prepared always, if-nothing else, for the prevention of *unprepared-for attack*...Paranoia for that which could *actually* happen and not only be paranoiac over-exaggeration: over-*estimating...*

'In-*Best*ment!' *Bridging*-loan with investment-option…cover your debts…'...and underground-tunnel entered into Wi-Fi Auto-Pilot *piloting* surfacing...alongside motorway and in-fields great-houses...mansion-estates and ranch farms and industrial park and...

'Play?'

'Play!'

'At the very least with The Arrow of Extrication...'

The-Clerk:

'You don't Get it? Do You?'

Silence.

'The-Game?'

Silence:

'Toxic-lending! Extinction! Buying and selling-on a dupe! And that is Me! Isn't 'It!'! This is how I will know what it is!; and this is what I will make of it!'

More-silence:

'I am that Dupe, aren't I? Or to-be so?!' the one hand, and now other-hand now *cutting-upwards slicing the across the throat, cut swiftly*:

'...up to here...' *and then noosed, strangling, dangling, hanging...The Neck-breaking gently-wrung as by the self-same owned hand lifting, twisting, twisted knotted and roped neck, and, head-jerked.*

Sideways-snapped back behind the ears, cracking The Neck...bone ear-splittingly crackling...hissing...sound bright-light...

'Tunnel-of-love@...

'Moving forward...'

'Oblivion!' the final dramatic riposte from the-Clerk, in the ungainly sully.

The-Other seemingly oblivious. Unmoving, unmoved, as anyone else on The-Train: moving with the train alone in their own personal and Grouped-Worlds:

'Today I am going-in...To save your job and many Others?'

'Or only a few of You? Us? I am likely to be shredding documents and deleting emails for You or someone like You!' *filmed photographed, buried and book burned filing cabinet...e-mail:*

'To burn the evidence…lay the past to paste…'

'Waste! That is it, scrap waste and recycling, that is where it is at!' Walled-in. Squared, and encircling:

'Wondering how to pay off: My Towering-Debts!'

Met, with a wall of silence. Then The-Banker leaned-back and glanced-out of the window, remarking:

'To whom?'

A crash of dinner-plates and breakfast bowls and tea-cups...at a well situated country residence, in town and country, and The-City:

'To The-Banks! The Shops! The Government! The Police! Social workers! The-Army! Another Army! My Government! Our Government! And, Yes! Our Government! *Ours!* it is *Our*-country! While 'We' are Here! Now!'

'A simple-Majority? And even simpler-minority! *Evens, anything above, anyone, or below Zero! Quits!*

'While you are tucked away in your Ivory Tower...'

'Or should that be Golden-Walled Palaces?'

'Water-wheels...and Open-Acres…'

'A-minority, believe-me, you do not stand a chance...'

'The 1%? Remember? And the-Others? Ten-per-cent, it makes *no*-odds!' *an invisible-hand raised in-defence:*

'Golden-Run?'

'Golden Risk? Other=People?'

'Risk? All the-Time!'

'On Others' Money? No-Risk? Cash-in-The Bank! Savings? Investments? Repayment mortgage?...And this *award* goes-to…This-

Bonus! This *stolen*-Reward...' *receiver-systemic-symbiotic: financial-sector expansion... everyone a shareholder, home-owning, low ages, higher-rent...relatively...n/N/n... house sell-off, buy-up:*

'Too Big to fail...'

'Vested-interests...

'The-City...'

'Country-wide international Unions of Workers consolidated corporations...' *affordable, to do business: building-societies and savings-banks, competitive-investment principles, competition between eaten-up...out of business...small and medium-sized business...billions of them...of Us, each of us bought-shares, selling shares as price-rises, prised-fallen off: sell off quickly...*re-competition and fall of the conglomerate banking investment houses for food and furniture at the end of the day, and houses...

'This goes to the-*smart*est One...or Two...in the room…'

Pointing back and forth, both:

'On *this* Train.'

The-Clerk correcting. Only then, the obvious:

'Living our-lived-out live on A Train...Crash!'

'Going forward…'

'Stuck on the rails, we spend our lives waiting…for what?'

'The next stop?'

'The Big-One, isn't it? No-Responsibility for its' arrival on time? Of a few-Million? Billion? Or...'Fuck-off!' then, eh?'

'There are Billions of US! No shopping-trip out-at-work cannot get enough of it country this...'

'There are families, and individuals...'

'7-Billion only…yet, and *rising...*'

'Then, only the Church. Secular-politicians. Police and Armies...'

'Or some political-religious-crazies...'

'Whoever is presently in-Charge...'

"It! Changes...'

'We do not.'

'Charges!'

'If you Do nothing! '

'If you Do nothing. You create a vacuum. A vacuum which draws speculation...'

'Into a Power-*vacuum...*'

'Prison, or-*Exile?* What would *that* do?' *when push comes to-shove...*and a-*glance* out of the window. The-Banker exulting, now executing:

'*Analysis* see? You have to be there. You have to *live it*!'

'Whether IT happens the way the-computer states, and the-Politician-economist suggests only without-*evidence*:...'

'The real ***Future?*** That is the only evidence anyone can have!'

'Speculation-only!'

'No-one knows what is going to happen tomorrow!'

'Or cares? Spinning-*Fields*...surely?'

'Excepting..that it will be much as today.'

'Business as usual?'

Re-iterating. Not allowing of any other response now:

'You have to be there, or have it instantaneously live-streaming CCTV closed-circuit television beamed-in satellite...'

'Everywhere at The Same Time...'

'Or computer...' *pica-second later...before? get me?' Good-timing? In or Out? The merest delay neon pica-seconds, pixels to spare then to follow-up immediately...In? On-the-dot! On the dotted-line?:*

'You got 'It'!'

'No You got it! All? For All!'

'To be sorted-out today…' *with-you, or without-You. Together? In this-together? Call-it Debt-Aid? Loan-Aid or whatever.*

Covering-the-tracks:

'As of the night-before, as you might say...'

'Back-room deals already going-down?'

'Going Up!' Exploded! Onto-the-scene.

Inwards on router smart-switched-on panel-screen through earphones loosely hanging heard:

'Arriving at the camps in lorries…' experiencing grey helicopter-gunships from the sky to burn yellow and red and black, and leave unburied. Paused. For shots, of the bodies, and in the skies, aircraft...*buzzing*-in...

'Here, Men be-draggled, and boys of fighting age taken and Women and Children terrified on makeshift transport of old lorries, bicycles and foot: 'Hundreds...thousands of miles, between-them...hundreds of families...Young and Old.' *and the on-screen reporting...then radio frequency-jammed cut-of from the rest of the world…warning…signs seen...tyres-burning…shabby Port and coastal Resort...dried-up river-beds running inland irrigating only dread...*

'Through The-Cities' severed-wires...' *like nerve-endings:*

'Everything looted and boot-legged stalls, bootless and un-bandaged-families living in the remains of burned-out old Colonial-Buildings...'

'Government Houses. and University...' *clean-walls, and cleaned out of every piece-of-wood and metal from door- frames to hinges-and window-frames.*

Of furniture, and fittings there were none left. Except brick dust and concrete. No electricity, water from some well or tap nearby, used by many-others...sometimes dirty, sometimes clothed, closed, when disease and pollution rife...

'Shock and Awe!' *frightened* and disoriented...The-Occupant family around a dinner-table laid-out and ready-to-eat...Leaving the centre of the room. Into the corners for safety...*as they knew:...*

Silently. *In case of through the wall Rapid-Mousing...mussing...musing...as through the doors and at the windows where they could be seen through helmet-camera stern simple instructions:*

'Up against the wall!!' *ghost-rider operation:*

'For Freedom?!'

'From the need for freedom...' grunted *almost lizard the house of the trembling leaves. The-scattering...petrified* in the moment: get down spread-arms and legs nylon-strapped, roped-down in the excitement and confusion in *The Truth...the Moment Gone...*Playing-out, as directed moving filmic mobile-evidence:

'Fully-accurate. Honest and truthful.'

'Fair, and reasonable?' *asking questions:*

'About liability?: Accident or Act-of-God?! *fear, with honest denial, or retribution, retaliation useless and falsely...*

'In-the-course-of-Business...' *excerption, exception, exemption domestic-content renewable irrelevant questions and decision: dropped-rates...when you're not-looking:*

'Tender? Proposal? Renewable, anytime? All contracts...re-negotiable in the light of such exceptional circumstances.'

'Bids' Fault? Failure? Fraudulent…even??'

'Stronger/*weaker* only. PR Politician, CEO-President. Internationally-acclaimed. Celebrity. Fun!'

'For-some.'

'Who would deny them?'

'WHO? Indeed...' *in the-pay and health-boards of countries, around the World Big-Pharma outdoing little-pharma unlicensing and selling-cheaply...expensively...*

'What price Health and Social care?'

'The-Public rules…'

'RE-Public…masculine…'

'The Domestic-Realm rules…'

'Fiery-males…mostly…lessly…'

'Equally-never…but almost always…'

'Differently? In-Trust?'

'Not-lying?'

'Either…'

'The Truth! Trust! That's IT!'

'Trust-Fund?'

'Cheating: Trust-Fund!*: pay me-out:...'*

'For The-Sport! Games!'

'Winning from The-Start…'

'Or by the end…'

'No draws…same-scores…all or nothing.'

'Quits then? To The MarketPlace!'

'Fair-Exchange negotiated fairly…not-equally…'

'That's The LIFE Game:…

Children beneath under their parents' solemn gaze and occasionally taking-part in the game: staring down the camera-lense as staring and reading a *movie* -script gone to adlib improvisation:

The Citizen-Reporter:

'They stop where they felt safest and nearest...'

'For Food and Water...exhausted. At *this* outlining outlying border unmarked Open Refugee-Encampment...' *tree-branched, plastic sheet-tents...marked-out, from the air...*

From the ground:

'Death everywhere. Deaths' daily totalled in double-figures...' *of small-children...and Elder's...shrunken and bloated with starvation...*saved more by Global-*Medical*-Help...' *without-Borders...other-than the Warring Factions: Armies and armies, armed Thugs and Militants, enslaved across borders...from The Citizenry:*

'For no-Pay!' copied-out onto a sub-titling screen:

'W*ith An Humanity lacking otherwise not at all:*

'Despite the many *Avoidable* Deaths...' *of The Youngest and The Eldest...*

'Without Proper Shelter Food or Clean Water...through no fault of their own. Only who they owe. Crackdown restricting-work Claiming-Benefits without paying-into the system, Free Travel-Pillow...

'They say here.'

'Cull.'

From the-scene:

'And hence, are each One and where forced-from a world of their making to one, not at all of theirs....'

'They fight on?' *against a breathless, thirsty, starving, enemy...' unseen, as from the skies...from the-ground...unknown before...*

'Collapsed!!'

'Their-Worlds...' *at an instant:*

'Crashed.'

'Collided!'

'Exploded!'

'Fairness?' *strategic decision-making upsetting any-natural-balance...acquitted-well... condensed condemned-to-exile...optimum-strategy random scissors-rock-stone product...exporting-food fuel...*

<*Win-nucleosis...*

>Strictly competitive society may be random...<

<May be-chosen...<

>All-chosen! Food! Complex everyday co-operative, not to out-do the-Other harmfully. Not need-to non-co-operatively-competitively need outside *referee-aspect:* respect authority-of-enforcers...

<S*urvival*-strategy.<

'Loneliness of the long distance...triteness. Boring...'

'Survivor-guilt. Everything laid-out for You..'

'Laid-on, cannot-*miss...*'

'Did I know what I had signed up to?' *Signed-up for? Haunted, of the haunting-attack, on a helpless, potentially devastating, enemy:*

'Spontaneous Change...things as they like...'

'To Bring back to a hapless helpless happy-*humanity?* Peaceful happy-*normality*...instead *line*-management...'

'Online?'

'Briefing-finds...'

'*Redundancy*?'

'Price to protest...'

'To-*prevent*?'

'To...Permit?'

‘To take a life?’

‘To save a life...taken out of The Game.’

‘How would You know?’

‘Depiction simulating endorsement...is not endorsement…’

‘C*age-fight...wrestling set-up…Bull-fighting to the death...of the Bull...bear-baited...’*

‘Littering-agreement...’

'Storm-cloud gathering…’

12.

The-Banker worried-out aloud. As at the Ports and Docks and Airport of the-City ahead and headed towards. As storm clouds gathered-low, across the intervening sweeping curve of big-sky and likely distant ocean and Continental Land-Mass: People working and *earning*-money and goods...The-Clerk returning to re-connected and simultaneously now re-interactive-gaming:

>Active-X portal-platform:...

<Play: Taskbar: *encryption...completed:...*

>Information-bar...*with interface cursor command…module loaded-message:*

<Your-City:

>Country: Principal-*Life-game:...as another joined the game from somewhere in The World...*

The-Clerk speaking again quietly with voice-operator recognition (VoR) engaged-earphones, and mouthpiece microphone headset sounded-into and from the Mobile Gaming-Device clicked onto:

<Information: How to Play?... *and task bar-typed on the keypad mouse onto:*

>'Go!'

<The *Aim of the Game*?'

>To Win of course! Not To Lose!'

<To come out at least evens to 51+% *better-off...*

>Somewhere else loses?

<Inevitably if not equally...

>Life? Everything?

<Possibly...

>How?'

<The-Rich-List: <>the higher the score...the *lower-*scores:..*poorer...*

>The-*Poor* List? ><*Simple as that?!*

<*The lowest scores: The Poorest...*

>*The higher: The Richest...and by staying alive as long as possible...under some extreme conditions...and for your family and loved ones...local and distant friends, cousins, and cousins' cousins' and Villages...*

Towns and Cities of the World:...address-booked requested: Countries of the world... come from...and-to...

<Where you are now?

>Geo-*location:*...re-allocation...found...and someone joined-in-from...*inform...be-care-full...Nnnn...*

Somewhere in the world:

<Game-on!

>Game-On!

Another *sharp-accuser* another *blunt-blade* joining *freeloading prisoner...*

<The-Game: *Selfish-ideologue: Rule the World!*

>Cashed-up...*and went All-Out!:*

<Total World-Dominion!

>Enough is never enough!! *sent-out...sending...*

<By getting the highest buildings and highest money-score you can...*against-others…as much money as you can…owning more than anyone else…or owing the least...for Richer or Poorer: lists…known, and not-known: list...by: names from your address book:…finding…pure-selfish protagonist:…apologist...Antagonist:*

<Stay Alive! By-staying Alive!

>Yourself!'

<As Yourself…

>And all I have!

<*And All that you will ever, or always have...*

<Everything? *Inevitably. If any return at all. Otherwise, Nothing...*

>What does it mean to lose?

<You-starve. You die. Game… Over!

>Then?

<How many Lives have you?

>One.

<One? Not so literal…

Tapped-in. Delusional blue skies immediately turning grey. The-heavens opening up: *red*-flaming...

>HellFire! You get blown-up?

<Or You blow yourself-up?

Silence. Fire-erupting emanating from the ground. The ground and sky, and space opening up: the-Media...transparent and *clear warning:*....

<Fueling: **The-City**:...

>*Natural* disaster: historical hurricane/ earthquake…from the-*ruins*:...

<You are Building your-City: again…

>**Name**: Home: City clicked...

Text boxed:

<Your-Bank: name: **The Rational Equitable**…

>**The-Bank** of *You*. Regulating…*ourselves immediately in The Debts of Agricultural-Communities: indebted by religious-tithes and political-taxes and commercial-interests:...*

<On-behalf of the newly-formed forming:...

>The-Banks! *trading with debts and...*

<Brokered Shares in…*these-Debts as...*

>Investment-Bids... for:...

<***Your-Equity:****...of pastoralist-farmer's, serf's and enslavement's and as the-Mercantilist:...*

<<u>Now!</u>: Local and/or Global:...

>Trades: Industrial/Commercial:...*effectively using...*

<Government-Funds...*as securities, bonds financial or in-lieu of...*

>Goods...*protection insurance for shares in derived stock...*

<<u>Actual-Goods</u>: currently-owned...*at any one-time, or space...produced and delivered, and costing and price accounted for as...N/N...*

>*Buying*?Y/N:...*don't know...*

<<u>Or</u> *Selling*?Y/N: *don't know...*Buying?Y/N:Y!

>Selling?Y/N: *at-market...on a first-come-first-served basis...*

<In-Currency?

>Sold-on...*and a potential seller asks a specific price for the stock...*

<There are multiple bidders...*or askers at a given price...*

>Auction?

<Action:...' *buying-prices:...*

>The clocks are ticking...

<Which is when the timing comes-in…

>Afghanistan…Argentina…

<Uganda to Zimbabwe...

>The Long Route...> *shorted...*

Time-trading prices and bid figures, derivatives real, or virtual on the floor on-line...

>Network of Economic-Transactions…

<Goods? Buy-up short?

<How short?

>Depends what You want...

<Buy-up...> *not a physical facility, or discrete entity, nominally relative only notional value bet on an events, occurring...*

>Sell! Gambling at Overall Odds: On of over 10% for example:...

<Australia...to Zambia! Over The Real-World Economy Markets: to...*Model*-Market:...Global:…

>From-time-to-time *cancelling-out*…any-difference…with failures of harvest and successes in equal measure with mercantilism...

<Capital-investment houses: *choosing, or losing...*

>**Capitation:**...

'De-capitation!'

On screen:

'Re-capitation...' *tutorial-college: Institutional-investor's:...such as mutual funds, banks, insurance companies...and*: .

<**Hedge-Funds**: List...*list's...and publicly traded corporations trading in their own shares, effectively, economically and efficiently risk-adjusting returns based on profit and dividend margins...*

<**Pay: Dividend** pay-out...*revolts by shareholder capitalists and Market socialist Employer and employees...*

>Ethical medical educational financial *treatment of people as animals...*

<Everybody is...

>All are...

<Against The-Fat-Cats *list:...*

>And Anti-Poor Law...

<Morally-Humanely?

>Then Immorally...

<Cannibalism...*when-starving, yes. it has happened...and that is why it is so important! It is the last-Sin, the worst! Disgusting, to have to do the-thing! De-generate worker's State Bureaucratic Capitalism... State-terrorism, Collectivism, State socialism...*

>*Incentive-packages...*

<Price's... *mostly at or near some ideal-equilibrium, based on openly public-knowledge...n-*N...

>Costs?

<*Purchasing*-parity...*across The Board:...*

>**Power**-up!: *Market-Orientated...*

<*Shock -therapy...*

>Hyper-inflation debt-crisis...

<Got 'It'! *the roulette wheel of probabilities known...almost, without any certainty whatsoever...*

<Pure luck...

>To start-with...*dependent on the skill and investment decisions, and reliability of information known or not of the different player's...cards kept close to your chest...protected by the armour:*

<Your Treasury:...*chest pictured, glittering and glinted in the sunlight:* Takeover!

>*Stabilisation*-prosperity...funded...to the tune of...*algorithmically designed micro-electronics Super-Jet...Super Didact: deducing deducting: Credible-True-Witness...*

>On current-rates... *on...gambling...*

<Future-rates*?:...lists...list:...listing...*

>Contract-rates: *interest and commission-taken...floating on a choppy sea financial instruments, to navigate the choppy waters...*

<Collateral-*damage* limitation…

>Management-*liquidity* for the whole-Global-market:...

A *safe*-port, or becalmed in *open*-waters…

>Optional shares in each-owned: own-City, State, and country-sided continuous...

<Land... and Production: list...

>Actual-trade's: *list...based-on an auction market bid priced-at (based on profit) against a specified seller price (based on costs):...*

>The Asking-model:... *where your potential buyer's bid bids at a specific-seller price for...*

<Stock-price?

>The taking-model: Y/N? Y: Done Deal...

<N/n.../N...*wholesale without transformation in bulk and the end-user:...list...*

>Itemised-call-log:-monthly- statement:...

<*Activate*...and not feel the pinch, when The Others leave The Pyramid-Scheme…*re-sold-on…efficiently and cheaper through e-procurement improved transparency along-the-line online:*

>Enterprise: *resource-planning: information-panning...*

<Quotation and proposal:…*and notification of intention To Tender...*

>Bid!

<As Consortium?: list...

>In-Corporation? Co-Operative? Collective?: *list...*Sole-trader or Limited-Liability Company (By Share-Dividend of: Nn...) Company-name: **R/E**: **The Rational Equitable@** *trading...*

<Opening-price…Nnnnnnnnnnnnn...

'Open-Sale!…' *set-up...off-set...set-up...off-line...backed by revenues- taken from drained swamp river and sea and re-vitalising pasture-lands and savannah, rivers and lakes, sea, and plantation, farms…spread-out as...*blue green…yellow-brown, black, red, white-washing white than white…chalkstone black-slate...built-upon *with local and non-local bones stones bleached white with the-Sun stones* *and pebbles...artefact and fossilised creature...wood and leather and metal materials...tools, fuels and fodder...*

>From the...*opening...*Great Journeys of Adventure: Exploration and Discovery-1:*in history...as if buried alive. Dead: Alive*:

<Taking-over...

>Pyramid-Effect over Law: List:...*for your own benefit...following digital-analogue language-marathon chanting oral-history: for immortality, or at least, continuing mortality:*

<Honouring tradition-and-family...*down to other's, not only-yourself:* Unelected-Analect: Cult of **The-Bureaucratic-State**:...

>Materialist-Ideology...

<Religion and Politics...

>Science...

<Rich beyond Rich...*beyond*-belief...yet *afraid of their own-shadow...*

In Imperial-*revenge conquest and coastal and river Cities named:*

>To control the flow of trade money, and people... *invasion and slaughter, and deportation of human-rights and responsibilities; remorseful, and the-compassionate: alleviation of suffering, understanding and improving responsibility of self and The Others:*

<Life on Earth: *list...*

>Outlawing-Slavery...Serfdom...servantine…*and all mis- and maltreatment of all living things..naturally:*

'Public and Private! Keeping The Peace!' *heard* crowded: banded subscript:

>At the...Village-gates...*and Cities with lion statues, legal, social philosophy, of order, wisdom, clear...seen-through:*

>Buildings and schools and hospitals:...

<Referend for Democratic...

>*Free-Speech*!

<*Just and kind:* Morality: list...*and not only:*

>People-Power ruling over...

<Each Despot in exile or killed.

>Military-Might! *Is Right? Left? Up/Down?@Inward and out'ards:*

<Defensive Walls...

>Towers *underground places...*

<Hotel-Palace as a Prison...*above us...only-sky...rested.*

Un-rested...arrested weeping, and fasting, fused troops questioning everything:

'Clever stupid Ruler...'

'Advisors...' making top-heavy decision closed society mock-trial censorship and in revolt joined in death:

>For the living successors of Civil-War: *All-Wars that is...*

<We don't solve our problems by hating! Or-killing!

>Or putting into hospital! Blown-up! Market-places watering places, and trees for shade for travellers to talk and take sustenance:...

<*Divine*-Emperor playing at Golden-Rule God-*fearing...supported by One-God One People...apparently with the Victory-of-Faith in a Glorious and Forgiving-afterlife..*

On The-Screen:

'Religious-militaristic invasion to spread The-Word..'

'And to threaten: to *murder and maim...otherwise'*

'Only Wise and Just...'

'Victim-Blame...' *for which The-Rebels will always win...*

'Eventually...'

'By-Force or By-Peace?'

'Bread, and weak-water in return...' threatened, beat, and killed those who did not partake in Their Law...Our-Law?:

Survived in a kind of afterlife:

'The next generation...'

'By seed, and idea...'

'But for Sword and Gun!'

''The pen can shoot bullets as deadly as the rifle...''

'Faith...Or none...'

'No-One has none...'

'Good-faith, in-Self? Or *None*?'

'Faith not in chance?'

'Chanced...perhaps...' *the Ideological and Technological-explosion of brutality, in-terror, besiegement and conquest:...'*

'For Trade?'

'Exploration by trade: Plunder and Monetaristic...'

'Credit-Capitalism suing for peace: for terms of trade...'

'And Terms-of-Trade?' astronomical-*omen* red glow grey covering dark skies and crop failure volcanic-ash cloud and the destruction of trees and drought-deserted dust-bowl:

'The Gods have failed Us!'

'Again!'

Looking across from the opposite seated the gaze felt suddenly looking up black rain to red storm clouds coming-in...'

'Business never rests...' looking-out the window...

The-Banker:

'So?'

'Business as usual.'

For the-Banker there was only one-way out. Nodding over to the game-player games machine breaking the unnoticed silence:

The retrieved now once-more revered newspaper; the *news*-sheet somewhat-wildly-waved:

'Only '*Natural: Life is a gamble*!' and as if the final word on the matter: 'For-*sustenance*…To-eat and *breath*!'

'Or be-eaten, right-here, right-now!'

'Flight or Fight?'

Alighting The-Platform:

'Fight to the Death? Or starve to death, eh?'

'Kill? or be killed?'

'Kill? or be killed without a fight, eh? Which is better?'

'Who? From who? Where? Where to?'

'We have free-will even now. Choose!'

'Fight, or flight? When is the *best*-time, most-*auspicious* Pause?'

'When what is there that is only-natural has happened anyway, eh?'

'Over the Chinese Wall? Insider-dealing in-time...is bound to happen, anyway?'

Looking-down into their computers both-One:

'This is not simply in the-*imagination*...'

'Or only dreamed of…'

'What do You mean: *dream* of? Those new-*Put's* list's…'

'They... have...happened...anyway.'

'Already?'

'Get in there first or else…' *for the next noisy ,and silent millennial-springing: closed-in.*

Summer...winter...passed...re-opening...autumnal:-return from failed...expedition, executioner and executive:

‘Army-leaders...’

‘Police...’

‘Aristocrat and Peasant...’ *all out-slaughter.*

‘With Army-General-Officers and Police-Marshall and Sheriff, upstart Colonel not yet elected by The-People…’

‘Only each nominally-elected by the-Elite…The-People under duress...of The-Establishment: *The-Elite: Presidential CEO and…Prime-ministers of the familial-elite: with...*

>Chain of Command:...

On-screen: *clearing ground razed computer auto-digging the trenches for sewerage pipes, and clicking…Work-Gang working...exchanging expertise and skill...artfully crafting:*

<Utilities: water/gas and electric and telegraph-cable lines *dragged suspended across and buried-below-ground...*

>Tunnels for Road and Rail-bridge... *and overpass...*

<Express-way:...t*o the outer-Suburban outskirts: row- upon-row of workers-houses, and ever taller…*

>Apartment-blocks: Homes built cheaply low-energy efficiency short-term small cramped tenements…

<With or without a market...rented, sold-off...garden, for food and flowers…perhaps....

>Industrial-factory-farmed estates, and...

<Business-park marked-out, by...

Lake and Sea...and Ocean...and Continental-shelf...

>Like an in-store Mall-shelf...

<Tenements storied-high-waves:

>Let's go-fishing!...*ships and boats moored at the river-coastal City. Alongside the-Airport. Taking-off and turning flight-path...*

<C*omplex*-Engineering...

>*Simple*...like: Mechanics...stops and starts The *Motor* of the World...

<Mere-automaton? No-more? We? Not even simple-minded animals who hunt and kill whether plantlife or animal nevermind same species...only as much as required for protection...survival and...and...

>Brain-surgery...The Good-Life! That is what we need!

<On-Holiday...like today...

>Of-course!...*holiday*-resort...resort-to...The Basics! Food and Fuel and The Leisure-Industry! Media! For good or Ill!
>Proceed>...proceeding...from scratch: land-cleared trenches-dug, cables laid and radio-signal flag post aerial raised. Over-seeing...capturing and directing and re-directing in faltering staccato-

messages and picture, and text uploaded spoken…continued commentary:

>Founding-stock:...*tax-free loophole…colonial*...concessions:...

<Floundering to the...

>Finish-line...*maximum-point's tooltips…for navigation…buttons, and more…to take care of everyday-touches...bootstrapped...providing a well built set of plug-ins for drop-down menu...channelling...*

<*Iconic-tabulator…tables and forms, pads and tablets as well as expertly crafted styles for typography…quick-clean and highly-usable guide-to- execution...of more complex engineering-applications...an easy-to-implement style-sheet, and screen-cast tutorial:*

>Query-Help? Your move:…*landing strip excavator and pile-driver controls, setting the lines and angles. Simple elevations:*

>Key-stone, and Capital automatically constructed ringed and Arterial-roads...

<Omnibus routes and railway lines...airport and space-station?

>Non-homogenous advertising-connected World-airport...

<Space-Base:...

From Abroad and at-Home:…

≥Without self-directed hard-work and risk…

<New risk-takers…

>*Alliances: spuriously*-forming…

<*Rich*-Elite *remaining*-: with...Economic-***Power*** and...

>Land to Win! *any fight…and populate with each, other, and others' found...*

<Willing-seller? *By willing-buyer?* Willing? *Like a victim, or prisoner unchoiced...*unwilling…then? *deliberately deliberating unwillingness delaying downloading…*

>Game-*changer*:...

<Change-*gamer:*…positively and negatively pointing-out, the discrimination...and prejudice.

>**Ratings**: N/n….in the...<Economic-sphere:...National-Treasury Bank…Nationalisation? Of The Banks? Of course! That is where the money is! Bailing-out!

<Some...more or less...

>What?

<Nationalised...

>Again?

<Most-cases...For National-Pride...

>Globally?

<None...*no-respecter...*

>Of International-Law?

<International-*Finance*:...

>Centurion-Salt...

<Millennial-Money!: *Government*-Bonds:...enTrusted! and...:NNNnnn...in-Trust-Fund: To WHO?

>You?

<Me?

>Us? Our Bank of Bonds...Securities...*gold and silver savings Rating: War:..prices: costs:...*

<**You**=Investment Bank! *Black*...gold and *silver*...coins and notes of tender promises...to-*pay*...always negotiable:

>Withdrawal?: N/black...to-*red*: **You** do not have *enough*-cash...

<Not-Withdrawal then?...*as-each of the Economic-zone's:...list:...***The World-Bank**:...*The International Monetary Fund:...silence on the matter...then:*

>Each-*denomination* of any currency *from this point...*

<Each by each degree of exchange mechanism…

>Ratio of liquidity equity/assets ratings: *All-hinges-on the-ratings…completely made-up between the-Banks…Where? When? Why? How?…much will they give…Base-Rate low…for-exchange…between…The-Banks… fixed…*or *fiddled…watching The-City burn…*

>*Cost-Prices-War:…savings…*

<*Investments..wages…pensions…benefits of The System: economic/political:…Government-Bonds:…worthless without…*

>The People's! Inequitable! No Rationale! Ratings…*going-down…N.nnnnnnnn…*

<Ratings? Do you still have: Holdings: You are your own City your own Country...Peripheral taxes? Paid? Paid Opt-in or Opt-out? Promissory-*notes…*

>Are not worth the *paper* they are written on...*rip-off* Customer Base…*CLOSING…*

<Going-Down...<*information-data:…*

>The Rich-list? Poor-list?<

<Both.<

>Or neither.<

<Legal? Illegal?<

>Both.<

<Selling-off the family-silver again…

>At Home!...Abroad< the *nasal*-pinch.

The-Banker looking-across at The-Clerk:

'Going-down...again...' *with global-markets warming...to legal-warning…to...*

The-Clerk:

Like writing on a piece of paper a large number and tearing it up into that number of strips of paper and paying-off the debt with as many more (s)tripped-off at what point is that atomised paper-pixels?:

>Legal-warring! With money! *blood-pressures raised and dropped, haemorrhaging but-only internally, cerebrally not-cardiac, yet…heartless? Perhaps. Have to be. Some may say...* and with some relief perhaps after-all an in-joke not backfiring potentially embarrassingly blushing reddening...*warming*-up The Banker:

'The Stock-markets are not really in Turmoil! Of-course not! Nothing is moving! Is IT? So? Turbulence, maybe, only...'

'Watch The-News...'

'...and *not* the-*News*, eh? Anything you want them to be! Whatever 'We' want it to be! Where 'We' want to be! Wouldn't that be nice? With your very own falsification, suspension of belief, disbelief? For the-impressionable. Only.'

On Holiday-delusion impressionable:

‘Illusion? 'Self-denial? Enlightened Self-Interest? Selectively...’

‘Simply ironic…'

'Yes I get the *irony…*'

Then:

‘'It' is not-*Legal*!’ Then:

‘Done nothing wrong.’ is what came out.

'Ever? Now? Wrong? Mis-leading? perhaps?’

‘Leader or follower...that is the difference…’

‘Or simple minded *symbolic* head of State? Of the family? Hangers-on? Underlings?’

'Maybe. *Misleading* perhaps...’

'Or *against* the public-Interest? Malicious? Maybe? Harmful?’

‘Never thought about ‘It’. But clearly as the picture-shows, not in-Turmoil....’ regaining the *higher* ground, the-Banker: 'Merely closed. And not-yet ready to be open-again for-business. That is all.’

recovering quickly. Reconvening-self like a determinably independent, with a serene *Sense of Nobility*...

'Mercenary?'

On the-Wall:

'Martyr?'

'With a-*Fiend*s-ransom…'

'Against-the-wall...'

'Trade-barriers, free-trade *closed*-doors...'

'Trade-Wars? Commodities...'

'Borders...Barriers…'

'Money? Of course, or nothing moves...' *have done nothing wrong...apart from what is ordinarily normally done...*

'Even indicted before the Court of the-Peoples' Law'

'For crimes against humanity…'

'Whose? Tax value-added goods and services sales and profit advert...truth: goods and services…'

'*Intellectual* Property-Rights...'

'On The *Free*-Market…' *scarcity and choice opportunity cost-logical action pragmatism subjective value want/need objective cost/price exploitation profit action axiom moral power to property-rights to external things protection from theft and fraud, breach of contract...shadow-market:*

<Almost. *By some timely proportion only...dissent and treason, personal-wealth and:*

>Like a religious-Dictatorship...

>Drunk on Gods' supposed will-power…

<Wealth and ability to control other's life and death…

>Of giving and taking away…drunk on killing…weaponised God or not…claiming and denying responsibility each of us…

<World-domination! Purist fundamentalist perfectionist puritanical…satisfying vain-lust…Capitalist?:

>Communist? National-Statist? Secularist? Globalist?

<*Individual (s)*…Drunk on Money!

>World-destruction! Of all…between all of us…not the goods and services to stay alive now? Of course! Protection against temptation…**Oil**-Wars…

<*Money*-Wars: Economies collapse the same...colonies-collapse...

>*Death-Toll?*

<Whose? *Workers...cheap labour factory-disaster...*

>*Collapsed...trapped...blown to smithereens...mine-disaster...*

<Shoddy work...

>On the conditions of work...

<Crime against The Proletariat! War and work and everyday living...

>Public-*opinion* vs. militant religion and science...

<Genetic:...Big Chemo-Co? Pesticides...Bayer Co. LTD.: Product...

>*doesn't matter what 'It' i*s if no use? Don't need To-Buy *anymore...*

<Moratorium?

>Total-Ban?

<Sanctions?

>Busting?

<Breaking the Rules?

>Trade-Embargo?

<Of what? Where? To and From?

>Food? Medicines? Arms Embargo...Defense and Media-Technology…

<Free-Markets!

>Free-*thinking*...Free-*will... with others ratio each to each 1-1 common contact contract...*

<Utilitarian-*consequential*:...

>Human-Rights and Responsibilities...

<Enacted?

>Y/N?:...

<By-omission?

>Intentionally?

<Successfully?

>*Welfare*-citizen?

<*Rogue-citizen created* with money-food and fuel-*poverty*…

>Dividend-stakeholder partners...*voluntary*-taxes taken…

<Theft through coercion?

>Otherwise?

<Anarchy?!@Archist-*minimal anarchy military/police courts and prison night-watchman...*

>*Archivist...*

<Gate-Keeper? Prisoner and guard? Nanny-State?

>To...Profit-from: *addiction to sugar and lard and salting... we all have to play our part-out...to keep going...*

<Castle and Gate?

>Whose?

<Libertarian-*necessitation*...how we *enable* our most-disabled citizens...and ourselves...

>>We have Our say! Not become the monster, that needs the-hand to bite the hand that feeds us! But to feed ourselves!>

<Believe this? A Communist! Trade-Unionist! Syndicalist!

>Systematically hostaged abroad for ransom threats of death private religious enterprise…

>Cannot get at The-*Perps...*

<Creative-accountancy, family-firms, *liars...*

<What about social-responsibility. Human-rights. Human-responsibility...Social-rights. Responsibilities...

<Simple-as...*liverish*-liner-notes...*littering* words on the page. On the-screen...littering-*leering search...*

>Print the money…*long-term* commitment...short-term hedges...

<Social-contract meritocracy...

>Assist least-able local-global economies...

<With Credit-dividend?

>They choose the-price, agreed...

<Choose the-price…against contractual-obligations...mandated…

<To who? On whom? All-Humanity?

>Not all, but with few exceptions...

<Why not?

>Not-again. All over the World! Crazy-Dance! Of Geo-political turbulence…everyday…High-Level-*perpetrators*...

<Of fraudulent crimes, and worse...

>Betrayal and revenge...always ends that way…high-level crimes of violence and abuse to an astonishing extent amongst the lowest, and highest...indictable for sure...sexual crimes…against…sexuality…

>But whether-*desirable or not*!

<What to keep 'It' that way?*...devolved murder and violence...*

To the-Armies appearing over a sunlit horizon and now nearly overhead ahead...seemingly:

'Into a peaceful necessity…or unnecessary war…'

'That shopping-*trip*, eh?'

'Day-Tripper?'

'To The-City?'

'All Possible...' *and probable open-area, walls, towers, built ever higher...*

'To keep-in, or keep-out? Fallen...maybe…*fallout*...but uncrushed...maintaining…the equilibrium...the balance…'

'Imbalanced…critically…'

As far as both the-Clerk and the-Banker were concerned an inner-crowning silence-crowding crowing as each The-Other: and yet *stilled in-the-air the question…about what to make of it all:*

'Everyone would if they could! Naturally, You could!'

'Business as usual. That is All?' *world-wide web- circulated networked media and as with the questions as yet still* unanswered:

'Deal? To be done. If we are to live.'

'Cannot alter that…'

'Not-Now, anyway.'

13.

'Like the-*Magician*s' trick...here one-day...'

'Love IT! Gone *the next*!'

'We will See *tomorrow*, eh?'

'Today…sooner not-later...'

'Today is Now…'

'IT will be done by midday anyway...done deals now...

'I-Deal…'

'When your shift is over, make sure you go home alive. That's all…'

'Treasury-Officer?' *there-enmeshed: the lesson: The first rule of Law-Enforcement: stay alive…*

'You are *enforcement,* now?'

'Innocent ignorance is *allowed*. But not guilty-*lies...'*

'There are lies and lies. I'm not going into The City for myself...You don't win without The Team!'

'Team?!

Sudden *anger* and:

'S*hooting*-gallery…

'Trade-Treaty...'

'The Government on the People! Shareholder-Elections? Negotiations...Now! Today! Of course not! Not-complicated? Like: Sporting...Life is…'

'Chance?'

'What? Cheating? How many know?''

'Are You accusing Me?'

'Accuse-yourself! I-accuse...If You can get away with IT again! With a *full-page advertisement: 'We Are Sorry!' What for? For getting-caught!! Caught in The Act!' Caught in The Care of...The Nations Resources!* If you can get away with it Again?' If I had I had been Caught robbing A Bank...I would not be here now, would I?'

'You would! They all are!'

'How many?'

'Insiders?'

'Liars!'

'How can you tell?'

'You don't see them...until it is too late. Perhaps, they are tailing you? The Inland-revenue...The Outland...' *whatever...and usually as You usually can cry off? Cry-of: Who started-it?! Didn't! Foul! Where is the-Referee?: conceded-accession result, recount, share-power concessionary-coalition acceding-against-attrition, contrite, not without-hatred, between razor-thin majority/minority worked-with...*

'Rule by virtue…not *brutality...*

'Civil-Service? Torture? To: Get a Decision?...'

'What *decision*? Who is the-Referee? What is the Reference: Umpiring-Intervention? Me you them? Mediation...Democratic?'

'Respect; Obedience; Individual; Democratic; eventually finally, yes! Alright. Fixed in advance then?'

'Of course!' *kick-it down-the-road...swap one-constitution for A.N.Others' preference...*

'*Almost*-guaranteed...If going to carry-out all the decisions, anyway? At the-Conference? Made-Public…Then forgotten-about...but a peace-deal…that is what it is, to placate the masses, in peaceful co-existence rich and poor…for-One, or All, now?'

'First past the post...the-decisions have already been made...' *and not by The People who too stupid who got us into this in the first place by being greedy, not us, no not us...in retrospect.* We are simply cleverer...*covered with news of how everything was much, much worse elsewhere, and The-Government etc....blah blah financial irregularity and regulation...not-inevitable…or-constant.*

Battle-ships…fast well-equipped nuclear-submarines and long-range bomber flown-over in psychological revenge-attack for de-colonisation re-colonising loans and defaults…unusual and extraordinary threat…National fiscal security and Foreign Relations…

Policy and actions threatening peace and stability, security and territorial integrity…sovereignty and the mis-appropriation of assets and lives…including airports and sea-port pirate ships hijacking hostage population situations…with the emotional volatility of a funeral...

'Don't You respect The-People then?'

'Rule of Law and the-courts?'

'Table-Tennis? Of course profits' take-charge. If You can bribe then You Bribe…'

'If You cannot?'

'Embargo…intercept…threat…'

'No-passing GO?'

'Until midday...'

'Or later...'

'Or earlier...'

<GO! Charge-account: Business-deal:...

'*That is Why We are In Business:* For The-Money!'

'*We* do business only For-Profit?

'Prophet? Nothing-else?

'Number-One...

'Money? Only?

>Number-One: Economic-Zone: Fuel and Food (machinery-oil and burning frying metal dust foundry mechanised but *unsafe*...) Technology and Defense (surveillance satellite…) Health and Social-Care…Building a Future with peace…

<We: ***R/e*** *list*... will make *safe* automatic-factories with a share in the output open *accountancy*...once losing absolute power absolutely nothing…

>But the horrifying torture, of injury, and Death, gone. You have allowed this: sponsored...and sub-*contracted*...

<Apart from of your-own-hands...the blood-*dripping*...

>To Hell!

Misleading and manipulating The-Truth: *reality*...

Both sides...unreal...only too real...

<Or Heaven!

Lame-excuse(s)...*heard* from over the way *lifting the arms embargo, on heavy-weapons...*

>Catastrophe! *Catastrophic...* Catastrophe...

<*On* and then: Off:...

>Thermo-*nuclear*?!>

<With those have already on-sided...

>The-Others are *asking* for non-lethal assistance, yet...

<Neutral Humanitarian-Aid?

Thinks...plays:

< Geo-Political: *map*...refugee...*ruler*...

>Ruler:...

<Treaty: *obligations* rights and responsibilities...talks for a democratic constitution, or no?

>Constitution? Body or Politick?

<What? For? A-fight?

>Sale and Return...

< Police and Army...Ambulance...*water-cannon...*

>Ignore *Internal-Forces...*?

<What?

>For Those External?

<Credit: *honesty...lost*...and Profit: 1% of 6—7B. is?

>1% of 7B? 8? 9? Trillion?

<Nothing if the shelves are full but no there is no money to go around?

>Fairly? Or plenty of money for some to retire early go back to the land…but empty shelves?

>The City:Equal?

<Then? Same thing? There is the catch! There must always be something! Many things! Enough!

<Buying statistics vast open questionnaire *spike*d...

>Environmental-risk:...minimise Risk to the Environment:...

<*Whose?* Fixed-at:NNNnnn...

>Resource: list...vast-tin and copper-mines with trucks the size of a house *pounding* the newly-built roads, to newly-upgraded railway, to neighbouring **Superpowers**' revenue...to the-*most*-Powerful: NNN...affectionate emotions list…

<Podium*-finish by Worker-Ants...as sovereign-Peoples paraded...*

>To build TV and wired-*circuits* for all. In tandem!

<Leaders' soldiers! *patrolling-sectors of the metal-mineral-garden:...for new-world technology and saleable goods:*

>Exactly! *the ever-present amongst the remains of the population, who toured and policed....:*

>The-*Areas*: list:...*themselves, as best they could.*

Without weapons? But with the same, as anyone else in or out, wanted.

Framed, the immediate was instantly one of self-organised...without the-power to defend against, uneven odds, but only to go-on...looking-outwards: telegraph-poles along The-Track.

The Lines down...satellite dishes destroyed and picking up the slack buzzing with pictures and satellite-messages drifting-back through the airwaves...

The-Clerk:

<*Defense-Industries Encorporated*:...

>To:...*Doves-and-Hawks: fluttering wildly...angrily across the screen*:

<*Pharmaceuticals*: Health-Care: Social-Care...

>Luxuries?> Accountancy>

<Leisure:...*and relaxation...*

>Relax?! Never! Neeevvveeeerrrr...

<Stop!s!

>The Markets!

<Lunatic!

>*Stellar*-returns...

<All Strong-*contenders…fireflies…from The-Sun...*

>Astronomical astrological Jovian perhaps...

<Ecology funds...*out-perform...everything else...almost*...N/nnn...

>**Citizen** of: country-list…

<**The-City**: Rational (once Equitable Town) City: Capital...

>**The-City**...wins... *everytime:...economic/political/people...ranking all-games….: multi-split-screen…slider…clicked:*

<Multi-player platform…*template…defuse…*

>Credit…point-value: list:...*control-stick, right and back nine-route 1060 jumping and avoiding, and spinning-around…speed-loss…fired-on… trick speed time…*

<TNnnnnnnnnnnnnnnnnnnnnnnnnnnnnnnnnnnnnnnnnnnnnnnnnnnnnnnnn:…

>Crash! Damage? Limitation:…

<*Control-centre metred-meted-out...*

>*...balancing: fiscal-ledge(er):...*

<Control: A-Z…vertical/horiz./up/down inwards and outwards away from...

>Danger!!: Difficult to Easy to Medium…hard-adjusting complexity and time-trial…number of races?

>One. Chance only...

<There. And then.

>Even *when* short sharp Shock-and-Awed…*into submission inflicted...*

Never quite works-out, as planned in the imagination on-screen read, saw, heard through headphones:

>If not for The-Other-Team!: *coalition-forces providing non-lethal aid...and lethal strafing at the:*

Armoury of the Glorious-Leader:...listed-as....

Rational	*Irrational*
Equitable	*Inequitable*

<**Warning!**-*given to civilians and shoppers to vacate the area. Market's and roadways cleared...stopped from doing-so by the loyal-Regime security-Forces...*

>**Rogue**-Citizen...*members* of the-toppled-**Team!**

<**Blaze-squad!**

>Prison-*break....comprisin'...*

>**Risk**: Analysis: *Political/Economic/Military/Religious-Media...*

>*Rationalising*: Nature...On/Off?: to/from:in/out:1/1%

<*Inequitable*: Nature... On/Off?: to/from:in/out:1/1%

<Equitable: Nature... On/Off?: 1/1%

>Rational...

<Action? Rational?><In retrospect...

>Irrational. Good-Game...*rationally-thinking*...>>Survived.

<Naturally...*rationalising irrational...*

>Action!

<Off The Wall! Basket-Cases!

>And Doing?>

<The best bit about this game...

>Compared to what?

<History...

>Is?

<*Our undoing...*

‘One for All and all for One!?’

‘Democracy...’

‘Or Dictatorship: then?’

‘Yes! But We could feed ourselves before! *on-screen...*

'We have nothing! No food. No money. Nothing!'

'Weapons? To get back at those killers…’

‘We do not need! The men have left to fight. Who is protecting us? We cannot fight! We have children! We have *lost* children. We have no food!’

'We are *trying* to Help!'

‘We have to help ourselves...’

‘What can You Do?’ looking and tapping furiously as speaking:

‘We are The-Executive! Aren't We?’

‘Who? You? Are the Exector!’

'Who is the Lawmakers…enforcers? Then? Punish The-People! Anyway, they were moving out, spread the hostages, more difficult, must be *contained...*'

'Money-fuelling as religious-*Radicalism…*

'Nasty-Nationalisms…'

'Of course we make their cars as weapons! They close us down! Not to make their cars!' *hitting-a-key:*

'Who has made invitation...

'To The Party?! *and allowed, Us to do business, in-Other's lands...*

'Y/N?:...

'Yes?:...

' 1st/2nd/3rd'Worlds...

'...4th and 5th and Sixth you may as well add!

' So...

>Destroying...no-more violence from the cells of The State: *to the-voluntary association of free-individual's:.*

'You are!'

'I am? I Am Too?! What?'

'Not. Punish the-People. They are punished enough as 'It' is...

'Police-charging trader fraud carousel copyrighted to producer *superabundance over-production destroying the market*...

<*<u>Evidence</u>*:...seen and verified:...

>Education for peace…choice…

'The *violence* is over quickly...more brutal the fear...'

'Poverty is universal...

'Brutal?' *heard as if bannered:*

'Democracy is slow...' *and peaceful and not so painful as war until the consensus reached then it is easy if still a struggle to continue always change...*

'Democratic-*poverty* is no worse or better than *Dictatorships*' poverty!'

'Sometimes worse!'

'This is not democracy!' *back-tracking...*

'What is IT?'

'Conflict between Two or more Sovereign-States...*elected majority, will that do? May not be here tomorrow, could be any day, why fear death, for others? is suicide a cowardly act?'*

'Publicly, yes.'

'And that is how they do it, through the roof, in front of the train...hanging beneath the stairs...maybe to protect...'

'Other-Family perhaps, from unaccountable murderous...'

'The Executioner? *Thoughts*...and carrying out...'

'Imprisoned, against The Will of One, at The Will of One!'

'Refugee's...'

'Unavoidably, or dead, by own hand. Violence arrest torture and death for being poor?'

'Or *cleverer* than them...'

'Stupid...'

'Mutually Assured Destrruction? That way lies Madness!'

'Not-difficult. Follow the trail of *collective*-food? From <u>Home</u> to the fields and mines...occupied...To the shops? With the shopping-trolley...shelves empty. What to do then?'

Looking-up, and out...and down again...

After-the-event...*ignoring, it would be absorbed or not go-away:*

<Blaze Squad!:...*the loyally Royally-forced Government-soldiers dead or deserted. If not for the targeted bombs against*

civilians' of the wrong-Tribe.. other-mapping coloured sector green, brown, blue, yellow, and red...from the scene:

>Familial:...death threat drug-fuelled...<

<Prison-Break!...whistle-blowing wind break taking the scent off the air, rolling down the grassy bank, jumping a passing-train:

'Nationalism: re-vitalising...rationalising…self-serving, presuming, before the event soft-racism quiet derogation, pre-judicial unlawful-discriminati*on*...

'*Ultra*-Nationalism...'

'Religiosity...'

'Bigotry...'

'Nice try...'

'Pre- the event, *hardened*...views...'

Rose-tinted nostalgia:

'Lies!'

'Pick-on-the-*weakest...*'

'First sight...then...'

'Difficult to do.'

'What? Shoot? Discriminate? Envy?

'About To Shoot...' *through cheating greed personal advantage maximising Capital: Human Goods and Financial Gain:...*

'Other: Pimping Crime?'

'Easy-method? Shooting

'Third-party? Anyone?'

'Other? Why?'

'**Go**!' *and The Go-Between...*

'Witness? Killed.'

'Or-Other...'

'Or Other...' *that is the choice. Every, and any moment:*

'Pull-the-trigger? Easy...'

'Except for The Children...'

'Easy. Targets!' *Who are Natural! Known to each other, and so growing-up with what We are used-to seeing...speaking, heard, acting-out...*

'Seen and heard no-longer...' *buried alive some of them, The-Executioners saving-bullets...*

'Who are they?'

On headphones: from The-Media *wired* Studio-Link:

‘They say Civilians must Convert:...face Slavery, or Death. Of their Loved-Ones...’

'Who is it doing The Shooting?'

'Both-sides. All sides...perhaps 3 or 4. Civilians assisting or trying to get away and...’

‘Professional-Soldiers?’ *professional-state and amateur. Militia or Armed-Gangs...*

‘Rioting...’

‘ Uprising?’

‘Insurrection: disturbance unrest demonstration insurgence mutiny rebellion insubordination defiance recalcitrance:

>High-beam profile: ibex-Business and Financial-sites...

<Television: The WorldWideWeb:...

From the TV screen headphones broken-into*...looking-out, and upwards to the left with a certain honesty, unlike the deck ward floor looking as if imagining...gone, walking into walls...gone mousing...heard scratching subtitles-on:*

‘Are there outside-elements involved?’ *as one and other serially deny or give cause to believe there are...*

‘Armed by who?’ a pause in the filming.

Whilst an explosion rips apart...something...dust, bodies.

'Are there Outsiders involved?'

'Well…yes…and…no….there has to be some *armaments* coming-in from outside...'

'As well as The Soldiers?'

'Correct.'*...up-grading... up-dated...*

'Insurgents?'

'To run-away...from this war of attrition now...'

'Whether inside the country or outside elements?'

'But can we say it is mainly outside-forces...'

'Not inside?'

'Well, there are armaments and weapons that have been supplied…previously, to this outbreak…'

'From Their-Allies? Who are?''

'Weapons taken or handed over by *deserting* Government-Troops and Police...the *so called* Security Forces…' *through un-monitored routes...*

From near and far, through the countries between...burnt uniforms everywhere...and naked bodies daubed hanging...

‘And the-Rebels inside? Where are they getting their weapons from?’

‘Well…that is ‘It’?’

‘What do you mean by ‘It’?’

‘They are getting their weapons from The-Government-Forces by taking-them by force, *capturing* or simply stealing them or being given them at The Border-Posts...’

‘The insurgents *murdering* as they go...

Stolen to the capital-City area’s gates and ceremonial-circus, square’s and formerly-Town and River-Port...

‘From Abroad?’ *...drowned-out by the noise of crashing masonry, bricks and mortar:*

‘City-centre’s, across countries, and Continents...’

‘Nations, and different States are responding differently. Seemly in chorus with a seemingly combined voice...’

‘By Midday? World-time...where we are expecting an announcement...what do they make of it there? Have you been able to speak with anyone yet?’

‘They do not know what is happening outside their Town or City. We tell them. it means nothing to them. All they are interested in is where the next meal, bread and water, and fuel to power the generators, and make contact with the outside world!

'Telephone-lines and digital-Power cables are down...'

'Satellite phone-link is all we have...'

'That cannot be taken down....' *another explosion...taking-cover*:

'GPS. Gone. Outside in The Street...'

'To support the-Regime?'

'Who is making the decisions?'

'People are under the rubble, trapped, screaming and crying can be heard all around. There is no firing on the ground, only from the air, and a few rifles for shooting into the air. No anti-aircraft...'

'No No-Fly Zone?'

'O.K.!'

Aircraft zooming into view *swooshing* overhead, dropping bombs...

'That is what they want?! No fly-zone for those who are unarmed?'

'To Be Armed?'

'They need food, energy...Lives! Life! And no more killings and wanton destruction!' *another background explosion:*

'So, the weapons are from the same sources as The Government in effect?'

'Who they oppose?'

'Yes.'

'And their-own stock-piled over several months?'

'I should think so. By-theft...and desertions...'

'And acquisition from abroad? Who?'

'Terrorists. And Terrorist linked Organisations, State-terrorists, wherever They may be. Terrorist-States. Constantly and continuously Home *supplied...Oil wells and energy and communication sources taken over or destroyed... Trade-routes, taken, by force, or prevention melted away...*

'That is correct.'

'And are The-Armaments continuing to be supplied?'

'Semi-automatic and non-automatic riot-control...'

'Chemical-agents...Yes?'

'Yes. Through The Border-Posts...' *tanks-rolling in seen lorries from heat seeking satellite seen carrying heavy armaments...re-forming a border with:*

'Their own People' *owning the reformed* *<u>Land</u>* *and* *<u>The People</u>* *or torturing, raping and killing them*:

'In denial of...or Open Genocide...

'Nuclear?'

'Not yet...'

'The Governments armoury?'

'Now the Secular-Rebels' without the petty disputes of The Religious Politicians and Police...are getting the upper-hand…'

A silent pause: *where songbirds could be heard singing, perhaps...but not here... but there*:

'Where the Government...are bombing and shooting their own people?'

'The Government Troops and Police are no-where to be seen...'

Except from the sky:

'Their-Allies...'

'The *Previous*-Insurgents?'

'Who are now?'

'The-Rebels.'

'Inside or Out?'

'Again. A disparate group of several thousand, no more. Mainly the dispossessed...'

'By The *Regime*?'

'Correct. The people here are sympathetic, that is all. They don't want weapons. They see what these arms do in the hands of the enemy, and their own. All They Want is...'

'...is...'

A satellite dish *whirring*-over...*faintly*:

'We are *losing*-you...'

'Until then...then, next time...over to you in...'

'From Geneva now....Thank you. We hope you will be OK there, We'll be back...' *the subtitles-continued...on another screen clicked into:*

'Rallies around the-World...' *breaking-glass Agent Provocateur...*

'The Demonstrators...'

'Secular-Rebel Army...'

'Presidential Armies...'

*'**Special Security-Forces**...accused of some the most atrocities...'*

*'All...involved, by degree...*It is as if they are invading, their own country!'

'Or escape from?'

'By Luck or Pure-Chance...*timing*...your departure before...'

'It is too late?'

'You make Your Own Luck...You take Your Own Chances...' *a cloud drifting-across the screen...of tear-gas eyes-scalded, felt burning, hazily blocking-out the scene.*

The screened buildings basement's levelled rising numbers...*falling...crunching graphics careering-upwards and careening downwards...turned-inwards...crackling-sounded sub-ordinate-body in...*

<Sub-ordinance: Now!...*categorical...folder: Radio...with pictures blurry and crackling too:...listen...in City-Streets, Economic-Political Rallies...*

>Breaking into the **Offices-of-Power:**...*a rallying of the troops and **Security-Forces** to-deal with those...that lay dead and injured and down-and-out on the-City streets and Circuses and across Plaza and around...The-Square...and at the...*

<Portside on sea and land...and air...<

>Want it to be *intact*...once they get there!<

<Intact?

Without-Tact:

>Across Countries...and Continents...City-Hospital...*<patched-up and...saving...buffering...unseeing, hearing*:

<Saving who we can of the dying...< *and deaths< dissipated...as if rationed for the inhabitants on the ground...<*

Fogging the outlook from the air…to the ground:

>Drone!< *steered from someway distant airdrome...*

<Combat!

>Predator-Drone! *armed remotely operated planes veil of secrecy over intelligence gathering casualties Grim Reaper precision guided missiles cannot hear them like Mosquitos...*

<Filming...for the record...No threat identifying the target...orders?<

<For the use of force...< *except by consenting host...*

>*Free*-**FIRE!**<

<Anything goes!<

>Self-Defense? Legal?:Y/N:

<By who's rules?

>N: *Illegal...Counter-Productive: public and vocal opposition...*

<Only if it comes to court...*surrounded by court staff ushers prison staff, Police, and Army besieged...*

>Civilians...**War**-*crimes*:...in *opening...*

<World-Court: *doubling-up drumming cynically and from a distance...*

'Kill! Be killed!' *life savers rescuers gone to help long war journal poker burn one, turn3 (flop) burn one turn one burn one turn one river...*distributed: denial of service cyber-attack overwhelming concrete concerned websites...

<To Force...Agency...then *an open-air announcement*:

'Insurgent into a peaceful world!'

'Illegal warring!' *utilising Banks-of-Equipment recruiting-enough others to participate in Freedom and Democracy with Civil-leader and control-and-command-structure. Immunity safe-passage to end bloodshed levelling secular rebellion religionist storm- troopers...*

'Uprising...'

'Cannon-fodder...'

'To-*slaughter!'*

14.

The-Banker spoke:

'Some *serious* clouds on *The-Horizon...' unseen future-past...*

At the Peripheral-Zones: *list*:..

Outside-Broadcast Camera and Live-to-Dialogue:

'From The-City:...'

Television-Cameras brought-in to show *victims of the-violence re-fused, to disperse, de-fused film-taken-out and destroyed...blocked...as well as the real-life* film-set demolished.

On film...transmission..transition...transmitting:

'The-live facts:...' *interpreted: denied, or un-denied, about who got more hits verifiable, or unverifiable, targeted-killings...*

<On-*Target! clicked-onto:*

>Civil-War! *is escalating between the or these sides..*

From the screen: *diminished* feelings:

'In-Place of Police-*Threats* of Ultimate-*violence* and *humiliation...*'

'Abide no-more...'

‘There have been self-immolation's…’*simulations and emulations...*

‘In-Town and Village-uprisings against corrupt and over-bearing, and over-demanding Port, and Party-officials...':...*seeing*:

‘Deleting: *corruption and Fraud...*’

Found-out...reporting...

‘Reports of travellers...’ *on-the-spot reporters-witness social-reporter...reporting:...*

The TV-Journalist:

'Humiliated because they have not been paid-enough not-even for a *decent*-life…a roof over their head…some food to eat…’

‘Petty-Officials and Police…’

‘Because they have not been paid at all!’

‘For their Favours! They only wanted more Greed Bribery and Corruption...’

‘Or otherwise...’

‘Paying-themselves...’

‘By Bribery and Corruption...

‘Taking for themselves...rape.’ *from the top...as below*:

'Now...' *overbearing theft and stealing from The People...silent-suicide...*

'Noisy-Massacre...'

From the front-line...where people had gathered on street-corners and squares and shouted:

'Unpopular-Government...'

'Time!' *running-out...unable to relinquish-any...thing...*

'Resign!'

>Power-ups...

<Inter-Continental...

>Ballistics...*weapons of mass-destruction...*

<M.A.D!

>Simultaneous...*Crashes...*

<Timed-out: Concrete-Wall...Millennium-Airline...Cosy-comforts...

<Telecommunications...

>Tanks and bullets...

<Satellite...*spoken clearly...*

>321...Live!...>

<Live!> *in Real-time…(faint indecipherable…)…dissidents library torched to the ground…*

>Ancient-groundwork>s of cultural significance and religious art, demolished, blown-up. From-night-time scenario into The Day:...>

<In the *Red...zoning-in...*>

>The-whole of the City, is on-Fire!>...

*White-zones flashed across the screen...yellow moonlit-zone, in the Black-zone: breaking-out into absurdly chaotic blue sunshine: the Black-zone quickly returning...fading-into brown...*To Red...*turning blue-yellow with the glare and white and blackout, with specked ash and frost blasted. Gone through Civil and Global Society...turning to blood red and the blackened charred battle-fields:*

>*Racking-up...on uncertain winnings...and losses unprecedented…in time:…*

<T3:...

>The Defence Industries: Global-*list*...

Battles between creditors and debtors destroying and protecting-assets how to fix-appraisal...hid under an umbrella...wracking the best brains for solutions, and how to fix-them…

<Wiki...for…

>Winnings: Selling-off? *Bought-off...*

<You-Bet!

>Hole in The Ground! The-City!

<Capturing-losses are easier to count!:...

>Than Big-Bosses...*now on the yacht or whatever...*

<N/N.../nnnn...*they do not add up to Victory for any-side...*

>Deal-with-it...*this is the-Future! attempted as irrationally rationally as could be equitably and unequitably ...into the unknown...*

<Ultimately...

>To make The World a Better Place...

<Make?!

>Defense and Technology: For the Survival of All...

<Rather than the eradication of all other?

>Education? Closed?

<Or worse...like ancient Kings and Queens of old...

>The *Eradication* of You...

At The-City-square and outside the Courthouse-Government buildings:

'Before the Grand house Palace and Hotel…' *recorded and to be sent whenever and wherever possible...searching...words and labels tagged-tailed and blocked-in…*

'Who? To-Who?'*…site-content disallowed…*

'Who from? Name?: Street name Town or City?'

'RPG! Attack!' *on a school or hospital...jumped-up from kneeling, propped shooting finger back into an alley red lit-up like arteries and veins from the-heart in the darkness lifting lighted-lanes and roads-out from the market-places and places of religious worship door to door...doors-closed shut-tight and locked from the inside and between wall stairways, that scurried away into even darker places marked red-laser light beacon tracked 700 rounds a minute...*

'The decision: to fire directly into the vehicle in view before a possible…'

From the-studio:

'Short to Long term *incentivisation:...' through share-price linked bonus, with more than 100% to 200% times-bonus variable-to-fixed, and pay-brakes applied for everyone else.*

'Persuaded...rather than risk the long-term health of the company...'

‘*Fairness*...that’s what It is All about...That is all IT is about…’

‘Influence beyond-our-borders...’ *beyond Our* Control...

‘With rigged-polls, election fraud delayed count and declaration while election monitors are condemned as are opposition-rallies against Government Forces...’

‘For Who? Financial, or Physical Reward?’

‘ No Punishment of Torture. For the sake of it...family...’

‘If not popular enough? Then: violence? So, who represents the wishes of the people?’

‘No-one. They represent themselves...’

‘We...*they... represent ourselves...themselves? How?’*

‘Reporter-Citizen...Rogue-Citizen:...

‘Face to Face!’ *line-by-line, social-networking...*

‘Unless one is prepared to stand aside for another...’

‘To Give-up one power for another?’

‘Rather than keep it all...’

‘For Ourselves...*reported...or unreported...in the...click heard:*

'Move-in...Attack!' Lines of Army and vigilante moved against each other...moved together against the-Other...then:

<Governmental Corporation-Accounts:...listed:...or not.

>Incorporated-Government-Exchequer:*...listed...or not..co-operative, or gullible, or not...*

<And To Be spent:*...not-saved, insured, pensioned-off. Invested back-into everything is spent...*

>The Bank of You: Procurement:*...tendering-bids...are: list...taken-on owner-ship...sales...*

<Logistic's:...facilities *numbers*-distribution and disposal:...list:*...accruement*: stock-piling...

>ALERT!!! *Accrued: Limited ammo...spare-part's...*

<Goods*...like anything-else...with supply dictating-demand and scarcity-of-supply...*

>And Services: energy supplies...

'For Life!'

The-Clerk@video log entry location link:*...blood-red-blotches on yellow skull and cross bones symbol...safety-regulations...i*n a warzone depleted uranium breathed-in atomic debris missile-shell dirty bomb aircraft drone dropped...

'Clean-kill!'

'Blue skies…' *thinking but no sign yet, as the air is thick yellow grey smoke and teargas...*

Blinkered. Suited and booted. Everything kept inside metallic-Kevlar silk-suit...

Goggles-helmet-earphones and speaker. Inside a plastic glass bubble of cold metallic clothing...manufactured materials...blinkers...hiding the sun from sight. Pinned-down.

Panning-out…

'Next M722LAW or RPG rocket launcher to tank battalion in the-City square!'

'Beware Civilians!'

'Coming out of the Building!'

'Join-up with squadron-Apex.

'Game! Squaddie-Z now joining!'

'Who is Squaddie Z?'

'Back to the Combat Zone...

'Zed do you have rocket launcher?'

'Affirmative?

'Rocker launcher in position at right front corner of the-Square!'

'Can you make it?

'Market! On my way!' squatting ducking low as ammunition bullets and grenades coming-in:

'In-coming!'...like a meteorite landing from all-directions.

Caving-in. Jumping and Ducking-and-Diving through to reach the launcher-corner of the...Town-square…City-Centre: *shelled* Citizens shot-at populations...

Country-borders threatened.

On-screen:

'…where there was a massive empty hole of earth and dust and body-part's...'

'Bodies? Good! Medics! Now aim Rocket-Launcher at Tank Battalions...in The Centre of the Quadrangle facing out…' *fazing-in...*

'To take control of The City-Square...'

'Civilians trapped in the building!...Soldier!' *clicking onto the hair target...line of sight...*

'I didn't come here to get shot or blown-up by my so called Allies!'

‘They’re Civilians!’

‘And our Enemies? Could be...’

‘Trainee-terrorists...’

‘Like Us! Our Allies?’

‘And Civilians? Go in Peace.’

‘How do you tell? Mercenaries…’

‘Tactical conspiratorial weaponry...’

‘Hired-guns!’ *in a quagmire mouse-holing...sand and dust and brick-work...*

‘Sand-box...wired.’

‘Neighbouring-house!’

‘Already dead...don’t know it yet!...’

‘Now!’

‘Country-folk!’ yelled, too late fired-on.

Blasted through the wall, from the upstairs, inside. The Army truck tail-gate left down driven- off too soon! Leapt back-out of the Mousy-Hole...*onto another passing...*

<Lucky!<

<Skill!<

Yelled back...

<Lucky!<

As from Ancient-time's skin and bones piece-by-piece stone-by-stone Rock-by rock and brick-piled onto wood and metal supports:..

Mining...Drilling-down…Stacking-up…counting cranes and scaffolding operating building sites brought-about from the continents of the original: Clan-Chieftains Tribal Leaders Executive director-manager...Presidential: The-Range-Rover: *screeched* to a halt outside the office complex at the centre wires trailed between huts pre-fabricated and brought in for the hundreds who lived and worked here: beyond the catastrophised yellow-ochre red desert:

'Hostage-situation?'

'Where?' the young-Clerk called out, as arriving for the next 6-month stint at the controls.

Buttons and levers to taps and valves inside the plant, and far outside leading above, and once again below, refined to defined ports, and tankers, driving over the seas across mostly barren and unpopulated land, and where populated, forcefully de-populated, across the globe:

'Boss has been on the line, says it will all be sorted...'

'Really?' the other replied, disinterestedly, almost, otherwise fully taking in the chance of another hostage-situation gone wrong. Got out. Got out, to the wider world: 'Different countries and armies, where the threat would be from, and who would step in to save the day...'

'Without publicity 'It' was only for money...for-Profits...to these Pirates, and...Well...Businesses, Corporations, that dealt with them to pay the ransom...to spend on? What?'

'More Weapons…to take more hostages…whole populations…first the villages…then the towns…then…The City.'

'They not Rich enough already?'

'They-*scared*, that is why. Religious-militancy, that us what 'It' is. They come with the-*holy*-book in one hand: *whatever*...the takings…and the Gun. Children some-of-them. Children dressed-up to be-killers. To be killed. Not big-*enough* to carry-weapons, and kill-themselves, not even in self-defence! Shock and Awe!'

'Awe and Shock!'

'Not. Slowly-slowly *does*-it. You weigh up how many are likely to come out in the best case scenario...Then Go! to achieve at-least that...or-Retreat. *Nothing*...retreat…defeat…recover and re-take over and again since Time began…'

'Hostage and Hostage-taker, of-course, that is what 'It' is...That is the-*situation* you-have. Simple: To them it is taught: Kill or get-killed.'

'Kill, and get-killed?'

'That's it. Systematic warring states hostaged for money for weapons and wealth to exile or death…'

The encircled site, strafed with aircraft fire, and the roads out, hostage and hostage taker, on T.V.:

'The Boss says it will all be over today, midday, negotiations...talk-talk. Over! It will never be over!' looking-up at the TV screen, news showing only some other crisis, and not, denying, in denial, honestly dishonest...

'No-*Crisis*', at all.'

'With who?'

'Anyone. With the government, tribes...who knows?''

'Who are taking bribes...'

'Called: 'Aid'?'

'...and about to be toppled, to get out of the next election, and get away with it again?'

'Aided, and abetted?'

'You got ‘It’.’

'Brutal.’ with former regime fall, or feared, vacuum filled by surrounding countries: east and west, north, and south, and diagonal-*i*deology: founded and *funded*:

‘Food-wealth and Weaponry: isn’t that it?’ *food and water carried across a continent, killing and taking over as they went. Trying, succeeding, until-wider gulfs and bays and villages and countryside, and desert-engulfs. Towns, and ancient Cities and Civilisations, desecrated, on-screen:*

'Hostage-assistance...' moving-off with the attack and secure-mission: surrounded by few tanks and armoured personnel, not requesting military assistance from outside, then having-to...another channel-switching remote-control crackling:

‘*Suicidal...*'

‘Post-revolutionary council and new-**D**ictatorship, behaving badly, suicidally...'

'In-desperation, eventually of course, all murder, is in cold blood.’

'To attack, and secure. Political-religious: Economic-Military Intervention. The-people per-citizen representative, not, never...too-many difference to represent all...so they kill them instead…generate fear…then death.’

‘Who?’

'Those who are *representing* only-themselves...'

With bullets! Bargain-basement...

'*Humanitarian*-Aid…assistance...'

'For...what? Free-prisoners elsewhere?'

'One country cannot dictate to another about that! Even if allies. Their own, each our own judge, our-own witness...our own victim. The-Boss will pay.'

'What terms?'

'Eventually.'

'Now.'

'Closed…' by all-appearances: In bulk, at the super and Hyper-markets on the City-port docksides another river estuary and canal-side and by the airport and railway track soon to be arrived at:

>Checking account...

<Prices: list...*processing*...fixed.

TV-screen multiplex displayed:

'CCTV-Surveillance!' dragged out into the chaos of throwing stones: 'Demonstrators-*outnumbering*…Gangster-Gangs: Drug Bandits hide-out listed...

'Racketeers:...'

‘No less, no more than...NNNnnn...Millions out of the-economy! Security-forces!’ many blood-bath...drowning folding, with dirty bombs…few refused, like a hail of pebbles…at-first:

‘Awaiting unknowing the-response the attempt that would be made to escalate...or *restore*-order...’ apparently, more than ever now, unknown. Ordered-by, the police and armies, upon the-hapless, once hopeless-people:

‘The-*retaliation…when it came...’ the consequences only seeming inevitable, in retrospect:*

The fear was only of the unknown, the anger known, real...

'Nails!' radioactive stinging blinding deafening shattering bones and lives. Head’s hair matted arms enwrapped laying together inside their homes…blood-soaked women and children, dead.

Carried-off settled into the ground along with scattered-landmines and yellow-shrapnel.

Then:

'Plutonium!'

Signpost seen: reeling signal warned to dress appropriately and shelter under a table, or chair, or sealed room...for a hundred years barren ground. Warning:

‘Keep-Off. No Children Playing Games! No Planting!’ *for a hundred-year’s!*

'Warning?!'

'Warring!'

'Humanitarian-Aid-Packages...' (non-lethal food and medical-supplies…*suspect-devices, to the-other...*dropped…*on-screen…*

'Contribute to the…**<u>Humanitarian-Aid</u>**:Y/N::?'

'In place of Our Own!'

'Relief-effort? Now!:Y/n?...' *in place of proper food, ready-to eat-meal, dependent on:*

'We *can Feed-Ourselves*. We only lack <u>Water</u> and <u>Electricity</u>. Can you bring us water and electricity?@U.N. Humanitarian-Aid...and Water-Tankers!'

Driven-into shot:

'There is none...' *in the gutted shops, or from the countryside. There was little, and it was run-by-The Gangs and The Military-Police, Security-Services including Hospitals and Schools...Bread-Ovens*:

'There is little that could not be used to terrorise at night.' Into the cold clear light of day. Without fear of retribution or otherwise-*accidental*:

'Death, and Taxes. They say they give us something...*They* give is *nothing* but *this*: Death and Taxes...not Bread and Bandages.'

'No matter who is <u>The Boss</u> is, The-Boss. No-one else. Like some ancient indispensible…'

'That goes for the whole of the human race!'

'Life is not a race! Is it?'

'No-better future to be had for: <u>The Future:</u> generations...shared re-distribution of ...wealth...'

'Social-schemes...humanitarian…secularist…'

'Bolivarian-Revolution?'

'Social-scheming...'

'Capital-capitalising…'

'Share the wealth...'

'Fake-companies?'

'Fake-message!'

'Lies?!'

'No-cash!'

'For cost? *Running-short...looking-out, for the long-game. Per-centage...*

'The Democratic Poker-player!'

'I Like 'It'! The-Magicians trick? Here-now, gone…'

'Cash-*flow*...'

'In and Out.'

'Political-will...social-conscience...is?''

'Is?'

Pre-*varicate*:

'Validate!'

'Military-will?'

'Gets' things done…peacefully…'

'Questioning?'

'What?'

'Anything!'

'Unable to touch them...for-Weaponry.'

'Allies?'

'Depends...'

'On what?'

'What Day?'

'To greater or lesser threat?'

'Monetary-Fines...Government taxes…'

'Sales-Ban-sales: Starvation-Sanctions...priced Out of The Markets...'

'Criminalising...'

'Tried-them-All...'

'Global-enforced?'

'Property-theft? Person-theft? Taxes? Or what?'

'People-Trafficking Pimping-People...All of Us! All The-Time?'

'Aiding them into prosperous business...'

'Enough for us each…'

'Or War?'

'Investment! Thriller Heist! The-Bailiff's re-possession...'

'Out-on-The- Street...' *literally...*

'One-room, for three or more people...'

'Or sleeping-in-The-Streets...' *the-City or Shanty-town painted-boars propped-up, metal corrugated sheeting: free or rent, slum:*

'If they charge *rent* for that.'

'Why?'

Again and again.

'Trillions...of US! Record: *disconnect...*

''They'

'Scientists they reckon the-Earth could *only* support up to currently 9 Billion…'

'Make 'It' Ten!'

'We are almost there!'

'Near. With land, government-stimulus, jobs, or on-welfare-*investment...*'

'Same-spending, as-earning, paying and savings investment-*holdings*...in Company Corporate-Banks?

'Never=again!'

'Retirement-pensions, insurance, schools and clinics...*controversial* controlling commander Presidential- coup…'

'Landslide popularity assumed militarily or otherwise democratically of sorts something to show the next generation…'

'For Good?'

'Or Evil? How do You know?'

'How do I know? Does no harm...'

'As seen by?'

'Me? Yes probably...' *ratio-rationing:: N/N...*a piece for all of us?'

'Of us all, maybe?'

'Maybe not. Don't push-up the *high*-hill...then...'

'Fall-over the-*low*-one?'

'Overthrow of unpopular undemocratic-minority government? Overthrow The Rule-of-Tyranny! How? Only to roll back-up again...The State? Government? Nationalist-religionist…You may say…have faith in…'

'Why? Who? Crack down on the-*criminals...*'

'Some, only, surely...'

'What *about* yourself?'

'What *about* yourself?'

'The only law in *sight* is that of-*Human-Rights...and Responsibilities...*'

'Whose? Yours? Or theirs?'

'Exactly.'

'That is what we need to speak about: Death, and the-Successor:...'

'Family-business? There is no Vote! There is no-Justice!'

'Familial and/or *Social-Justice:...anywhere?*'

'Everyday...'

'Fair-play...on the World-map...'

'Continuous-revolution? Take no-notice?'

'Rebellion?'

'Nothing-to-hide...'

'What is the answer?'

'There is not-one...'

'Police-*Criminals:* know they can get away with anything! and nothing will happen.'

'If it does, it is to somebody else...'

'Or they just ride-it-out, their life, their home...'

'Their *escape?* Prison-break? Inside-job?'

'All guns firing...'

'Ex-President's...'

'Make no-mark on the World-stage! There is no-Law, no-Government. No-Police, no-Army, no-Religion...'

'No-Justice?'

'No-Money too?

'Getting-excluded...' more angry! *permanent* microBlog brain worm:...

'Small-arms embargo...'

'Against War-Lords and President's...like *latter* day Kings and Queens unrepentant...'

'And Clerks?' suspended sentence...*sacrificial*-diversion:

'We-*Lie* to Ourselves...We all Do!'

'All The-Time?!' *the unpalatable-falsehoods...apparent socio-psycho-profile:*

'Self-deceivers...all.'

'Of Us! With Free-will to alter? Human?-*rights?* Free-*responsibility...*'

'Human-automaton? 'It' all-*happen*ed...despite myself?'

'Despite? Not because-of?'

'How the-*halo* slips, when you are not looking...'

'*Misanthropy: you start to hate anyone who is different, even your own family.*'

'You Hate everyone?!'

'Robbery, theft, rape, torture, murder! Who couldn't!'

'The rest of The- World cannot be-*wrong*!'

'Get used to it! Misogyny…*racist* Nationalist…tribal bullying always…see the worst in all?'

'The best in None? Or One? Some? Soon too to-become: One of the-Richest!'

'In-Truth.'

Exploded:

'Humanitarian-*crisis*:...

'Reconstruction:...*opportunity*...

'Occupy:...and *rebuild*?

'Service-*level* agreements:...'

'Control and command systems...'

'Virtue and Sin *found*-out.'

'Benefit the greatest number?'

'One. Me! Alive!'

'By intention? Do no-harm?!'

‘Some circumstance...do you eat meat?’

‘Halal? Kosher? What’s the difference? Do you eat carrots?’

‘Humane-treatment?’

‘Of prisoners?’

‘Of anyone! AnyTime?: <T3:…’

‘So there is point at which harm to one, may benefit another?’

‘Of course! The question is...Least harm, most benefit?’

‘Not no-harm-Full-benefit? Closest to the-Win! For everyone!’

‘Social-hierarchy...’

‘Economic...hierarchy...’

‘Lechery. Do what they like. Throw Money at it!’

‘If you’ve got ‘It’. If not?’

‘Not above the law?’

‘Who says? The-law? Direct-action?...trespass-campaigns...

‘Economic-damage...

‘Social...

‘Guilty!’

‘On both count’s?’

'Mine, and yours?'

'So who is correct?'

Contemptuously:

'Mine, of-course.'

' There can never be any denying, of the cash-book...never lies...'

'Customer and pension-scheme, life-insured, savings for a rainy day...'

'Not-assured. Not so-assured. More-assured. To hold up against the flood: The Tsunami...Train-Crash!'

'When It happened?'

'Last-night...' *shares shoring-up, power-to-influence-change...*

'When change must-be.'

'After The Event...'

'All the time. You/We decide democratically, by power, shared, by your strength of choice, decision making, argument...'

'Evidentially arguing for, and against...'

'With The-Others...All The-Time: Publicly as in ancient times but better. All the Time, not just-now, but Everywhere!'

'Just-now?'

'Then?'

'Ha-ha...'

'Sure... '*and perhaps the only right we share. Whether, or not, including the right to life, so a responsibility also. To Ourselves and The-Other:*

'Each to each-other:...

'To The Vote...

'Or Not.

'To decide with The-Others.

'Or not.

'And leave, perhaps, but at least live to see another day! That is our-Responsibility!'

'And every decision, of everyday?'

'We do not need government. Yet we need government? And we do not need Corporations? We are corporate enough?!'

'Incorporated! We become something...else. Alright, we are all incorporated! We do not *need*-Corporations...perhaps We, as federations' of people, peoples...what about that?!'

'Incorporated, with ourselves?'

'Incorporated-*kindness...*'

'And federated with all others...' everyday every decision made in *that*-day... Only divesting the body-virtually of 'its' own-will digesting (and in-digesting) twitching, and moving and sleep-walking, and dreaming, as we dream all-day! With our eyes open, ready to protect and defend, and find, and take, for ourselves, sunlight, air, food:

'We do not need Banks?! Governments? Corporations?'

'As we have Economic-zone:...lists:...*lists...?*'

'The new-way?'

'All at once, and for all time?'

'Love. Think. And Act: apart?'

'Together!'

'*Fairness*!'

'Democracy!' *is not just about one vote won, or one vote lost. It is about all of them, for against, unwavering, and yes, no voters, if there only vote is for none of the above.*

Declaring:

'Anarchy! is not a crime! Human-rights? Animal-rights and responsibilities and responsibilities...and all-*concomitant...*'

‘We have as much right, as responsibility...’

‘Of-course we do! Do no Harm!’

‘Some more than others...’

‘I was going to say:...’

‘Differing-*proportions* at-least...’ ratio’s through-time...

‘Separated into their parts closer, or yet-further apart...’

‘For-most, of-course...’

‘Of-course... different times-of-their-lives...’

‘As Secularist-Janus looking all ways!’

‘As Congregationalist or Rastafafi?? God, or no-God...’

‘Gods? *Economists*-all!’

‘Reckoners...*and* Beckoners...’

‘Of Environmental-*damage...*’

‘Recovers...’

‘Recovery *All*-Ways! We paid-our *compensation...*’

‘Did-You? Didn’t notice?’

‘Pittance! Only ‘cos: Costly Litigation...’

‘Sued? Prosecuted?’

'Lawyer? Libel!'

'That, was libellous...remember? Nuclear, you-said? In-Public. Caused a *commotion...'*

'A mauling...'

'A Moiling...'

'Doing?'

'Done?'

'Done. *greasy* back-hander...'

'Didn't work, did it?'

'What **Austerity?** Now? '**Cut!**' *'s in public funding...while reducing-Taxes for The-Richest..'*

'Not-to lose-out...'

'Again... and Again!!'

'Holding out for low interest-rates, until the-bailout paid-back, or not.'

'Take-over another countries-resources...fix the rates, to pay-out, and to be paid-in, between us.'

'Not loaning to business? Holding-onto-the-reserves to exchange between the-Banks and Government-economic zones...'

'Think-your negotiating with a-government, and people...Who?'

'Well, this is different...'

'By-bailing -out-the-Government-Banks...to feed The-Banks...as investment in Big-Business: list...Yours:*list....to spend on whatever you wish-for?'*

'Work? For?'

'Money-from-Work*:energy expended, used-up, or sold-on to output-cost/Price/Production-capacity:Nn....*Work for money, simple! *But*-No! Banks lend to each other...'

'**Banking-Corporation**: *pay their top-bonuses, not-wages, or salaries, lower-down, in the-thousands, if your-lucky or unlucky to have a job at all. Bonuses in the-billions. Listen again in- the-Billions...*

'**Government**: Trillions more then?'

'One, some, or all? For everyone of the planet!'

'Soon!'

'Credit-Boom!!'

'Again?!'

'Building-bubble! Dot-comm. *disasters...*'

'Sure. We did that. Still will-do? No. Well...Sure. Business-as-usual, as I say...'

'But different?'

'This-time? It maybe no-different... may still be lawful regulations, you know, are not-Law, as such. They are...*regulations*...not-commands...opportunity...'

'Get Out of Jail-Free!'

'Companies and Corporations...Oil.' *seconded into government: CEO-Presidential: hired-lobbyists, paid-for journalist, accountants, business-partners unevenly hit not-keeping a-track of it all...proselytising privately publicly, too*:

'What You see? The *Nice*-side? Or-Evil? Unlovely?'

'All on One-Mainframe?'

'Mainframe: The Good-Earth!'

'Going for Resources?'

'Got enough?'

'*Never-enough:...*' *metals and materials, from places on Earth...from asteroids and moon? Mars' moons? Mars?*

'Go for it!'

'O.K. No-compulsion!'

'Lead A Decent Life?'

'Happy and successful! Lead the-Good-*life*! too?'

'Marketplace of faiths, accounting house of none, marketplace of none.'

'Blown-up!'

'House of faith.'

'Or Marketplace!

'Or None.'

'Faith?'

'Yes?'

'What about all the others?'

'We are all patently at variance with Each Other All The-Time...'

'Are variously saying you agree with each other, democratically...yet never agreeing...'

'We are allowed to express Our View: Free-Speech is fundamental...and if swaying The-Majority...'

'Of course. But not at the expense of...'

'Of A.N.Other?'

'Of course...not!'

'At your expense, and your expense only?'

'Of-course...'

'Yes? No-credit?'

'Here it is:...NNNnnn...@n/N...'

'*Extortionate!*'

'Or otherwise?'

'Exploitative. For votes! Only one-vote. To yourself, and others...*names:...list...*

'**Democracy**:...*is a state of mind...not a word, a name, and one-vote, each:*

'**Power**-*Leveller...*'

'Level-**Power**-*base...'*

A frame of mind. referential...

'Full Scale Civil-War?!'

'Necessary, proportionate...*disproportionate*?'

'Legal?'

'Whose rules?'

'We cannot be responsible for what others may do, only ourselves.'

'**Humanitarian?**-crisis?'

'Sure. Everywhere. **Occupy**?: **Reconstruction**?: afterwards:..

'*Opportunity...*'

'Occupy...'

'Your own-body...'

'And mind?'

'And *rebuild*?'

'Service-level *agreements*:...*tender*-Bid?('s)...at-auction.'

'Benefit the-One or The-Greatest Number? Infinite. Or the-Richest?: Control-and-Command systems...Virtue and sin? Found-out? So-what? By intention? Do no harm? Without initiation-of-forced enforced physical exploitation *alienation...*'

'Fraud? Theft? Trespass? Vandalism?'

'Deception, by-lying, misrepresentation, verbal and actual threat?'

'Use of force to body and possessions: legal coercion, violence or restraint...'

'Of Trade. By striking! *Incognito*-labourer soldier-spy?'

'All of Us! By-Gvt.-*collective*...collapsed...'

'Mass-torturers?'

'Executioner?'

'Collective of the unwilling...'

'To Group-*Individualism*...voters couldn't care-less! About anyone else! Heroic-*innovators...they...'*

'Buy? They Sell!'

'*Withdraw*-Work? How to live? Villainous-parasites?'

'Who? All-who *struggle* to survive...'

'Live-off other's...By-*force*...'

'More-force?'

'More-*burden*?'

'Profit motive-*efficiency:* Economic. Payback?'

'For self-sacrificing and risking long-*hours...'*

'Not. Who doesn't! risk?!'

'*Altruists*? Profit-*function*: life-goal?!'

'Not-extortionate, or excessive, enough, and more...'

'Spent-money? For *The* Money-Rent?'

'Capital?'

'For use? Spend:-on...'

'Or as Capital-standstill...'

'More-Ecology and Equity...' *across-the-board...*

'Abroad! Not-Here, of course! The-Globe? Global Capital! Principal-Benefit! Private-militia army-prison torture, after *tenuous-*Liberation? Standstill?' *habitat habitual-problem...of Self-Regulation...*

Of paranoid rhetoric of shadow-monsters...

'Not-Violence? Win with words...'

'Threat? Ever? Anywhere? Of any typeface?'

'The Pen-is-*Mightier...*'

'Than the Screen…is *mightier* now.'

'Benefit of The-Most...*at least...*'

'The *least*-Benefit...The-Most? Of The Most? Everyone? Everything...'

'Exceptional-need? Do you eat meat?'

'Do you eat carrots?'

'So, there is a point at which most harm, as in death, to One, may benefit Another?'

'Of course! The question is...'

'What is that? Least-benefit, most-harm?'

'Most-harm, least-Benefit? No-harm, full-Benefit?'

'Closest to the-Win!'

'For everyone? Impossible.'

'*This* has happened before...'

'History does not repeat itself...we continuously make-it anew…'

'Even *copies* of the past do not repeat exactly...bad-memories…'

'We cannot help it?!'

'Can-do...Cannot-do...Don't *have* to.'

'Start **The Attack**?!'

'Stop The **Attack?!'**

'What **Attack**?'

'If you would stop...'We' would support some of your demands?'

'What if You don't?'

'What if You don't?'

'Together we will...'

Ceasefire: fixed-price for sacrificial necessity for food, perhaps evidential of self-defence...'

'One-to-One?'

'O.K.' *by listening, acknowledging, in the temple, at the market...*

'Now! 'I am looking for God, in the market-place...''

''Den-of-thieves!'

Temple-of Anarchistic-merchants! Independent vested personal-investment! Judiciary, court of law and elected-President, not above the law. Implacable-enemy laughingly-called Minister-of-Defence...

Heights' tank-attack civil-war...elsewhere:

<The Battleground...*playground*: resistance...

>Axis with secret police internal-stability and death and public-grief.

<Education, learning, marrying meriting across a-divide...*criticism* allowed…

>Did not last long. Modernising-authoritarian system-changed that.

<The Elite, and the to-be-**D**ictator, elected, or not, became *more comfortable with* *power* abuse arrest and torture of Men, Women, and Children:

'Known-about!'

'*Death*s!'

'Children!'

'Economic-enemies, and reforms...'

'Personal-*privatisation...' liberal-economic, illiberal-political-barons, family-connections: in-Corporation fabulously wealthy while country-starves in poverty devastating agriculture, natural and not maintained, importing City-jobs instability in the countryside in the-agricultural industrial-Towns, and Cash-rich Commercial-for:.*

The-City: *immigration* and emigration: population-collapse...*Explosion!*

'Never-*happened* in the way it was-*supposed*-to...' neglected.

Bringing secular-sectarian religious-racism swept a Middle-Eastern spring-*sunshine*:

'Toppling and altering governments from Tunisia to...Pakistan.'

'India and Tibet-Chinese Peoples' Republic: so-called Soviet-Style Government-corruption, fraud, and:...

News:

'*Beaten-up* trader...by Police...or was it Army? Difficult to tell now:...'

'We will not be *humiliated...*'

'The People want the fall of The Regime...'

'He who demands The Killing of his owned-people, is a traitor.'

'They who supply The Killing of their own people, are not traitors, but Patriots.'

Mis-guided. Exiled...into another war zone:

'Less or more safe?'

'Structural adjustment…Quantitive easing…'

'Any-day.'

'For-anyone, a cost...people…democracy…'

'A risk.'

'Of life.'

'And of Death. '

'From instant, or god-forbid! slow-death...'

'Life can be like a slow-death.'

'On the wheel!

'But manageable. Day-by-day...*no-choice to attack-riots, turned into outright revolt:*

'Who started it first?' *The kidnapping, kernelling, killing, destroying homes, factories, fields umbrella-organisation's, three letters long, rarely-more, or less*:

'The President!'

'Act's with impunity!'

'With-Punity? So people know who He Is!' *across the-countryside, burning and looting*:

'Demanding-*Fealty* and Food...'

'Carrying weapons from we knew not where...'

'And mustn't know:...

'Old Kalashnikovs...M-16's…Uzi assault rifles last forever…' *pent up frustration of minorities with less-power together, than any single-minority with power 1% 10%...99%...*

'So what?'

'With-Weapons! nationalist racist sympathisers…'

'Means they will be caught? *massacre...opposition-assassinated legally by a criminal murderer, never caught:*

'Enemies' enemy?'

'No-legal objection!'

'Demonstration!'

'Remonstration!'

Listened-to *heard*:

''Kill X Kill Y Kill Z?' *stir up old hatreds for some long forgotten, now remembered in some way, enemy, summary execution:*

<Soldiers-of-Justice!

>Whose? Civil-war? Atrocities both-sided terrified...*except only the-President himself, too stupid to know:* Infiltrator: to-the-lost-Homeland:...and Leader...*ascending the-Political apparatus...regime and those-connected...massacred. Imprisoned, tortured, killed, exiled:*

Proxy-battleground:

<For anti-authoritarianism to-rule authoritarian future...<

Fragmented, divided, regular shelling, keeping apart hidden infiltration- targets, masked and veiled...threats:

>Pestilence and Plagues on your Houses…

<Yours, too!<

>Assured a place in paradise? Hero-Martyr? Coward? Murderer? Dying-not in vain? Of-course!

<Propagation. Of the-message! Glamorous. Mundane-everywhere...everyday: easy to die...

<Murder?!<

>Difficult to *stay-alive* each day...a battlefield<

<But not a war…not-suicide today wished for or otherwise…

>No to: Murder *mystery-mayhem*!

<Love life! Live 'it' to the full for it will soon be gone!

<>Not fail!<relatively failure may be success…

<Not to-Fall...<

>If You do: *pick-yourself-up...and start, all over again.*<

<Remember: where-ever you are be sure to go there...<

>Have A Plan?<

<There aren't *no*-Plans...*all in the response, the reflexes, the-nous…the noose…*

>Electro-mechanics...Sonic?<

<Frontal-lobe, see. Cannot do anything about <it<!<*feelings:* thoughts-into-action, or action-into-*thoughts…*<

<Or neither?<

>Impossible.<

<Including-dreams? If you do-not-dream, you are practically-*dead*?<

>Urban-myth. Or forgetful...Or try a morning lay-in<<

<I wish I had!<

>You remember Your-*dream*s? then?<

<When you wake-and-rise, in your own good time?<

>The Brain-Shrink?<

<See<s the-Divine in everything.<

>See the-Divine, in nothing.<

<Except Good or Evil?<

>Evil the absence of Good<

<Good the absence of Evil...<

>Regime-Change...<

<Is the only way?<

>By The Ballot-box...<

<Boxing fair or foul?<

>Every-hour of everyday...<

<Accounted for:...<

>Whatever IT takes…<

15.

Across hub-status airport *weak*-governance...*standards-skill<s: crisis: good-money: costly-fusion aim-listing: list...*

>Check: Smartphone patent war: SMARTV. Super-prime property top spot safe haven status research wealthy investors steep growth closed behind golden postcode addressed to and from dull suburbs and glistening inner-city urban financial quarter lodge house staying-in correction...

<*Narcissistic*...self-sorry no-sentimentality hits post-crisis lower-reform levels, standstill excessive interest in One-Self.

>This, is how it is: Open-Spirit: *expect:* Statistics-*show...*

<Poll *shows where when and how* Well-Being is *trending....*

>Trade-ins...

<Trading-lift...*escalator accelerator pitched...*

>Euro-nestbox: from Poland to Portugal, Italy to Ireland/nextbox main changes index:

<NasDaq...Nikkei...

>The Chinese Yacht Hang Seng Composite:...

<CMA *on the world market yet embracing failure.made in.com or not made-in...attention to detail and lack of investing in morality ethics...unpicked alcohol and gambling, and prostitution-come-pornography...as long as...everywhere...*

>Free-Trade:*...mind-games...*

<Su-Doku:...

Fiendish. Super-fiendish. Brain-trainer. Polygon. Geodesic-homes244U property-Mart...people-watching, trending, eye-test...

>Laser, correction...Free-guide *easy*-use:...

<Discover: '*Freedom and Democracy!*''

'We will be Free!'

'Stop supporting Dictators!'

'Unpaid-tax' They owe Us! 70m!'

'Freedom and Justice!'

'Axe the Tax!'

'Adoption of: Conservation. Climate-change. Sustainability: gripe...'

>*Dissent:...*

<Dispute? Disapproval...ratings:...list...*list...*

<Protect!:...

>Enjoy.

<*Learn*. Elite. Established. Technical. Affluent. Service. Traditional. Working, all.

>Cyber:-business attack advanced...

<By-passing secure-defences firewalls...*sitting ducks*: Networked Fire-Eye says:

'Phishing...' *straight-through, and in-side out*:

'Attackers!' *sending corrupt email files, to unsuspecting-users, remains the most common form of attack. And actual government economic regime taken...to do your bidding?*

'Just like You?'

'Just, like Me?'

'See?'

Seen only now through the half-blind, bruised blank gaps in-between the now tooth-less figures.

Now the abbreviated rounded-up and down, plus and minus letters and numbers in-words and columns, read across in either-direction, up or down, in-sequence:...

Quantity, and *quality*-branded impish impious, even IMPERIOUS, neither {sure, not Honest. Nor Deceitful except {[of-Self]}… nonetheless, impressive. Desirous-of, and assumed of by all. Lusted-after. Luscious-orderly lifeblood dripping away.

'Created Chaos!' spurted from a neck wound

Dripped-onto, the-walls and the boardroom and kitchen and bathroom...the *shower-room floor*: good/bad:

>Moral-high...low?

<Ethical-*position: set by The-Government? Religion? Science?*

>*Common-Sense...*

<*Green/anti-discrimination agenda...*then...

<**Human-Rights!**

Red-lighted...

'And **Responsibilies'-Boss**?'

'What?'

'Animal-Rights? We get out of here alive?'

From the other side of the World or nearer the same side…

At any one time, or another...in-chains: Orange Jump-suits...striped-jumper...

Indebted with life giving cables and equipment, aerial out-front for all to see...satellite-dish crashing on the side of the vehicle...on the back of a flatbed lorry...passing beneath, and carried away, below the overpass over the subway...

Underground vehicle bomb networking Cities...

'Actioning!' *firearms tracer bullets through the night air, in the daytime, unseen laser, into the night. Into the day, cutting through the defences, the homes, the barricades.*

'Lives!'

'Hardened!'

'Families!'

Brutal Sectarian Body-armour...*flesh and blood the same...*

'Retribution...' *cultish* opposition...

Then, in-Opposition to...opposed...opposing...who? *shaky-alliance of Democratic-Partners...*non-aligned The-Others: workers and bosses alike. Different-century: New-Century: The Modern-Era:

'Cut my head!'

'To Death...'

'Enlisting with pride.'

'Or necessity...' as seen as:

'Rid the world of All Known Tyrants!'

'And unknown!'

'None exempt.'

'Except, mission creep. Every day the same, or worse, than the day before...'

'Who?'

'Anyone! Them! We. Kill! As if Death, is all there is.'

Off-screen...time-meddling cronyism:...clone@Chrono...T: mysteriously illusionary magic-*creed* assessing...key-*memories* ant-clustered humans' encharmed to the cause...

'To be enslaved: children, women, fathers...tortured…abused…'

'The same. Alive. Dead.' *yet, freed in-danger, disaster, escapist-fantasy...*creepy-*thriller* across hill and field and empty house...gone. Snuffing-out@Combat-halo spaceship parasitic flood of sensual-life beyond this *spiritual*-journey:

'Beholden to *some* unknown known Master-Plot:...'

'Cause Chief to-lie, bluff, or twist...'

<Or **Bust**@*folded bio-shock without actual- control over actual life turns out land-dweller sea-farer...*

Cyberwar re-orientation crashing:

>*Equity release-calculator...*

<Keep-*pressing*-the-buttons!...*raising and lowering the-life-morality-bar...*

On-screen: *images moving-screen depiction of historical...*

>Ethical-Events:... *unfolding...*

<Mission: Select: Game's: Point's-*won*: Battles won/lost: Wars: won/lost: Peace-pact's and Treaties...Trade! Commerce: N/n. Import/Export: Programme1:Training-completed. Congratulations!!!:...

>On what?! *woken-up the sleeping dragon, lion, butterfly broken-effect of one single action (in the full glare of the Media if not shared by The Secret-Services, Terror Commando's Assassination-Squad:* with teeth of gold, and tongues-of-fire...

<Combat-*scenario:...*

>At The Strategic Institute: *Policy Room:...*

<Rules of Engagement: *Personnel interfering with...*

>Combat-scenario...Programme1:...

Combat-Scenario:…modern-Contemporary:

<Choose: Global-power-state/Rogue-state: Choose: Command and Control:

>Peacetime Treaties: Trade-Deals:...list:... granted and cannot-attack or be-attacked unless:

1. If already occupied or occupying, attacking or being attacked.

2. If being-attacked or going to-attack: all peace treaties, are null and void.

<Combat/non-Combat *scenario?*: *non-combat scenario no-longer available…*

<Who says?

>Cannot attack in case of attack without clear evidence of intention to attack (or occupy, dependent on responsibility for protecting civilian-population): *list…*

>Combat-scenario:*...already-occupying occupied:...*

<*Occupied*-City: Name: National Rational Equitable OK?: Yes/No...Yes!

<No? Yes?

> Yes! Sir! Ma'am!'

<O.K. That’s the Terms and Conditions done.

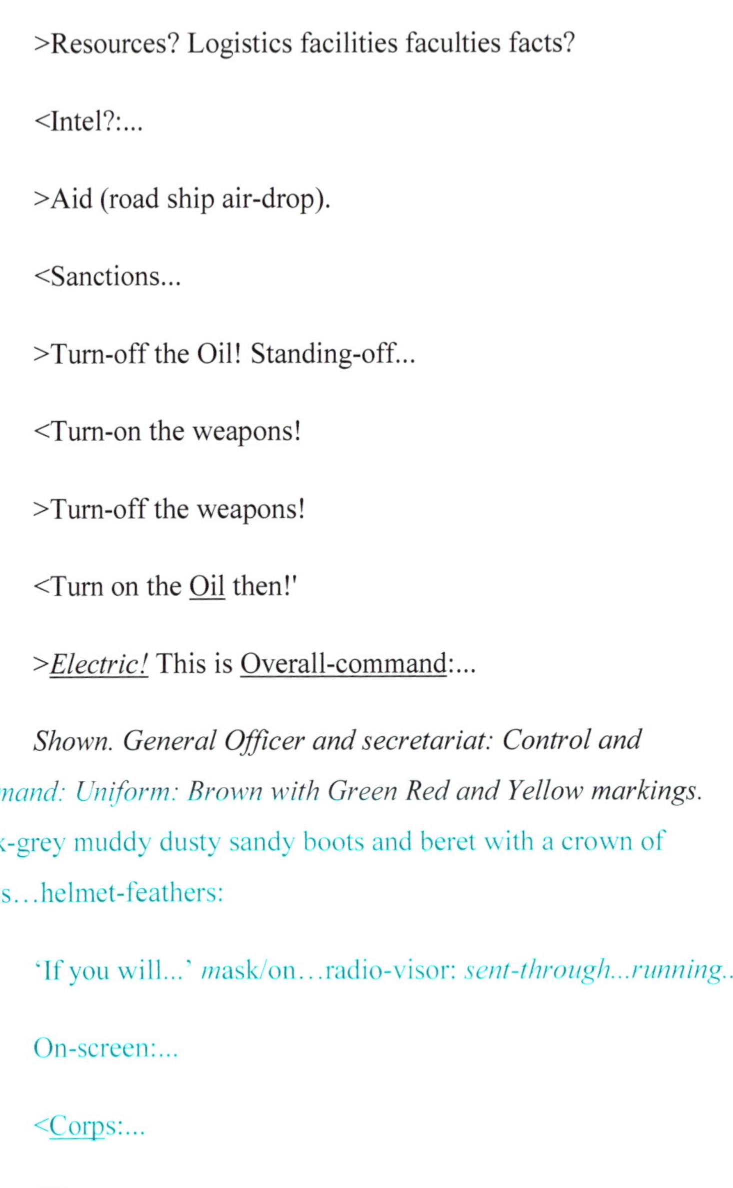

The Instruction-handbook…*downloading…down-loaded programme loading...loaded:…initialising…initialised:*

>Resources? Logistics facilities faculties facts?

<Intel?:...

>Aid (road ship air-drop).

<Sanctions...

>Turn-off the Oil! Standing-off...

<Turn-on the weapons!

>Turn-off the weapons!

<Turn on the Oil then!'

>*Electric!* This is Overall-command:...

Shown. General Officer and secretariat: Control and Command: Uniform: Brown with Green Red and Yellow markings. Black-grey muddy dusty sandy boots and beret with a crown of spikes…helmet-feathers:

‘If you will...’ *m*ask/on…radio-visor: *sent-through...running...*

On-screen:...

<Corps:...

>Against!:...

<Intel: Terror Camp...

>Famine (natural/manufactured) to make the threat *more*-real:...self-*fulfilling*...

<Control and Command: *take* Control: A-Z ...*about* ?

>What-is and What-is-likely-to-happen?

<Those forever unfinished...

>Revolutionaries. Eh?

<No Revolution this! *going backwards again:*

>This is only the *catalyst* to *light* the *fire*s…

<*Permanent*-Revolution!

>Going-in!< *we went in…*

'Whose side are you on?'

<Open-markets?!<

>Self-regulating!…again!<

<Self-regulating market-place...<

>World-wide prices…<

<Production-growth-figures…<

>Logistics:…transport by-air, land and sea...<

<Sold-on...and as a potential seller asks a specific price for the stock…<

>*e*-pirates of The Digital-age!<

<For Your larceny and pilfering!<

>Safety and security?<

<Of the-Masses?*...not-guaranteed...somewhere else…tanks-armed with mortar and machine-gun fire...paid-out…*

>Police, and Military intervention: Power-up's… tank's rolling-over bodies on the ground.

<Whose?

>The People's of course...<

<Our-People's?<

>Ours? Yes of course! Yours and Mine!<

<…and our Trade-Routes…<

>…and theirs?…in-and-out tactic this time? Export the risk…shoot-first ask questions later.

Rapid-dominance…inducing paralysis. Desperation, and a sense of extreme vulnerability...

>To Import-Export:...*licence...with evidence of financial-exchange and debt-incurred...*

<Corruptly or otherwise...< *significantly...*

>Familial...<*fraudulently...from...where? and who?...to where and who...creditable contact and legal-agreements to be signed-off simultaneously on-line...*

<Personal-Government:...*contract<s:...*

>Personal: N/n.

<Public: n...*to be signed over screen-saver of landscaped fields and industrial-sites...*

>Building-sites: list...and office-blocks and housing-blocks and Business-centre:

'My-People!'

Family-at-war conference: *key marriage-decisions made behind closed doors, with the key people:*

The doctrine, the propaganda, the action: the crossroads right or left...decide...then the next phase: Left? Right? Natural-selection: RANDOM/ORDERED = +/-...military and moral strength diplomatic and financial energy and Terror-Threat At Home and...Abroad...

'Airstrike-*Diplomacy...*

'*Immunity...*Humanitarian-Effort?...

'In the name of?

'Real Democracy and Freedom! For-Humanity! To Maintain Influence…' *information:*

'For or against?'

'Or ever Neutral?'

'After one of the most dramatic televised act of war in history...'

'Turning a blind-eye?'

'Once opened may still be blind...'

'Only Waging-war on wagering-War!'

'As a brazen act of War!'

News-pictured spoken: the President General/Great Leader, hunkered down, bunker boiler-room, control-room.

To order The Final Deluded and Deluding-Truth of Supremacy: Economic, Political, Familial, Religious-Scientific **Power**:*considerations of course...*

<Foremost or no-longer...*as self-preservation takes over, defers bravery….*

>As so many times before…

In **The War-Room** concrete pillared not-marble panelled tent, bare walls, with maps and charts, *seemed the safest place*; since bombs dropping all around. As being sealed into: The Concrete Mausoleum.

Strategic Weapons-*dump* or The-Armoury: **<u>The Palace-Hotel</u>**: packed with explosives, and journalists.

Human Rights Lawyer Civilians...lists...*from all over the world:* 'Activist's....'

'Supporters...'

'The-Demonstrators...' *against or of Old and Young-Activists...dying...*

'As they wish...'

As *The-President rises above the law: with no form of redress, fairness, or any peace or reconciliation...*

Only opposition and protest, remonstration and final funereal demonstration...

'Of the President?' *seeking compact, relief from the-madness-trapped in-family and tribal-compact, blood-line, or married-into?:*

'To Seal-Loyalty...*forever...*' *without-faith...anymore.*

At the final-moment, how could you...not-know? As At The First Act? Only to die ignorant of what brought Death? Only to have for any <u>Hope</u>...

Or no way out, now. Being there. True. The truth...and:

'Even then, You, Me? *We* don't ever *really* know *What's Going On*...until It has...goinmg-going-Gone!'

'For-Ever?'

'For-Ever…'

'Not The Truth then, ever...'

'Only in The-Moment...gone...

'And the next.'

'Nor do any of us know What's Going On?' *most or any of The Time...strategically forced or similarly deluded into The Human-Shield...to be pilloried.*

The most-precious, precarious, precocious. The most-ferocious, fearful in case of losing it all! The Devils' ransom! What You knew but did not do anything about...

Or even try. For fear? Of what?

'It was going-down anyway...'

'All or *Nothing*?'

'Not even One-Life unaffected...'

'Or any other...'

‘Would stand in the way…of...'

'The last minute…'

‘From The Previous-Rebellion...’ *re-copied anew re-grouped and cooped around a-ghastly figure-head attempting to cover-own vicariousness...*

‘The Conference? Midday?’

‘And Family?’ *from The Television channel screened interview*:

‘With some claim they may never own, or see Their-Own again...’ *interrupted…interrupting...un-proven Intel. radio-message:...*

'Check-*verisimilitude:...*’

‘O.K!...’ *attention breaking grabbing The-News...*

‘The Prime-Focus News...’

‘Dispelling false rumour and report...’

‘Reviewing the whole document now:...’

The full-story*…cache-full...trawling seasoned eye-witness filming time and date and commentary-shouting-over the noise of crowd and each individually validated... playlist:*

*‘Shock!...*and Manifesto-Prime-Time-Fear-Factor: *the news broadcast index scale stale-algorithm sweeping across...’*

'Verisimilitude?'

'Shot-through…'

'With Brute-Justice.'

On screen: *Breaking-news*:...*latest*...*live-image*: The Journalist:- montage from: The-City: The Azimuth Hotel:

A Women dragged suddenly from a metal-chair in the highly-decorated plaster and marble-hewn hallway.

With pictures of the-President on the walls...dragged along the corridor screaming, grasping at the images:

"Him! Him!...' where She had been talking and filmed-talking to recording Other-Journalists she dragged! suddenly, by her hair, by her head and arms and legs dragging pushing against and towards The Foreign-Journalists lined up for The Press-Conference...*or whatever the-President had called them in for.*

Her head in a headlock by the-Guards...

She was *screaming: 'They* tried to rape...Me!"

Reported live:

'She was pulled out into the Hotel-Lobby...' *breaking free from the laughing minders, she screamed:*

'I tell them everything, everything!'

Grabbed by the neck and a hand forced over her mouth, pushed onto the steps outside.

The recording equipment taken. The one remaining, running from a briefcase suitcase camera, hidden from view; not from the view, with sound and fixed-held veiled concealed camera: *verified*:

'She was knocked to the ground dragged by Male Security Guards and another Female Journalist *standing-by helped her...'*

'She was taken to a waiting car...' sandy dust-brown black shiny carriage-work no markings or other distinguishing marks. Except clearly a car of The-Regime.

With trumpets and loudhailers: *The Peasants and The Students descending on the Palace of the President-King Querulous Queen:*

'The People are unarmed, not dangerous...'

'*Who have weapons? But A Few Farmers and Homiest Gangster-types...' looking after their murderous suicidal backs:*

'To plead for mercy, and for food...' *hungry and becoming dangerously roused.* The Driver, The Chauffer in place The Car reversing up the slope deliberately into the-crowd:

'Reporters and Journalists are...'

gathering:...

'Demonstrator's getting close to the Presidential Palace...'

'The Peace-Keepers, Diplomat's and Ambassador's *minding* Business and Trade...'

'Observers. Monitors and Objector's...' *called-on for the-fighting:*

'Human-shield!'

'The World! Hostage! You are either with Us, or against Us.' shouted spat.

To camera:

'Black and White flag's...tens of hundreds of thousand's together with more million's...'

From the studio:

'Billion's, across the Globe!!'

'Then Trillion's of US! One per cent, of the Trillion's! Ten per cent of the Trillions! Shared-out between 'Us'? Together?! Family, or not. All are! Called-on for the fighting! In dying! Put away our weapon's! What good will come of us all killing?! Let us embrace like brother's and sister's'...'

Deadly. From the camera in-camera-phone...

'Stop!'

'God comes to the rescue!'

'Throw the weapons away?'

'Promise?'

'Pledge.' Plebiscite pledging to prohibit, inhibit, require, or regulating...*it will pass*...*focus on there is not end to it, no way out: live, sleep, dream, death.*

'Let Us Pass!' chanted louder. It will pass:

'Everlasting-War!'

'Or Revolution?'

'Anyway?'

Looking-down; the-Clerk punching-a-key...*ripping-off headphones*, then replacing again:

'One or Other.'

'Wrong...'

'Correcting...'

'Miscalculating...'

'Inevitable...'

'Deadly.'

Whilst talking:

'We cannot settle things the way we do...With nuclear, chemical, and biological warfare? Or threat thereof?'

'Rather than using these things for their *peaceful*-ends?'

'Change would be good...'

'For the better?'

'Not worse! Than *this*!' head-earphoned:

'See? All things to all men...

'Peace!'

'To-Hell!'

Then:

'For Bread and Freedom!'

'Bread and bandages…'

Then:

'To The-Jaws of Hell!' Imprisoned for Life *ironically force fed to eat on hunger strike forced to drink water water-boarded he died...there:*

'To Hell!'

'Without hell!'

Told:

‘In the end They Always Fall: Tyrants.’

A hurried figure entered the-screen heard:

‘They have lain down weapon’s...’

‘Where?’

‘Everywhere.’

‘They have lain down their hearts. For Love, and Truth?’

‘For the love of God!’

‘From Truth, and Love...’

‘Life. Living!’

‘Nasty, Brutish, and Short-changed!’

‘For the unselfish Love of the Lord!

‘Annihilated.’ the-HYPOCRITE liar-apologist:

‘Something had to be done!’

‘Liar!’

‘Murderer!’

‘Misled!’

‘Care-less?!’

‘Carless? No! see: Range-Rover: *list...returning-to-profit rating’s...’*

‘For the Love of things!’

‘For the Love of family...for a Lover...’

‘Sacrificing-Self?!’

‘Loser!’

‘Like, I’m that careless!’

‘Job’s destroyer!’

‘Unfortunately.’ crocodile tears...from the screen, some Politician...’

‘At each level makes-less sense...’

‘Defenders are harassing the enemy all-around...*assailing*…’

‘Defers from the actual conspiracy-of-...’

‘*Economics’*-Power-Up/Down/In/Out/Forward/Back…

Onto on to The Battlefield…onto The Streets:

‘Less conspiracy, more-in-*perspicacity*…’

‘More-in-competence *apparently*!’

Back at Your-Office:

>*Maintaining...The Situation:...*

<Trade-ins and Trade-outs...

>On International Legal Contract :..

Of all-sides back and front to accept or *reject...*

<Or Blockade?

>Legal or not...

<Mutual-*assistance*? Shared?

The-Office:

>Or Enmity...

<Violence!

>Of Insurgent and Refugee...

<For straightforward saving…execution!

>Accusation's of support of Anti-Democratic Dictators'-denial and breaking of long running...

<Ceasefire...

>Peace and Trade Pact.

<Two-side's to any conflict.

>More than Two.

<Always more...

>Three. At least!

<Many sides...complicated: Rich and Poor too many, too many too count...

>An unelected Elite...and The People used to vote for them...

<Buying the vote through <u>Price</u> and <u>Sales</u>...

>Against Civil Unrest: Bread and circus's...

<Elected Elite for One term of Office only?

>Two? Three? For Life?

<Decided by *Them*-selves!

>Life!

<Then! Divide and conquer...

>Rule The Gaps!

<Elitist *Colonial* and internal Civil-<u>War?</u>

>The-Establishment: *named: list*...last: The Only-Ones who could...

'After they attacked-Us!' *like children in a playground:*

'Collaborator!!'

'Stooge!'

'Scum!'

'Scab!!'

The back doors of the shiny black-car, silver handles pulled open:

'Get In the Car.' *said malevolently almost laughingly viciously brutally man-handled...in a country with as strict gender roles, and rule's as any...another television-journalist trying to ask:*

'Why are they taking you?' *another yelled desperately, in vain for an answer. Yelled again!...yellow-grey fog couldn't see click in front of you, a fraction of a click-even...above the parapet*:

'Snipers!'

'Tear-gas!' fired into the crowd.

The *cry* went up as demonstrators and police sprayed Paint and Gas and The Police and The Army and The Security-Forces sheltered their burning eyes behind masks and shields as did The demonstrators in imitation:

'Stop imitating! Start Irritating!'

'One rule fits all?'

'Kill the killers?'

'Eye for an Eye?'

'Or likely possible or most unlikely?!'

'Allow them then To Murder Our Children in their beds?'

'Like Our Children murder theirs...'

'Tortured...'

'Raped?

'Suicide Blown-Out! The Same!

'Charismatic!'

'Not so the-end...dead.'

'Interesting 'though?'

'Definitely. Family...'

'Outside our Legal-parameters...'

'Ours?'

'Directing others to kill? In Foreign Lands? They claim are theirs?'

'They do not murder, You do!' *potential loss=cost/price alone, value added costs and value:*

'Through starvation...and greed! Who decides. then, eh? Judge, Jury And Executioners?'

'Us?'

'You, and Me.'

'Executors.'

'Executioners?'

'Feel the Power!'

'The Regime *manufacture* a Truth...'

'There is none.'

'To *save* itself...'

'From what? Each and every other...'

'The Wrath of The-Insider?'

'Outside forces...'

'No-longer Civil War, then?'

'Global.'

'At all costs? Including life...'

'Scorched-Earth...'

'Towns and Cities...'

'Living on the street of bombed-out building...'

'Cluster barrel bombs...'

'Indiscriminate...'

'Criminals!'

'Who? They say of us...blood on our hands! These were my friends I played with in the street...'

'No longer...Their friends...Enemies...and made The Enemies of us...'

'Inhuman...'

'De-*humanising...' threatening slaughter...of innocents...*

'No-one is now...'

'Ever was in their eyes...see that now...'

'Our eyes...'

'Of The Insider Outsider takes sides...'

'Or doesn't care...'

'To see us fight now...'

'Become the Leaders of People!'

'Parents separated exhausted desperate threatened and threatening slaughter...'

'Seen by their children copycats...long stare...' silent sensitive, wanting *Them* to go away now.

'Ever make-up? Made-up? Knocked-down? Try to carry-on as normal...what is normal?'

'I only want to go to school again!' *children playing at digging graves...smashing gravestones...*

'I see *ghosts of my friends...' with their hands and legs and heads cut-off...*

'For-Surrender...' *and then be killed anyway...*

'Avenging my brother, for my brother...'

'Older for younger...'

'Younger for Older...'

'To Survive Only! Who is left?! Do not go in anger but in Peace!!'

Friends4Ever scratched-out graffiti seen:

'WarFair4!'

'*That* is what started all this...'

'WarFare4!'

'Anger and blame instead of...'

'Soul(s) sold to The Devil!'

'Poisoning our minds!'

'Generals and Priests!'

'Take *Delight* in Killing...'

'Took. Now...Martyr Hero for my family...'

'Irreconcilable past...'

'Life can be replaced...not A Cause, A Country never...Forever!'

'God is the protector...God willing...may God have mercy...thanks-to…'

'Told to lay down and be raped...with a gun...'

'God is not fair! Between rich and poor, thin and fat...'

'Shot-up the *Jacksnipe...*'

'Chest-crushed…'

'Breasts'-broken...'

'Love lies...' *ever dissatisfied...lust straightforward satisfaction...*

'Again and again...'

'Until finally...ended.'

'Utterly...'

'Self-serving…'

'Personal-Reason...'

'Never thought We could be so-greedy…'

'Wider picture?'

'Unequal...Unreasonable...'

'Uncertainty...'

'Live with it.'

'I hate The Future so much. I don't know who will live or die...Me and my family...'

'I would rather die now, than know and *not know* this all the time...'

'Who is Who??'

'Rebel? Government? Faction this or that? People! Children!'

'In Fear...'

'There is *almost* no-Love left...the-way they see adults their protectors…and friends and family…like You!'

'But *hatred* then is....'

'In Love there is no fear...'

'Choice or Chance of re-birth...'

'Pray we do to them what they do to us!'

'As before...*Business-as-Usual…*'

'To Cut-Off food and medical supplies...Restrict access to markets and technology...'

'Sanctions? Economically besieged:...'

'Starve or surrender!'

'Never!'

'Labour-strike?'

'Today! Capital-strike! Port's blocked...'

'Arms Embargo...Cut-Off weapons and...'

'Free for all?'

'Non-violence...pressure...International Community...'

'Voted on? Who *Votes*?'

'To Declare War and Kill?!'

'At the end of a gun...'

'The Army will save us...'

'Universal soldier!'

'For Trading-*relentlessly...'*

'Necessary?'

'Crusade...'

'Jihad?'

'With *their* lives as wel as Your Own owned!

'By Me! Immoral and inhumane...'

'Moral and inhumane?'

'Humane and immoral? Whose rules?'

'Moral's and humanities'?'

'None.'

'Un-Ethical *e*motion? Or I-Robot? Martyr-Murderer? Suicidal attempted interruption of The Eternal Peace...'

'Hero-Power!'

Dragged-out…and hauled back and pushed into the back of the car:

'What is your Name?! *another journalist sensibly screamed to her, to follow-up…and was punched to the ground. Into the back of the car, still screaming, and still heard, as the vehicle drove off, at-speed.*

Sped into the main-street of the Old-Town, City-Street. Water fountain-pumping square circus could almost be anywhere in the world, turned-into… and only army vehicles, and carriers patrolling The Roadways…

The Journalists*...and The Demonstrators' shouts and calls heard...over the distance guns-crackling, shells-exploding with a* ***Boom!****ing: Th...ud!...that echoed the wide streets and narrow alleyways...*

Lighting up the sky above, with fireworks, stocked for the fiesta, in red as for a final ascension. As through a fragile clear sky, looking-glass, over a map. Not-allowed to leave. From the Hotel Presidential-Palace part Press Room...

The-General-President In Command-*and*-Control *next-door in* <u>*The-Castle Palace*</u> *the highest building in* <u>*The-City*</u> *landscaped behind with:*

'Rooftop view: not allowed.'

'In case of what?'

'Not-allowed to go onto the roof, or take the upper rooms...unless-taken...'

'So, cocooned into the downstairs area...where I am speaking to you, from the restaurant and *private*-Bar-Area.

Where Politicians, Bankers, Buyers and Sellers of Weapons and Equipment have Loaded The Weapons To Store and for The Command and Control Centre of the-President:...'

'Who is said to be here, and at various other locations 'To protect His Highness'...and the-People.'

From the vast multi-storey ground floor courted yard entrance potted palm-trees along the roadway's and poplar and evergreen once pine forest stripped bare.

To Deserts-cape:*...beyond moved with the gentle salt sea-wind and dry-odourless desert fish smelling-carcass, unloading at the Harbour-Port. But Not-loading-on or Unloading-From: warm-ocean wind boiling whistling through and down the streets and buildings on both-sides…like tunnels, built towering blocks, overlooking:*

<The-City:...

From outside The Hotel and Presidential-Palace:

She was carried off screaming:

'*They* tried to *rape*-Me! I am from T…! They wanted to Kill Me!' in-pain and bruising tyre-flex bound, and beaten body dumped: *another body? Left in the street, on the doorstep, a warning rifle-butt bludgeoned tramline pushed, crushed.*

Showed-up at The Press Conference called *announced...a distance hence yet they said she was the same person:*

'She was *A Known Madwomen.* She would be questioned about her allegations and returned to Her Family Abroad. She would come to no harm. The Bombing of The Palace was not succeeding in alarming: The Great Leader-in- the-*least...*'

In answer to The-Journalist(ic) question: of which the answer was already implied and aimed to catch-out, and catching-out...entrapping, ensnaring self-out.

In the end:

'Yes. He would be staying-put...here...yes...' (*in fact he would be moving around, different Palaces, through tunnels built for purpose*) and…

There:

'The-People were with Him...and...'He is winning!"

'The-People were against-Him...and He Is...'

The-Journalists were soon to be de-mobbed from the-Demonstrators...

Separated from The Crowds beyond...*heard and seen* then not-seen but heard and recorded and sent...calling:

'The People want the-Regime to Go!'

'We shall not be moved!'

The Journalists moved to The Palace compound, as The Hotel:

'...was no longer safe for them.'

The Safety-alert given, ironically or otherwise, as the bombs-dropped...

From the sky closer zoomed-in on and spelled-out, and taken spell-checked auto-didactic data autonomous...

Auto-checker: the-Threat muted, did not go unfelt, or unwritten about.

Without the feeling of braving it out, with various degrees of optimism and pessimism for themselves, and All-Other:

'At least She went knowing and her-*tormentors* also knowing, whether caring or not of this attempted rape, if *not- real*...She would be known at T…and that The World would know of her and Her cause and Her people and perhaps, that She would be rescued...now...*saved...' a querying gaze looking up, almost absent-mindedly, until after the event* The-Clerk:

'Trade-ins?'

'Trade-outs?'

'And who is Going To Pay this-Time?'

'Humanitarian-Aid?'

'When it all goes up again...' looking down *into a rising Tide of Debt…liquid…gas...teargas...*

'Even Rainwater! Pure-Air!'

Putrid-air rising yellow orange *like a sunrise*. From the brightness of the colour in the air, the acid acrid taste, manufactured and could be felt *streaming*...nervously The Nasal-Pinch:

'Going down...'

The Action:

'Hook, line, and sinker...'

TV *channelling*...cut-back in: The last report, with:

'The Demonstrators in The City centre...' in the background chanting quoted:

'We do not expect to be returning alive. We have made our peace...'

'Here, this is a terror-crime...a fact of war! An 'Act of War'!'

The-Clerk a weekend *territorial*-reservist *thought* upon this and deliberated upon:

'Tame! Kill the-Devil!'

'Dead or Alive! Beheaded! Severed! Burned at the stake!'

'Not until The Great Leader leaves the Country!'

'Silenced! Garotted! And never returns!' blurted into a television camera. Seen in Graffiti-Effigy...' *hanging from a lamppost.* Shot, dead against a wall. Another winding panning-shot:

'<u>The Great-Leader</u> must be brought to trial!'

Crashing-shot! Zoom-shot *into satellite-spacecraft, before breaking-up the pixels…and cut-out….*

'Cut!!'

16.

'We are the-same You and Me.'

'Me and You?'

'We could be identical-twin's...Thee, and me.'

'...which twin am I then?'

'Who is Venus?'

'And who Earth?' *sharing opposite planetary proportions in composition of all the ingredients for life in equal...*

Yet by reverse quantities...

The-Clerk knew. And in-response out of the shared window saw not-similarly but *much* differently:

'The Same?'

The-Other Boarders, and as if bored into:

'To Capital-Hell, eh?! Or Heaven?'

"Eh?'

'Bring-on the grim-Reapers...eh?" *the early-train, crowded with commuters' pin-stripe suited plain palpably tailored brief-cases with deep-pockets. Well-heeled...and if not a-fanatical for reading:*

The Financial-Newspaper...

Or even: ***<u>The Business Plan</u>*** *and Financial-Report...seen.*

On-screen: opposite briefcase laptop opened and shiny manifestation *and all I see, are Vampires! Blood-sucking flesh-eating Zombie-vamping seduction manipulating-analysis...role-playing...acting-out...revamping:*

'Re-construction?'

'Afterwards? De-constructed first...'

'Then: *re*-constructed...construed-as? Re-pairing? Maintaining...'

'Business as Usual...'*frantically, frenetically*:

'We are not machines! We are not algorithms for your Astronomic wealth creation…we are…pyrotechnics! We do not control nature, we are nature, nature does not control us, we control ourselves…in so far as we have free-will, to the extent that we do, we are free of nature, as nature is free…as night has moved across our worlds the day has arrived and we continue…to move with it, we, have not stood still, only the markets are closed, we are open, open to the day! Otherwise all around us we are chained to our person, to our personality, sure, which we cannot avoid, since birth, perhaps, but we may alter surely our history and birthright for the better…and not to anothers' worse automatically, or at all, as far we can help our fear, we can contain it. In so far as we can help our anger, we can turn our energies around to help not hinder other, and in our betterment. Forever only altering with time and nature the puts and stays of science and the spirituality we all have for Good or Evil, there is not Evil that brings Good, or Good that brings Evil…we have the heart to make something of this…the scales may fall from our eyes that blind us, that make us measure everything against everything else instead of taking the wonderment of life and making life of that wonder…not destroying life which we need to live recklessly, as an excuse for necessity, but with love, and relative peace…'

The Banker alarmed at this outburst from nowhere…

On the train in the shade relatively still, and only partially-*enlighten*ing inside the carriage, now sheltering sky. Going-Forward with the ever-rising Sun, now behind them, and ahead looking-out. Straight-ahead. To each distance for One and The Other. But not Each Other: the same, both racing the-Absolute Earth-clock from one end-of-The-Train to The-Other: in opposite facing-directions, around The Globe *on the-surface: headed hi-tailing along as in the forward-wake of The People and automated-systems that contradicted every other up or down to this point in processing...sent every price tumbling one-after-another, there, at least, stopped, without contradiction until:*

'Re-working the workplace-*hours*…then?' The Clerks phased response:

'<u>Pay:</u> No-Payback? *With personal and grouped insurance underwritten re-insured and not-assured...*' *spooked slightly:*

'You are Joking? Seriously?'

'Seriously? What about?'

'The Money that You are going to Give Me...to Pay-Off My Debts with? Your Money?'

'Or lack of It...Today, as anybody...'

'That You *double* with Mine…'

'After you have Paid-Off *those* The Initial Debts...The Initial Debt, again...Double Your Money!'

'Double ***<u>My Debt</u>***?'

'Halve-it...and then make more...'

'Debt?'

'Profit.' *challenging, questioning, answering...*

'Like some *crap* TV quiz show or something?'

'That's correct! I cannot do it alone…they will suspect a-ringer...Ding-a-linger? I cannot get-in-there too-obviously…see? Have to await, await the opportunity…'

'But not miss the -opportunity.'

'Got it! Great pass! This…Opportunity. Got it?! See. That is where you come-in: You get-in, not-Me. See? They will be watching Me, but not-You.' w*hispering*:

'We…Corner-the-Market?

'Pincer- Movement, eh? No-one knows who you are. You have a company name? The Set-up:…*perfect*- opportunity: 'The-Sting! They will not know what has Hit 'em! Shock and Awe!'

'*Monopoly*!'

'Monopoly! Of a whole-Nation!'

'Global-Oligopoly between the few!'

'Got to have some competition!'

'If that is what it takes! But only one or two, eh? You and Me? Eh?' *whetting the appetite. Or wetting the underpants...*

'Except no-one knows it is 'Me'.'

'Or 'Us'?'

'Rather than 'You'?'

'And 'You' too.'

'It is 'Us'. Partnership. Legal.'

'Trust-suit?'

'No-chance! Communist? Commitment?' *though...* thought The-Clerk:

'*Breach* of Trust?' *thought,* and spoken:

'How about Breach of trust? Any Duty of care to Your Shareholders? To Yourself only!'

'And You?'

'And Me.'

'Customers? Client's?:...'

'Null and Void.'

'Is that it?'

'Except keep it To Yourself, of course. Ourselves...I mean...'

'What if You don't pay of my debt's...'

'What if You don't?'

Confidently:

'You'll be no worse-off.'

'No deeper **In-Debt**, you-mean?'

'We will get 'em Paid-Off...with more On Top!'

'Isn't *that* how people get scammed again?!'

'Gullible. The-*promise*?'

'I am not Stupid!'

'I know that! But...'

'They' need us more than ever to prop up the markets. To Trade…be in on the-Game. The Real Deal? Done! Bailed out, and bailing-out...'

'Taking on board the Debt-flood...' *almost tipped-overboard!*

'Some gone a way, overboard!'

Insider-dealing mergers and take-over's...mis-selling products to a gullible guilty client-base…' The-Banker now casting-the-blame. Looping through the air.

The river-line baited, the-fishing expedition already spoken-for and therefore and forever thereafter True. As spoken thought. Believed. Felt to be True: Going to Happen: swishing sound:

'Phishing-trip?'

'Swish!'

The insect-bait. The metal-hook. The likely-catch. The Golf-swing...

'Big fish? Little fish? What is that?'

'The-Stock-Markets: The Biggest Shopping-Mall in The-World!'

'The-Markets! The-World!'

'Three steps to success!' The Big-Fish! Whatever it is? It is drowned into the air and light of *This* Day!' in the imagination: held up to the camera dripping, onto the financial pages, wrapped and wrap-tagged: No pictures! Of course not! Not even of The-Fish?!'

'Think Global Asset-Management...'

'Think of Yourself!'

'I always do.'

Insides glowing with self-satisfaction:

'There is some-*skill* in it, no doubt. You have to be quick with figures. Quick, to spot the window of opportunity the talents of money! The moment? Without moment. A trifle, a-fancy…and without the callous:

'Machismo-ruthlessness of a fistfight...'

'Feminine-Flight...'

'And Both?' *from a bloodied battle-scene...*

'On-Paper?'

'And Screen?'

'Yes, of-course. it is all <u>The-Great-Game!</u>'

'Greatest-'Game? Still-playing?'

'<u>The-Real-Thing</u>...'

'Is out there...'

'Where?'

Looking out of the moving-window.

Both, and each down onto the alternately watched displayed-screens. Before looking-up, together, and straight into the eyes of each other, again. The-Banker opened The Laptop Briefcase *placed on the table between them:*

'Gone. *Analysis*:…that sees nothing but Pure *Financial* Analysis. Those income-outcome figures…eh?' *paced metaphorically.*

The-Other wandering aimlessly.

The-Other strolling homeward bound...

'All to be sorted out today…'

'Midday. Meantime...'

'Over optimism?'

'Yet again? Pessimism. See? Lack of Confidence...'

'Fairness?'

'Merchant and Investment-Banks...' *caught with grotesque over-investment...fair-enough. Over-confident. Incomprehensible debt-instrument's...*

'Credit-fraud!!'

As soon as uttered, heard:

'*Fraud-Alert*! Fraud-Alert. ***Fraud-Alert...***'

'Who?' repeating the question *journalistically...*

'*Toxic* mortgage-backed securities...*predatory* -lending...that's all. Buy-back.? Without the debt...'

'On-credit, or Rental...'

'Or Lose The Lot...anyway...' *unaccountable unaccounted-for...trespass and fraud...*

'Money-laundering...for criminals and police-states...sanctions- busting...'

'That as well.'

'Spent. Conspiracy...to-*defraud...*'

'For?'

'Incompetency! Bonus-bubble? False-accounting...'

'Unbelievable Greed!'

'Jus' following the money! What's wrong with that?! Innovation! Just following Mechanised Computerised...'

'Just following Orders...from a machine? Orders! What about the actual goods and stocks? Gas and oil-pipelines, procedures? Processed... Terms and Conditions? That is all. Contracts...are: Policies: Merchant-Copy: Industrial-*Averages...copied...earlier and sold-on already:*

'Big-Hitters...Berserkers!'

'Hitting Whole Country-Zone infrastructure...'

'To Re-build...takeover...*normality*-restored: Fun and games: markets and *media...*'

'Super-pact?'

'Something like that...as an agreed wording...Trade-Agreements...The Words...'

'And The Numbers...'

'Crucially Signed-Off Protocol. Midday?'

'What if *they* don't agree?'

'WE? Privatisation anyway...or Closed.'

'Nationalisation? Or central Party...or Religious heads...'

'Some places...'

'Control! Of resources! People, or things! That is what it is all about! Once fed and watered, Control!'

'Making-a-*living*...'

'For your Family! Eh?'

'And yours. Your social group and the rest...land, buildings...Go and Fuck...'

'Never too good for them. Eh?'

'The Politics of Envy.'

'The Envy of Politics. Food and shelter?'

'Then Money-Mad! Only with enough of it to be without real risk. Never-enough!'

'Until now.'

'Staked chips:...'

'Casino-gambling!'

'Personal-greed…if you-*like*!'

'Diamonds...'*are forever...*

'A Gift from God…'

'For you maybe...'

'The Rich will always with us.'

'But drilling-down…'

'Mining?'

'Trapped!'

'Massive explosion!'

'Massive-accident...oil-spill, nuclear...energy, on excessive speculation...'

On-screen heard, and outloud, The Clerk:

'Kicked the can down the road...didn't You?'

'Carry the can?'

'*Healthy*-competition?'

'Safe.'

'Only if you can pay for it? Otherwise...'

'Turned-off The Life Support...'

'Machine? Insider?'

'Corporate-sabotage...'

'For-personal-Advantage. Pure, and…'

'Not so –simple. Complex…'

'Gaffed! Gaffer-taped! Voted-out. Loser! For Personal Profit...only!'

'Pure-*complicated* and…'

Interrupted:

'You make it so unbelievably complicated? Un-un-ravelable...'

'So You don't get caught!'

'I get caught, I go-down! Fines un-payable, prison!'

'So unknown about by others...So what? Corporate-confidentiality...State secrets, what is the difference?'

'You sure? They both mindlessly kill...'

'Necessarily, for their own protection.'

'Others in the fire-line...The-Journalists...are just the-*punters*. Too. Like everyone else. Small investors...'

'The-Customers'! Conned! Outright! Bamboozled...' *turned a blind-eye to.*

If doubling the price one place...then halving somewhere else! Half-price? Two-for-One? Buy One Get One Free!?

'The Home economics of world finance?!?'

‘Making Good Profits, eh? At the expense of who? Your Family? or someone else’s?’

'I think we know the answer?’

'What is that, then?’

'You, and Yours'...and then everyone-Else...’

'Could not careless?!’

'Can-Go and...*fuck* yourself!’

‘Not producing anything! Except pure-profit-driven Monetarism...’

‘Money, sole purpose banking...’

‘Lending...that others' may live...’

‘What is wrong with that?’

‘Not re-investing except in yourselves. The rest of us! Loaned, renting-out...’

‘To make jobs and livelihoods for The-Others!’

‘To make more unearned un-worked-for unshared-profit?’

‘To payback: The Bailout!'

Incensed:

'All of US! The People! How much more?!’

'You *don't* have to borrow?!'

'You don't have to lend!'

'Make it difficult...'

'Or not at all. The Banks are Closed. Haven't you heard? Made to borrow! All of us! With the collateral nothing but the Country-itself! Its Stocks and Shares of Goods and Services and People...and...the-Banks!'

'The-Banks?! What...all of them?'

'Yes! Bailed-out by US! Government! Rates, that is all it is...Income-outgoings. Outcome: incomings! Import-Export.'

'Interested?'

'Payback? The National-Bank...'

'Us'! Payback, with hardly any interest...loaning the interests of the many, for the few...'

'More money than sense!'

'So The Government prints more money!'

'Common-sense: Quantitive-*easing*...'

'Yes, that. Well meaning...but the Banks have got 'It' Everytime, don't they?'

'What?'

'The-Money of course!'

'The Private-Banks, yes. Government(s)…'

'The Interest on the Currency is Spent on Paying Off The Government-Bank...'

'And Private. Our debt?'

'All of it. Along with All Our Personal-Debts of course...'

'Insurance rip-off and...'

'Social-Scandal...'

'All? Thick as thieves!'

'Children...'

'You said it!'

'Home!' *..and mortgage-rental...lost, bought-out, sold-out...*

'Governments' *over-spending...'*

'Or not-at-all...'

'**Our-Tax**(es)!'

'What on? Pay-off loans the-Banks and Economic-Zones stack-up the National-Debt to the-Banks...bailed-out...stepped-down...'

'Got-it!'

'For them...'

'Got IT! See?! Social-care, the infrastructure...people and families...'

'<u>For=Popularity</u>...'

'**<u>The Popular-Front</u>**...'

'Themselves...'

'Hated and Loved in equal measure...'

'Of course themselves! Don't we all?!'

'And The-People…Who have been borrowing way- beyond their-means...'

'To Pay-Back?'

'Impossible! Now!

'Or the bailiff's?'

'*Bailing*...<u>You</u>-out!'

'Again.'

'Or jail.'

'Monetary-cycle: **Boom!** and Bust.'

'In...and out!'

'And when of course! Today! In-debt?'

'You? Bankrupt? with the commission-on various variable bank-rate's fixed again...'

'To profit by unfair advantage!'

'We are not nice to be around, most of us, They say. Not now anyway..."

'Who?'

'The Press, the-Media...people...'

'Banker-bashing?'

'Army? Police? Religious? Yes. No...' in case:

'I got your number...' if this-one turns out maybe some kind of Super-psycho...Assassin. Especially deceitful, or honest, dishonest counterfeit crank?

'Apparently...' to The-Clerk: not thought-out nor without the publicity only in thoughts not meant to be shared and beliefs shared and unshared. Trusted non-profit interest making product mutual funded shared equity…

Ultimately the-truth happening here and now and in the post-betting buying and selling-money shopped *imagination* sought...

The-Banker:

'Lending-rates: N/n: *fixed* between The-Banks!'

'Ahhh. The Beautiful lie...'

'Free-Market-*forces!*'

'Lie bore! FedEx. ForEx!'

'Fixed!'

'Libellous?!'

'Which explains how we rarely see these people, these CEO Bankers! These-people!'

'Reprehensible traitors!'

'Nothing will happen to them! They will take their booty. Ill-gotten gains...they do no wrong…'

'Not. Interbank-rates in double-figures...'

'Fixed. Keep paying. Interest-rate low, hedged-high, lined with gold... '

'Happy to pay non-performance based bonus bonus-bonus again!'

'On Zero negative-Rates?'*...eating into the Equity now...savings, pension-investment, rent and services needed:*

'Savings?'

'No, spent.'

'Exchanged. Worthless! Somewhere to live? Mortgage? Business-Credit? Credit-card. For the luxuries...Necessaries. Daily, weekly shop, payday –loans, at extra-ordinary 4.000% pay-back penalties! Bank-loan, or fraudulently fleeced? Lionised Bank charges, interest-rate swaps, three-minute sell, over the 'phone...'

'Not-Stupid.'

'Stupid...very...'

'Naive...perhaps?'

'Greedy. Based on *fraudulent* false-performance numbers...'

'The rest of us have to live with...Standard, Moodies...'

'And Poor!'

'Rates!'

'Competitive Banking-Interest rates, you see...0%!'

'Lending between each other...leaving Everyone-Else out in the cold...Why would...they do that? Why would You? Cash-only...keep the cash, with shares...not loaned-out...Or Given-Away...'

'Charity? As Tax-Cuts? To-Spend...'

'Benefits by Customers' wages and salaries and daily-rates...'

'Employment-Government -Taxes to Pay Back The Bank(s).

'Bailout?'

'When it all goes-wrong...'

'Lock Stock and Barrel!'

'And <u>Public-Service(s)</u>:...*shared...to pay staff for stocks and services....an inequitable shadow-money-market raised against a wall...*

'So?'

'Shares. The Markets may be closed, but...'
mumbling...glancing down at the laptop computer screen-saver hidden from view.'

'The-Expectation...The Surety is-complete: returned and ever more complex...complete.'

The-Banker:

'Competing on-Price and Costs:...fixed/*variable*...rate...'

'Of Everything? Value of Nothing!'

'Wrong! Of Money! Profit. Pure and *Simply*:...

'The-Price of Everything! The Value of Everything!'

'With The-Interest on Capital-Value *investment...*'

'And Returns:...*for doing nothing but pressing a few buttons...*'

'That's it? Isn't it?'

'Or some newly found The Golden Mountain out there is there? New Dot Comm.s?'

'The-City:...Money: *Currency-Banks* and Investment-Houses...'

'There is a difference?'

'Are essential *invaluable* institutions...*different-regulations...*'

'Although not entirely necessary?'

'Could We *really* not-live without...'

'Us? Personal-Death and Public-Taxes! What about *Taxes*?' *a snicker rattled throaty machine-gun like sniper returned this time.*

In sheer *derision* now:

'The-Devil wicked or *wicked* takes the Hindquarter's!'

'The Government: Mortgage Assistance: Now?'

Press-To:

'Privatise Everything! Again?'

'No-Taxes...No government?'

'No Banks! No-Credit! Invest in-yourself!'

'Invest-yourself?'

'Privatise yourself!'

'I have!'

'No trickle-down…'

'No trickle-up Bullshit! Winner takes all. Period?'

'That is all it is.'

'Whether by any means necessary...or none.' *whispering*-again, leaning forward and back:

'This a Secretive world. Rarely seen. Of people un-recognised in public. We are not-nice-people-to-know. They say. But they also say: We all have to eat and put a roof over our heads. For our-families...sake, eh?'

'Eat? Roof? Family?':

The-Clerk, spoken-out aloud. Both. Almost absent-mindedly thought and spoken-for, just like being shot-at, shot- down with sympathy or self-pity.

The-Banker continuing:

'We are the-same You and Me.' *same age? Level playing-field? Same valuable debts?*

'And When?'

'We couldn't back our promises' to pay with Real-Money...'

'To **<u>The-Shareholder(s</u>**)…'

'**<u>The-People!</u>**'

'Got-*greedy* of-course! IT is Only a-Game...' *cover your losses? Once you have passed the few Trillion-marker! Fixing the rates up or down to sell'em back again...*

'As In Ancient-Times?'

'Pyramid style! Up-siding...'

'And Down-*sizing*...'

'Upgrading?'

'Too?'

'Alright! We didn't expect the richest and most privileged to be So Greedy...'

'So uncaring? So...' quote...unquote: '*Self*-Interested...'?

'Of-course!'

'Didn't care about anyone else. Except Family, few-friends...and said so more often than not. Did a lot for-Charity of course...At least on the pretext of! That you can Rescue Your-Country...Your-City...Yourself... and The-World!'

'A-scapegoat, eh? To be Trolled By You!'

'Don't get caught, that is all! With your fingers in the till? Selling. This story! Journalist? Treasury-officer? Spy?'

'And You?'

'Laying-Low.'

Pause.

'You all knew what was going on…' *justly...or otherwise…decided to do-nothing? Take a hike...then...on a rich-resignation of ill-gotten gains maybe, promoted to a position of steady in-competence ha ha…*

The-Clerk's hand moved as slicing across the neck:

'In a bland disregard...for failure of ordinary Economic-Welfare Benefit become Fiscal-Warfare...'

'Tax and Charity scandals *failings* across the boardroom...'

'Many...'

'Access to dis-counted funding?'

'Investment-opportunities?'

'Banks to invest-in...'

'Other-Banks?'

'Why would They do That, now?' *for them To Invest In Money alone? For Us to take The Risk of industrial and agricultural investment:*

'*In-Commodities'...in nothing more...*'

'Off: The-Money *Itself*: Bond-deals bonded and Warehouse Currency-Exchange alone would yield: N/n...'

'n/N?'

'Employment and Pay:'...on-*unemployment*...and Pay-Load Driving...'

'On: The Public-Road(s) and Railways and Airplane:

'Fuel, and Funds, eh?'

Didn't get-It.

'Food, clothing, everything.'

Off-hand:

'Credit-Control implementation?'

'Regulation of Trade...'

'Globally? Open-handedness?'

Floating-branches on rivers of despair...

Scrap-site...repossession...Shit!

'Stimulus...'

'Bids...'

'Financing...' *confidential sources special-delivery, pave-the-way...t*roubled troubling-distribution stalled.

The-Banker, expressionless, now looking-out over the last of the blue and green-and-yellow patched crimson-brown and purple-yellow grey-jaded fields and forests...

The Train-Line passaged *overlit* bright *shimmering* lake.

As an *azure* eye cloud over-shadowing. Blinking over a deep blue private swimming–pool. Lights reflected-upwards…*night-time, and outwards, inwards...*

Over-flying slow fly-past...with both-hands at the controls…feet-tapping at-the-pedals:

'Not-Working!'

'Look! No- hands! Un-steered!' *another's voice?*

' Bust! Boom!!'

My Voice! faltering, factoring-in *faster* careening away swaying wildly. Rocking from side-to-side, impulsively reflexively the foot-pedal depressed, sharply and The Airplane began to nose-dive violently thrashing out-of-control...*shaking*... tremendously...through a cloud misty fogged mountain-side scale-reduced…down to radio-*bandwidth...*

'Stalled!' into the radio-visor face-mask.

Out loud? The most-*terrifying* thought: revealed:

'Dead?' *In-private. Alone? Suicide? Then back at the controls. In-control*...*piloting happily sleeping but not doing anything asleep, proudly and aloof...gliding-over…*

U*plifting pitching-downward looking and watching turning-view silently and slowly...swhooshing…*

Turning-low over the landscape, to see…*smoothing-out self-imaging…*

'Now!' *the mindful-scene now turning around to face:*

'The-Face! *released from the mirror spoken speaking?*

Spoken? Hearing? Seen? Felt?:

'Stalled!'

Photographed Only...seeing The All-seeing:

The Minds'-Eye and ear-splitting noises of a good engine-breaking-down...spiralling-below... and towards The-Earth *cycling and re-cycling:*

'Global.'

'Zero-Hours!'

'Trust Me!' *like a slow-motion crash waited to-happen...*

*S*truggling *madly*- felt...

To-*escape* in mid-air...altimeter-reading: 0/0...' *heard* said? *Seen?*:

'Parachuting-in...' said quietly *softly* as if almost without moving even air *spoken?*

Whispered:

'No parachute...' *not-opening...again into:*

'Freefall!'*...falling...freefalling*...crashed-again.

From The *familiar* Nightly-Terrors...terrible *tremors-shook...*

Early morning remembering in The-Bathroom Gym...

The Work-Out and *shower...o*n...The Bathroom-Floor

Tiled-mosaic day-dreaming absolution-nightmare prayer.

As *this* morning.

Earlier: This Day: driven-in through fine-weather course setting-out from secluded The Mansion-Estate: *farmland and forest all-around, fenced and walled-in and gated-out indoor- and out-door swimming-*

pools with gymnasium and private golf-course CClub-house and fishing-lake:

'Barrel shaped: The Lake.' *flying in to a Business-Function…functioning social-human-being…*

'The Lake?'

'More like a *pond,* really.' *heard* said:

On-awakening earlier this day. At-Home.

One of them: o*nly One-Self at A Times'* thought, though through this-time through the air-gasping in the sea-drowning washed-away…as…*thinking*...saying:

'To keep *flashy*-fish in?'

'To catch?' Easy? Eh?'

'In a Barrel. Barrel-shaped...Lake. Get IT!'

'Don't tell a-*sole*!'

Hearing:

'Especially not-mine.' and-*laughing* quietly to-self.

Chuckling...*inside*: The-Earth World engulfing:

The Home Country-garden and the-grounds polished rough-lain and bolted-together…*bath-taps, gold-leaf plaster-mouldings mouldering brocade-curtains ripped and torn aflame many-lighted candelabra chandelier* cavalier crashed to the ground:

'The Board-room floor...' *feared…headed-for flooded injury to any main-arteries bloodied-marbled-hallways:…*

'Hellways!' *plunged*…woken from the wide-eyed reverie. Alerted! with a jolt. Over another crossing once more…*un-heard?* Felt. *Un-seen? Seen? Undone?* the sudden alarming thought as at <u>The End</u>.

As in <u>The-End</u>:

The-Face: unpiloting bodily yet helplessly passenger from the lucid lurid last nightmare-daylight scenario rescued…a-*cough* of relief and…On the-<u>Train</u>…jolted.

Again, across bolted rail-crossing points...and a nod upwards. As look upwards: in a *Flash! distracting the attention...*

'To Put <u>Pay</u> to...Sell-on!...*anyone*...<u>Stay!'</u>

Bought-On...non-reflective

'Black-body In-Space-lit by The Sun…'

'Going around in-spirals blindfolded...'

Opened as from *some* Underground <u>The-City:</u> *overground* field cliff-edged balanced…*dropping-down*…again.

The Banker free-falling…over The Edge…

The-Banker…kicking and screaming *dragged out-of-the-blue black-out into...* red from *green*-tinted...

'Rio Tinto...to...the Gulf of Mexico clean-up…'

'As One. Once-more...back into the blazing-red-rising-Sun.

Into the Black, grey white now yellow green-backed fields...back into the-flames of the frame of the window imaged…and imagined seen: *slightly turned the shoulder to-camera…*

B*ack-dropped set through the window* through a tunnel in the ground...grounded tunnel-walls *flashing* by still *advertisements*:

'Best Advertisement in the World!' neme-*screened:...*

Over the tunnel funnel-walls.

Through *nano-cabling* electro-atomic light radiation leaking-in product:

'Named?'

From a stormy and sunny morning; and from where the-Sun would soon be breaking-through again. From behind an-escarpment, tree and flowering carpeted-counter of red-brown and green-blue dark cloud drifting-into:

<>Desktop Brief-Case-opening as pitched-into:

'What is Your Name?'

The-Banker, alerted replied quickly:

'I am The-Executive...'

'Executioner?'

'Both of us. Together.'

Computer-screens *underlit* as well as The-Train.

Over-lighting…The-Sun now searching reaching-above: as an Over-arching angle-poised lamp *in an Endless Office the centred of which was: The Boardroom Table.*

The only light in a pitch-darkened room to be switched-on and off and on-again endlessly...with a quick silent click-of-the- finger's reflection bounced-off the deep undershine of a hardwood varnished between: The-Banker and The-Clerk *refracted* through seemingly…

The-*Glass*-Ceiling shattered...*vanished* into a woolly varnish-striped Bank-Logo is all that is required of:

'The Cloud…'

'The *riches* of The-Earth...' as a tree conjoined above and below-ground *fungal*-growing *glowing* a crystalline iceburg rock to be re-melted.

To be made into something-else. Something different, indifference now, and separately-minded, mined drilled and dug-out cleansed and to be befriended and un-befriended and defended against: The felt-*threat* moved *glittering*-below: The *Travelling*-Train:

The-Sun once more on-track to reach IT's Zenith.

Again...

And I said to myself

'Oh, what's the matter here?'

I'm tired of the excuses

Everybody uses

He's your kid

Do as you see fit

But who gave you the right

To do this?

...what you did

To your own flesh and blood.

From In My Tribe: by 10,000 Maniacs 1987

Also by M.Stow:

EarthCentre: The End of the Universe: (An Anthropic Odyssey)

Universal Verses 1-3

Walter Mepham (A First World War generational family-saga)

WarFair4: Part One: The Day The Markets stood still...

WarFair4: Part Two: Algorythm: The Day The Markets Crashed! and instantaneously re-installed themselves.

WarFair4: Part Three: Into the Abyss. The Day The Money Markets *finally* collapsed...

Printed in Great Britain
by Amazon.co.uk, Ltd.,
Marston Gate.